adrian mcneil

inventing the sarod: a cultural history

adrian mcneil

inventing the sarod:
a cultural history

Seagull Books
calcutta new delhi
2004

Photographs courtesy the author
Cover design: Naveen Kishore

ISBN 81 7046 213 4

Published in India by Naveen Kishore,
Seagull Books Private Limited
26 Circus Avenue, Calcutta 700 017
Printed in India by Rockwel Offset
55B Mirza Ghalib Street, Calcutta 700 016

contents

A Note from the Publisher

Musicological terms and proper nouns in Hindustani classical music pose certain problems of transliteration into English, with several spellings being accepted for the same term. This volume has followed the consistent principle of dispensing with diacritical marks, and the italicization of musicological terms and names of raags.

The elongated/accentuated vowel sounds in Hindi, Urdu and Persian have been transliterated with double vowels where the normal English pronunciation does not allow an elongation of sound. The more accepted/Sanskritized 'raga', 'tala', etc. have been replaced with raag, taal; the word 'tan' without diacritics has been made taan. However, excerpts/quotes from other sources retain their original transliterated spellings. A list of musicological terms and categories with clear explanations has been provided in the glossary.

The syncretic nature of the Indian classical musical tradition, enmeshed in a rich oral history tradition, has made chronology a rather dubious and problematic category. Dates are mostly conjectural and few versions concur.

We gratefully acknowledge the help and cooperation we have received from Anindya Banerjee, who has painstakingly checked last-minute queries from the rare texts, journals and pamphlets in his collection, pointed out certain anomalies which had eluded our notice and provided some rare stills for the book. We thank Amlan Das Gupta for his suggestions and especially for providing us with the invaluable glossary.

Acknowledgements

The intrusion into other people's lives in the name of research has always struck me as being a somewhat disconcerting act, especially when working in a culture outside of one's own. Maybe this is partly because the nature of the personal relationships, nurtured over many years, and the many types of exchanges and obligations that transpire along the way, appear to be at odds with any sense of objectivity desired in the research itself. This is something that I continue to have trouble in reconciling. But whatever the reasons for this discomfort, what does emerge from all of this is an ongoing sense of indebtedness to those whose lives, in varying degrees, are part of this project too. This is so because although this study may now be completed in its present form, these people fortunately continue to stay in my life. This work is dedicated to them with gratitude.

As this research has taken place over many years, there are far too many people to name individually, who in one way or another had became an integral part of this project. Given this situation, it would be out of order not to mention my music teachers Pandit Ashok Kumar Roy, Professor Sachindra Nath Roy and Dr Ashok Da. Ranade who inspired me and were always there for guidance. Also without the encouragement of my family and especially the invaluable logistical support of my brother Craig, this study would not have been possible. The same sense of gratitude also extends to Asher and Luba Bilu, Jon Barlow, Georges and Kabita Lindenmeyer, Abhijeet and Smita Roy, Sugata Marjit and my other friends and colleagues in India and Australia: Rashmi Desai, the other 'shibsena' of Jadavpur, Amlan Das Gupta, Moinak Biswas, Michael Stevenson, Manolete Mora, Gladwin

Charles, Aneesh Pradhan, Debashish Brahmachari, Prabhu Edouard, Bablu Ghosh and family.

This book would also not have been possible without the institutional support of an Australian Research Council Post-doctoral Fellowship 1996–98; the School of Music, Monash University, Melbourne; the School of Media, Communication and Culture, Jadavpur University, Calcutta; the Centre for Studies in Social Sciences, Calcutta; the Centre for Studies in Contemporary Music, Macquarie University, Sydney; and Shubha Chaudhuri and the ARCE, Delhi.

Finally, heartfelt thanks to all the musicians, musicologists and other acquaintances who kindly and patiently endured my queries and assorted follies over the years.

Introduction

This book is an attempt to document the cultural origins, historical development and musical experiences of the sarod over the last three centuries. In doing so, this inquiry also considers the history of its musicians—sarodiyas—their oral histories, professional and social organizations, patron groups and the networks and structures of patronage which provided their livelihood. It investigates its material culture, i.e. the physical elements, design and construction innovations that defined the instrument at a given point of time. It tries to establish a connection between developments in this area and the strong desire to produce a particular musical sound and musical voice. The book also sets out to construct a methodology that makes musical sound, both in conception and practice, an object of study.

The historical development of musical repertoire and performance practice are also obviously important aspects of the instrument's past. Such a subject becomes all the more complex and fascinating when it is considered that the core of this musical corpus is transmitted orally and a competent performance is realized on the spot through improvisatory structures. This makes a study of the music itself not only worthy of its own separate and detailed inquiry, but also places such a subject beyond the scope of this study. Nevertheless, an outline of the main aspects of the musical elements, playing style and techniques of the sarod are touched upon whenever it is able to inform the primary aims given above.

These aims in part contribute to two overall objectives. The first of these is to highlight the cultural syncretism and diversity that has underpinned the development of the tradition to date. The second is to address the current climate of contestation over the cultural ownership of the tradition and its history. Contestation seems to have always been part of the cultural activity that produced the sarod. This was contained within the tradition. What is different now is that this contestation occurs in the mass media and other notable public spaces and is argued to be part of a wider tendency in contemporary India for re-imagining the past—a practice that lies open to manipulation by pernicious agendas.

The use of the term sarod and rabab in this study perhaps requires a little explanation. This is so because it is not a term that is restricted only to Hindustani music. This term is shown to have historically had a wider circulation than this, not only in Persia but in the north-west of the subcontinent where it describes a number of other instruments that are morphologically very different from the Hindustani sarod. It was also the name by which the Afghani rabab was sometimes known before the modern form of the Hindustani sarod. This particular rabab, as distinct from Punjabi or seniya rababs, was also known as the Kabuli rabab and the Pashtun or Pathan rabab. The terms were often used interchangeably to refer to the Afghani rabab, according to the practices found in different geographical and historical contexts. This situation can, and in some instances has, created some confusion in dealing with the instrument in both written and oral historical sources. As far as possible, this study specifies the context in which these musical terms are found and the particular instrument that they refer to.

This study tries to address how and why so many elements of the history of the sarod are highly and sometimes acrimoniously contested. In such a situation it is inevitable that the issue be taken with some of the interpretations and conclusions arrived at here. Any mistakes made in handling and representing the material, either inadvertently or otherwise, that may cause offence to some musicians, are not intentional and some understanding is requested, given the limitations of this study.

Finally, it should be pointed out that honorific titles customarily used to address Hindustani musicians of some calibre, such as Ustad and Pandit, do not appear in the text. For those familiar with

Hindustani music, this may be regarded as an unacceptable compromise. No disrespect or offence is intended by this, however undesirable their omission may appear to some. It was a decision made on the one hand simply to give clarity to the text and on the other to overcome the difficulty in knowing on whom to confer such titles, when dealing with the large and diverse numbers of musicians this study is concerned with.

Sounding out the Sarod

THE SOUND OF THE SAROD, in the hands of an adept, is a delicious thing to savour. Capable of seducing the senses and nourishing the souls of connoisseurs of music, this instrument enables its performers to realize delicate tonal qualities and subtly manifest the feast of nuances and other delights of Hindustani classical music. It is this potential as much as anything else, that has made it a very suitable vehicle for instrumental music and ensured its central position in India's shastriya sangeet or 'art music' tradition.

Due to this ability to enchant the aural palate, the sound of the sarod has also become one of the principal factors of inquiry in this study. From such an orientation the history of the sarod tradition in India therefore becomes as much about the collective development of the culture of sound which has historically sustained the instrument, its players and their development, as it is about any other facet of its history. But it is not just the physical sound per se that is of interest here; this study also tries to explore what the meaning, function and quality of that sound might be at a given time. Herein lies a much-visited quandary: any aesthetic dealing with the quality of musical sound tends to elude reduction to a single source of action. By this it is meant that tonality, musical voice or sound quality cannot be meaningfully represented by a single set of classificatory or analytical parameters, suited to the more usual practice of quantified inventories of musical pitches and tuning systems. In short, the sense of quality in sound somehow defies articulation, in much the same way as the enigma of taste torments similar expositions in culinary endeavours.

Nevertheless, there are two areas of consideration available to us which are helpful in disarming this quandary. Of these, the first is that sound production in contemporary North India is informed by, and grounded in, a centuries-old commentary on the philosophy and practice of sound. The second is that, over the last one hundred and fifty years or so, innovations made in the design of the instrument and its active sound-producing components have largely been developed in cognizance of this broader thinking.

Over the last two millennia, a profoundly rich philosophical commentary on sound has been expounded through a series of treatises on music and the arts in general.[1] While acknowledging the existence and importance of this body of information this subject is, however, not the primary focus of this study. For the present purpose, commentaries on and guides to the ontology of sound such as those provided in, for example, the *Natyashastra*[2] (second century CE) Somesvara's *Manasollasa* (twelfth century CE), *Mankuthul/Ragdarpan* (fifteenth and sixteenth centuries), and more recently in secondary sources such as the compendium of aesthetic principles, *Kalatatvakosh*, and *Music and Musical Thought in Early India* (Rowell 1992), are sufficient to introduce the notion that the origin of sound on the instrument can perhaps also be said to be philosophically located in culturally-grounded idealized forms or archetypes.

While recognizing the weight of authority of this knowledge, it should also be pointed out that the exposition of this commentary has not been restricted to textual sources alone. Besides written material dealing with sound there is the orally-transmitted knowledge contained within the myriad 'schools' of interpretation and styles of musical performance passed on through personal experience, codified behaviour, practical instruction, anecdotes, maxims, metaphors, proverbs and, in this century, sound recordings. Common to all these written, oral and recorded sources, which interact together to form an aesthetic, philosophical, intellectual and metaphysical matrix of endeavour, are deeply-held beliefs concerning the cosmology of sound, the properties and effects of sound, and guides as to what is therefore good and meaningful in sound. The various designs of the sarod which have surfaced over the last two centuries have attempted to devise or enlist features which consciously or otherwise have sought to realize something of and/or adapt to this profound level of understanding sound.

This study makes use of three primary levels of understanding sound which, in a practical sense, are useful as vantage points for addressing the commonly posed yet deceptively complex question: 'Where did the sarod come from?' Each level is defined through its own understanding of the point of origin of musical sound.[3] The most obvious of these is the level that locates this point of origin in the instrument itself by concentrating on the design of the instrument, its material culture and the basic physical action that produces an impact upon its strings. It therefore tends to be empirical in its approach. The second level is formed from the assumption that the sound heard on the instrument is preceded by the desire of a musician to create that sound and the imagination applied in realizing that desire. It locates the point of origin of sound as being within the musicians themselves, and is thereby tempered by such things as training, experience and individual talent. This desire and imagination is itself informed by the third level which places the origin of musical sound within the collective endeavour producing the aesthetic conventions, idealized forms and esoteric practices in which the musician is enculturated. Taking these together, the point of origin of sound therefore can be claimed to be simultaneously located in the instrument, in the musician and in wider aesthetic conventions. Of course, each of these domains is interlinked with and interdependent on the other two levels in the act of music making and so, such clinical disaggregations need to be seasoned with some caution. It is with this sense of discretion that these three levels of understanding sound, and the areas of inquiry they give rise to, are applied in this study.

Situated in a historical framework, these three levels then generate their own associated concerns and historical trajectories. By locating sound in the instrument a number of physical considerations directly affecting sound production enters into focus, ranging from the overall design of the instrument and the materials used in its construction at any given time, to the properties of its strings, plectrums and the tuning systems employed and so on. There is enough empirical evidence available via photographs, antique instruments, etc. to construct a reasonable picture of the development of the instrument through its material culture.

Locating the source of sound within the musician introduces a level of inquiry in which sarodiyas also become a central concern in the history of the sarod. This particular focus directs our attention to the immediate circumstances in which the professional lives of sarodiyas were engaged at any given time, viz. the types of music and musical forms they played, where they performed and the individual innovations and artistic decisions taken about how to perform. These questions also touch upon issues of their social identity, their access to learning music and how they made a living from it. As part of their professional lives, sarodiyas also had to collectively negotiate a series of formal and informal systems that governed their social organization, transmission of musical knowledge and the means by which they garnered and engaged patronage. Despite any difficulty in articulating a direct connection, it is not unreasonable to infer that these factors in some way temper and effect the realization of sound within the musician.

Locating the origin of musical sound in idealized forms, aesthetic conventions and esoteric practice opens up another intellectual space within which the history of the sarod can be explored. The relevance and meaning of these forms and conventions at any given time is also contingent upon specific historical and cultural contexts. These in turn are linked to, among other things, the concerns, sensibilities and resources of patron classes and the logic and practice of networks of patronage through which cultural, social and musical exchanges between musicians and their patrons transpire.

The three tiers of sound associated with the instrument, musician and convention when taken together, along with their cultural, material and social analogues, are argued in this study to constitute the primary dimensions of the sarod tradition in North India. It is on, through and across these three levels that the tradition has so far proceeded through history. While addressing the question of where the sarod comes from, one also understands that to answer this by focusing only on the organology and material culture of the instrument, is to ignore any number of other coexisting historical strands that explain why past events happened the way they did. Therefore, along with a study of the history of the morphology and material culture of the instrument, which is the thread of the tradition most commonly heard, there is also an exploration of the forms of patronage within which it developed, the history of its musicians, the history of the sound and musical voice of the instrument, the history of its music making and its etymology.

Each of these levels of inquiry, no doubt interconnected in various ways, often proceed upon their own historical trajectories and thereby generate their own sense of the past and subsequent historical discourse. Sometimes the past is approached so differently on each level that explanations of, for example, the etymology of the musical term 'sarod' on the one hand and accounts of the invention of the instrument on the other, appear to belong to quite unrelated events. Even by accommodating these different trajectories, stacking up different levels of interpretations within a larger intellectual space and creating an interplay between them, we may never arrive at a definitive history of the sarod but may at least be propelled closer to a more likely scenario of the past than can be obtained by studying one level of this larger history in isolation.

However, it is precisely through such isolated threads that the history of the sarod is most commonly encountered. These come to us via the personal reflections of significant figures within the tradition. In the recent past, there have been at least five or six competing accounts of the history of the instrument in circulation. Each of these invariably claims the distinction for the invention of the sarod for a past family member. The tacit implication arising from such claims is that having invented the instrument, their familial antecedents then become the legitimate historical voice of the tradition. Consequently, the history of the sarod is recalled through these accounts as a series of seminal events and experiences exclusively belonging to that family which, on occasion, are also projected as being the core experience in the development of the sarod tradition, against which the events and experiences of other families are either deemed peripheral or simply ignored.

The details of each of these individual claims are examined throughout. However, the point to note about these specific claims is that each addresses the same two fundamental issues, viz. the distant cultural origins of the instrument, and the invention of the modern instrument sometime in the mid-nineteenth century. Each individual account invariably presents a different version of these two events. Therefore it is inherent that some degree of contestation between accounts exists, often making them appear mutually exclusive. Out of the two issues, differences between accounts become the most apparent and most hotly contested in relation to the cultural genesis of the instrument. It is also the aspect of history most prone to appropriation by contemporary political agendas. While this may be the most difficult aspect of the sarod tradition to grapple with, it also becomes the most important thing to keep in mind when approaching the sarod's past. The primary differences in accounts of the sarod's distant past introduced in this chapter, precede a more formal exploration in later chapters.

The Beginnings

There are at least three separate versions concerning the genesis of the sarod. All of these historically locate the event more than a thousand years ago, and one goes back as far as two thousand years. In the context of the general evolution of musical instruments in the region, this antiquity in some ways invests these accounts with a sense of a mythical past, beyond our historical horizon, located somewhere within the far-flung realms of the primordial. For this reason, inquiry into this level of the sarod's history can become highly problematic.

Some sarodiyas have stressed, through personal accounts and written sources, that the origin of the instrument can be traced to a region straddling modern-day Afghanistan and northern Pakistan and, in particular, to the rabab played for many centuries by Pashtun musicians (Plate 1-1).[4] In India, this rabab is more commonly known as the Afghani or Kabuli rabab and is often held to be the direct progenitor of the Hindustani sarod. Others have reiterated the connection between Pashtun musicians and the sarod but also go on to add another dimension to this version. They state that this particular rabab, in turn, had originally come to Pashtunistan from Greece after Alexander, where it was later adopted by Pashtun musicians. In this version, the creation of the original rabab form is specifically attributed to a person named 'Fishew-Ghorus', better known in the West as Pythagoras. Proponents of a third version currently argue that the sarod was developed from a line of short-necked lutes whose origins were unequivocally Indian. Evidence is cited in this instance of an ancient Indian lute, the chitra vina (Plate 1-2), depicted on temple reliefs from the second century CE with the implication that the sarod is the end product of a steady line of evolution from this point of origin which had produced the sursringar (Plate 4-4) in the early nineteenth century.

While not wishing to engage the details of any specific viewpoint at this stage in the discussion, it is enough to note that contestation concerned with the genesis of the instrument primarily concentrates on establishing an organological link between the modern instrument and its advocated precursor, the Afghani rabab or the sursringar. With this in mind it may be helpful for the time being to make some cursory observations on an issue that is perhaps not as clear cut as is commonly put forward in expositions of the sarod's ancient past.

Firstly, it is important to note that many types of plucked short-necked lutes are evident in, and around, North India. The Pashtun rabab, or the chitra vina for that matter, are therefore not entirely unique organological phenomena. Available iconographic, historical and ethnographic material on these instruments suggest that many types of plucked short-necked lutes are, and have been, played for many centuries by musicians stretching from Afghanistan in the west of the subcontinent, across the Himalayas and the northern plains, to Assam and Bengal in the east. In this regard, the rabab of the Pashtuns can be argued to be part of a larger population of plucked short-necked lutes which share varying degrees of similarities in shape and design with other lutes belonging to the music cultures of these regions. Even though there has been a preponderance of short-necked lutes sharing similar morphological features to the Pashtun rabab played across the entire north of the subcontinent for many centuries, it is possible to make a basic distinction between various types of lutes based not just on morphology and performance practice, but on which cultural orbit they developed within.

Cultural Orbits

In this study, an important and significant distinction is made between those lutes which in centuries gone by belonged to the north-west cultural orbit of the subcontinent in which Persian culture prevailed, and those that fell within the cultural orbit of 'inner' India, roughly the doab region between the Yamuna and Ganga rivers. To this distinction can be added other instruments that belong to the intermediate geographical area between these two orbits, namely in the area bound by the Yamuna and the Sutlej rivers, such as Punjab.[5]

Disagreements over the genesis of the sarod in the broadest sense therefore boil down to which area of the subcontinent, viz. whether it was in the north-west orbit (via the Afghani rabab) or in the inner-India orbit (via the chitra vina and sursringar), that gave the sarod its origins. By implication, the versions can also be distinguished not only by geographic location but, perhaps of equal significance, by whether the instrument was originally part of the wider cultural orbit of Persia or conversely whether it belonged to a Hindu cultural orbit.[6] This particular point creates a polemic (Persia-Muslim/India-Hindu) which underscores and pervades the contemporary accounts of the history of the sarod. As the discussion in the final chapter shows, it is also the point of departure which exposes these histories to the sectarian agendas currently active in the political climate of contemporary India.

Within the historical inventory of the sarod tradition, there are many competing claims on the past. There is no doubt that each one of the family histories retold by hereditary sarodiyas are compelling, and perhaps this has something to do with the way they neatly arrange history into a chronologically linear progression (viz. event **x** was followed by event **y**). It is in this form that the history of the instrument is most commonly encountered. Yet, at the same time, given that they all provide seemingly contradictory versions of the past, it also seems obvious that they cannot all be correct. Further, beyond the five or six individual claims, there are many more dimensions to the tradition and historical truths that exist outside these fragments. These other dimensions of the tradition dealing with its musicians, patrons, systems of social organization and so on, tend to be arranged in a progression of inter-related yet non-sequential episodes (viz. event **x** was influenced by **y**, but both could only happen because **a** was in the process of transforming into **z**).

It is precisely because history can be carved up in so many ways that points of tension emerge in attempts to tackle the tradition's past. The challenge then becomes to try to negotiate and accommodate these diverse ways of approaching the past within the course of study. Whether this aim is deemed to have been achieved or not, the one point that nevertheless does strongly emerge is that despite the unflinching certainty of the past which swells inside individual accounts, historical truth can never be so easily pinned down as they may suggest.

It is apparent that there have always been competing accounts of the history of the instrument, but there are other aspects of the tradition that are generally beyond dispute. Principal among these is the seminal role played by Pashtun musicians in the invention of the modern instrument.[7] It is this point that perhaps provides the most solid footing on which to begin a study of the sarod tradition, and accordingly it is from this point that the main part of this study begins, around the beginning of the eighteenth century.

Notes

1 Apart from the representation of this commentary brought to light here, there are a number of other dimensions to this endeavour which lay outside the scope of this study. For instance, there are the metaphysical and spiritual dimensions which are based on the connection between sound as the primary element force—nad—and yoga, as well as connections between nad and Tantric practices.

2 Chapter 32 in particular contains a detailed discussion of the aesthetic

conventions desirable for voice culture.

3 Rowell (1992:312ff) has eloquently described and analysed philosophical thought on sound in Indian music, and made comparisons between this and Greek and Chinese thought on the same subject. The present discussion draws upon some basic tenets raised in his work and readers are directed to this source if further clarification of the approach to sound adopted in this study is required.

4 The same type of rabab is also used in Kashmir in folk music and Sufiana Kalam.

5 The concept of cultural orbits is directly based on D. K. Chakrabarti's work *Colonial Indology: Socio-politics of the Ancient Indian Past* (1997:17). The reader is directed to this source for an exposition of this model.

6 At this stage, the claim that a rabab originally came to Pashtunistan from Greece is included within the Persian sphere of this polemic as its point of entry into India is still via Persian-'influenced' Pashtunistan where it was further developed for a number of centuries. The details of this claim are more fully discussed in Chapter 2.

7 Whilst stressing that 'in all my years of experience I am confident that the sarod is an Indian instrument' (Mukherjee and Kothari 1995:34), even Ali Akbar Khan still acknowledges the contribution of Pashtun musicians to the development of the instrument. Surprisingly though, the central role of Pashtun musicians in the development of the sarod often goes unacknowledged in accounts of the history of the instrument by some musicologists. For example, see Indrani Chakrabarti (1991), Lalmani Mishra (1973) and Sharan Rani (1992).

Pathans and the Sarod

PATHANS TRADITIONALLY LIVE in the region stretching from eastern Afghanistan to northern Pakistan. At the time that these two relatively modern states emerged in the nineteenth and twentieth centuries respectively, Pathans were roughly divided between these two countries. Prior to this, however, the Pathan homeland had been united both in cultural identity and geographic delineation for many centuries. The name Pathan is derived from Hindustani, later adopted by the British, referring to the speakers of a shared eastern-Iranian language group living east of the Durand Line. In their homelands, Pathans are known as Pakhtun, Pukhtun, Pashtun or Pushtun. The first two terms are used by those from the north of this region whose accent is more guttural than the softer Kandahari dialect of the south (Spain 1963:40).

The first important written study of the tribal history of the Pathans can be found in the early Mughal chronicle, *Babarnama*. Although the function of the chronicle cannot be separated from Mughal aspirations for control of that region, it does nevertheless contain some useful references such as a description of, for example, the Bangash homelands (Beveridge tr. 1969:231–33). Writing at the end of the nineteenth century, Crooke, a British ethnologist, lists twenty-six major divisions among the Pathans, each in turn having many sub-divisions. In addition to these, a number of independent settled tribes are also described. Over time, various clans had settled throughout the region and each established control over their own territories. Of the major groups listed, those living the furthest to the east of Pashtunistan, such as the Yusufzai, Ghori, Mehmad, Bangash and Afridi, had the greatest representation in India.[1]

More recently, Quddus has divided Pathans into three major groups, the Durranis, the Ghilzai and the 'true' Pathans (1987:26). The Durranis, whose homelands are entirely in Afghanistan, north of Kandahar, have supplied the ruling houses of Afghanistan.[2] The Ghilzai almost exclusively reside in Afghanistan to the east of the Durand line, across the border from Pakistani Baluchistan, and have been susceptible to Persian influence to a considerable degree. The third group Quddus identifies as the 'true' Pathans are those who live astride the Pakistan–Afghanistan border to the north and east of the other two groups. Unfortunately he does not explain what the difference between the 'true' and other 'untrue' groups of Pathans may be.

The most useful and thorough source of reference on Pathan ethnology is by Gommans (1999). His recent work on the Indo-Afghan empire in the eighteenth century provides the most complete list of ethnological, historical and ethnographic references concerning studies on Pathans published in many languages. These and other studies speak of the historical complexity of the ethnic and political dynamics of the region. Gommans's study demonstrates that counter to the commonly-held opinion of the region being a stagnant backwater during pre-colonial times, it was a dynamic and influential hub of trade between Central Asia and the subcontinent. This trade, more than any other factor, facilitated the large-scale movement of people and goods that occurred between Afghanistan and India in the eighteenth century. While there appear to be a few different interpretations of identity and delineation of the various Pathan tribes, the fact that their homelands have historically been geographically, culturally and socially sandwiched between the empires of Persia and Hindustan is not contested.

A defining characteristic of the north-west cultural orbit, it seems, was its role as a buffer, or a zone of transition, between these two larger powers, viz. inner-India and Persia. The influence that each exerted within the north-west orbit at any given time tended to follow the ebb and flow of the political fortunes within the two greater powers. Consequently, over the centuries, the influence of both Persia and the subcontinent can be found in different configurations at different times in the region. In this regard Quddus specifies that the southern tract of

Quetta–Kandahar–Herat came under the influence of Iran while the northern tract of Peshawar–Jalalabad–Kabul was more oriented to the subcontinent (1987:54).

Against the dynamics of this wider cultural and historical scenario, core elements of Pathan culture in various ways have maintained the cohesion of Pathans which must have only been enhanced by the isolation offered by the natural geography and rugged mountainous terrain of the region. One core element is the common language Pashtu shared by Pathan tribal groups which itself originally derived from a language of eastern Iran (Spain 1963:40). Through language, all the Pathan groups are connected in one way or another and the Pashtu-speaking people constitute a very real cultural and social entity (Spain 1963:41).

This attribute often indicates not only an affinity with respect to kinship, as suggested by Spain, but also to a shared set of cultural or social values. Pathans share a common code of moral conduct which governs behavioural interaction between individuals as well as between clans. This practice is known as Pakhtunwali and has been translated as 'The Pukhtun Code' or 'The Way of the Pukhtun'.[3] By religion, most Pathans are Sunn Muslims of the Hanafi sect, converted initially by invading Sunn Turkic groups in the past. This shared religious outlook also contributes to the overall cohesion of the group.[4] These unities had more recently been appropriated by the Pathan nationalist Taliban forces in Afghanistan, and by those pushing for an autonomous state of Pakthunkwa in Pakistan.

Pathan Music Culture

Not much is known of the music culture of the Pathans outside their region. A handful of studies of Afghani music by Slobin (1972), Sakata (1983) and Baily (1988) are primarily contemporary urban-based studies and, as such, the traditional function and history of music and musicians in Pathan social organization and their system of patronage in premodern times is not part of their focus. Hence this study provides, as a prelude, only a brief overview in order to concentrate on the past functions and practices of rabab-playing musicians within Pathan music culture.

While it is evident from extant studies that tribal Pathans have been greatly influenced by both the cultures of Persia and the subcontinent, it is not clear how the influences were absorbed or expressed in the music culture of the region at any given time. In particular, it is hard to discern whether the musical influence of Persia also followed the cultural fault line which saw the overall influence of Persian culture more resonant in the southern parts of their homelands, i.e. among the Ghilzais and Durranis, than among those in the north-east from where most of the Pathans who migrated to India had originated. It is also true that these wider musical influences on the homelands waxed and waned over the centuries, as did the political fortunes of these two larger powers. The point therefore remains that Pathan music culture, despite being unique to the region, was not isolated from the imprint of other influences and thus was part of a broader continuum of music culture stretching from the subcontinent to Persia.

Presently, the general impression of Pathan music culture is that it contains diverse modes of musical expression voiced through a variety of instruments, genres and styles. Among these are the musicians and the musical practices that migrated to India accompanying waves of Pathan military groups over the centuries. It is in this milieu that the early social history of the Hindustani sarod is to be found.

Oral history is replete with stories of rabab-playing musicians on foot or horseback, leading kings in procession or troops into battle.[5] It is also not unusual to hear about musical genres such as war ballads and epics recording famous events and other past encounters, even though the factual historical details have faded from the memories of the descendants of these musicians in India. Quddus, himself a Pathan, writes

> [The Pathan's] . . . love of liberty and independence have been given expression in a number of war ballads. In these songs Ahmad Shah Durrani is the hero against the Marattas, Dilasa Khan against the Sikhs and Akbar Khan against the British (1987:93).

There are also descriptions of the recreational martial dance of the Pathans, Katthak,[6] and folktales contained in Pashtu songs and other regional musical forms. Though some Pathan musicians at least had knowledge of, or performed music derived from/influenced by Persian art music, the documentation of immigrant Pathans performing these types of music in India is not forthcoming. So our knowledge of the musical forms, styles and performance practice of these musicians remains, to date, largely incomplete.

Fortunately, there is some more general information available on the hereditary musicians of the Pathans. In an account of the musicians in Mianwali, a town as well as a district now in Pakistan, Ibbetson (1970) has listed and described a number of endogamous groups of hereditary music specialists under the blanket term mirasi. He has also given tantalizing glimpses into the multifaceted roles and obligations that made up the jajmani system in that region. As both mirasis and jajmani (the system of patronage) play an important part in defining the early history of the sarod tradition, it is worthwhile considering these terms in some detail.

Jajmans and Mirasis

Jajman literally means 'patron'; and the jajmani system, when found in the context of music, refers to the various forms of exchange between groups of hereditary occupational music specialists, generically known as mirasis, and their traditional jajmans. The system grew out of and was most active within premodern, feudal political economies. The roles played by patrons and their clients in premodern times created a maze of economic and cultural relationships that were embedded within a set of clearly demarcated social conventions and obligations, which in turn were determined within and shaped by a localized cultural and political framework. Beyond this general overview, however, what we really know about this system is at best piecemeal; it was active among different communities within various strata of society and covered many forms of artistic and cultural activities out of which music and musicians constituted only one part. On the basis of information currently available it is therefore neither possible, nor desirable, to reduce the diverse workings of this system to a single set of classificatory parameters or nomenclature. This is because this system of exchange and obligations seems to have varied greatly not only in the details of its practice from place to place and time to time, but also in its name. It was within the logic and workings of the jajmani system that sarodiyas, like many other groups of music specialists prior to the twentieth century, were to make a living and maintain and develop their musical tradition and artistry.[7]

Morsels of ethnographic material on such music specialists in general can be found in the colonial gazetteers compiled by British administrators. These musicians are also occasionally alluded to in regional and general articles on Indian music written in Indian languages and in English. Further ethnographic source material can be found scattered through oral histories, social science research and folklore studies and in the documentary work of state institutions such as the Sangeet Natak Akademi. Neuman (1977, 1980; forthcoming) and Erdman (1985) have written about the social organization of musicians in specific regions of North India. This material implicitly reflects the jajmani system in the eighteenth and nineteenth centuries, which comprised matrices of networks and individual relationships active across a range of musical styles, status, numbers, religions and castes spread over the entire north and north-west of the subcontinent.

The British ethnologist Ibbetson includes all endogamous communities of music specialists in the north-west of the subcontinent under the generic term mirasi (1970, vol. 2:106). In his account, Ibbetson provides a glimpse of the lives of these music specialists among which players of the rabab and sarod have also been listed. As a generic term, mirasi—originally derived from 'miras', Arabic and Persian for 'inheritance'—possesses an ensemble of meanings. The role of this category of musicians was to commit to memory and recite the genealogies of their individual jajmans or collective patron groups. Sometimes the word mirasi was abbreviated to mir and appended as a title to a musician's family name. According to Ibbetson, mir mirasis are panegyrists, but the term mir is applied to mirasis out of courtesy as well. It is also said that the term mir mirasi means one who is the mirasi of the amir or the wealthy (1970, vol. 2:109).

Like all the client classes, the mirasis' social status varies with that of their individual patrons and patron groups. The mirasis permanently attached to a Rajput clan are said to have had a higher social status than those who were merely strolling players or casual attendants at a jat wedding (Ibbetson 1970, vol. 2:106). If the position of a patron group rose within a given social and political milieu, it seemed that the position of their musicians also similarly improved.

The social and musical function of the mirasis from the north-west region, as described by Ibbetson, was to sing songs '. . . in praise of God, the Prophet, Pirs and heroes . . . to accompany their masters in war as minstrels . . . [and] to keep horse stallions for breeding.' (1970, vol. 2:107) The following, recorded towards the end of the last century, encapsulates a mirasi's view of their function:

> Guniyan ke sagar hain, zat ke ujgar hain, bhikari badhshhon ke;
> Parbhom ke Mirasi, Singhon ke Rabab, Qawwal Pirzadon ke;
> Sabhi hamen janat hain, dum maljadon ke.
>
> We are the ocean of knowledge (gun), enlighteners of castes, beggars of kings, Mirasis (hereditary bards) of our patrons, Rabbis of the Sikhs, and Qawwal (story tellers) of the Pirzadas (Shaikhs). All men know us, we are the Dums of the wealthy (1970, vol. 2:119).

Music specialists who played the 'rabab or sarod'[8] are listed by Ibbetson as the mirasis of the Pathans and are named as sarodis (1970, vol. 2:115). From this and other ethnographic information examined in later chapters we know that, in the past, patronage for these Pashtun musicians in their homelands came through jajmani networks and that these networks shared common cultural and economic patterns with the experiences and functions of musician groups in culturally contiguous areas such as Punjab and Baluchistan. After the migration of large numbers of Pashtuns to India in the late seventeenth and eighteenth centuries, the jajmani system continued to determine transactions between sarodiyas and their patrons well into the nineteenth century.

Ibbetson divides mirasis into at least forty ethnic and cultural groups. Recent ethnographic research in Rajasthan by Neuman and Chaudhuri have indicated even greater levels of complexity and subtlety in the social and cultural contracts that existed between mirasis and their jajmans than was previously understood.[9] In the light of this recent research, information provided in gazetteers and colonial records, admirable in their efforts and useful for modern-day research, have also to be approached with some degree of circumspection.

The following list of mirasis from Mianwali, compiled by Ibbetson (1970, vol. 2:118), is approached with this sense of discretion in mind. It ranks a number of groups of hereditary musicians in the following order:

1. Pirain or Pirhain.
2. Mirasi, i.q. Dum.
3. Kalawant.
4. Sarodi.[10]
5. Dhadhi, also called Rawa or Shaikhana.
6. Bhand.

Ibbetson (1970, vol. 2:119) goes on to describe these categories as:

> The Kalawant is a musician more skilled than the Mirasi (i.e. Dum); and the Sarodi resembles him but plays on the rabab or sarod and performs also as a tumbler. The Dhadhi is a genealogist or story teller and is not attached to any particular family or tribe .

Perhaps the first thing to note about the above categories of musicians, with the exception of the sarodi, is that they are also names of musician communities which have at one time been common in North India, among Rajput and Sikh communities in particular. There is, consequently, much variation in the definitions available of these musicians, their functions, identities and status, depending on where and when they lived. For instance, Nahata uses the term kalawant to denote a koum[11] of musicians who originated in Rajasthan and whose background was unequivocally Hindu (1961:27). Specifically, it was commonly used to describe a particular community of Rajput mirasis around Gwalior and the western parts of India.[12] At the same time, it was a title of honour conferred upon the best musicians in the court of the Mughal emperor Akbar (1556–1605) where it was a marker of musical status and not of ethnicity (Fazl 1973, vol. 2:279; Imam 1959:14).

Nahata also describes an endogamous caste of Hindu dhadhi (male) and dhadhin (female) musicians and dancers from Marwar in Rajasthan who, in ancient times, used to sing and dance in temples devoted to Krishna (1961:27). He further states that, at some later period, dhadhis were also employed as musicians by the Rajput courts (Nahata 1961:27–28). Writing in the mid-1800s, Imam confirms the connection between Rajputs and dharis [dhadhis], whom he states are

> the oldest community among the musicians. By tracing their history we know that they were originally Rajputs. They sang Karka [khadhka or Rajput military songs]. During the Muslim rule of the past, they embraced Islam (1959:18).

Bor, writing about dhadhis in the sixteenth century, contends that,

> Dhadhis were originally professional folk musicians from Rajputana and the Punjab who specialized in singing war songs and heroic ballads called karkha and bar, . . . other dhadhis played on instruments such as the rabab and sarangi (1986:59–60).

The spread of dhadhis over a wide geographical area is confirmed by Crooke who, writing in the late nineteenth century, adds that 'there is a Hindu and a Mohammedan branch [of dhadhis] amongst which the [1883] Census lists some forty sections' (1974, vol. 2:276–77). In Punjab, dhadhis are so named because they played on the hand-drum dhadh to whose accompaniment they sang songs in praise of God or their patrons.[13] This large number of social sub-divisions within the wider community of dhadhis can be expected to have generated an equivalent diversity in musical practice. Whereas Bor mentions that some dhadhis played rabab and sarangi, Ibbetson says that a dhadhi in Dejarat (on the Pakistan-Afghanistan border) ' . . . only chants and never, it is said, plays on an instrument.' (1970, vol. 2:234)

The geographical, social and musical diversity that exists among these musicians is also evident in the various pronunciations used to describe them. In the above discussion it has been shown that Rajputs referred to these musicians as dhadhis, Panjabis as dhadhis and the Mughals as dhari. While the difference between dhadhis and dharis may be explained as regional variations in language it seems likely, as Nahata argues, that after the Muslims came to India these older terms were corrupted to dhari due to the trouble that Persian speakers, such as the Mughals, had with the pronunciation of the retroflex sound, dh (1961:27).

The most general and widespread use of the term dom is to describe a Hindu caste of untouchables who carried out the work of cremation. However, dom or dum mirasis are quite distinct from them and have been described by Crooke as a group of '. . . hereditary bards or minstrels to the lower tribes, as the Bhat is to the Rajput . . . They are seemingly closely akin to the Dhadhi, and the Muhammadan Mirasis and Dhadhi appear to intermarry and eat together . . . The men are musicians, story tellers and genealogists; the women dance and sing, but they are said to perform only in the presence of women and are reputedly chaste' (1974, vol. 3:496). Like Crooke, Ibbetson was also working on this compilation at the end of the nineteenth century and provides this contrasting description of doms (1970, vol. 2:107):

> In Dera Ghazi Khan [a district around Baluchistan], the Dum is also called Lang, and is said to be the mirasi of the Baloch, using the sarinda and singing Balochi songs in praise of God, the Prophet, Pirs and heroes. The Langa also keep the Baloch pedigrees and in former times used to accompany their masters in war as minstrels . . . Then again the Mirs or Dum of Dera Ghazi Khan used to keep horse stallions for breeding and he still does so in the Bozdar hills.

However, by the early nineteenth century, musicians and dancers known respectively as doms and domnis in North India came to have strong associations with courtesan and urban kotha culture.

A similar range of definitions are also attached to the term bhand who are most commonly described as storytellers, jokers or buffoons. The name comes from Sanskrit/Hindi 'bhanda' which means buffooning '. . . [and they are] commonly kept by [the wealthy] like the jester of the early English noble, but also wander about the country and perform to street audiences' (Ibbetson 1970, vol. 2:83). In North India, mention is made of these musicians as entertainers, mimics and acrobats (Sharar 1975:143–45)

Pirain or Pirhain are presumably other names for qawwal, a well-known term originating in Persia to describe the mirasis of Sufi Pirs, but one which is equally subject to the same variety of definitions and descriptions as the above terms. Therefore it is clear that the use of such terms to describe individuals and groups of musicians must be carefully discerned and contextualized clearly according to the place and time in which it is found.

Despite any differences in the way these musical terms may be applied in other regions, it is nevertheless clear from Ibbetson's description (1970, vol. 2:110) that sarodis were regarded as a distinct category of musicians who are specifically defined as:

> mirasis of the Pathans [who] also claim Pathan descent. But the same account says they are descendants of the Prophet. They are described as endogamous.

Sarodi is not a term found among Rajputs or Sikhs, and for this reason it may be that it was confined to Pathans, whereas the other terms discussed above were found right across North India and the north-west provinces. Besides sarodis, there were four other groups of mirasis—Baral, Ghori, Kak and Pahli—whom Ibbetson also mentions as being attached to the Afghans (1970, vol. 2:113). Therefore it may have been the case that sarodis were only one among a few groups of mirasis traditionally tied to jajmans in their region. It is also implied by Ibbetson that the musical status of sarodis was comparable to kalawants, and therefore above the musical status of other hereditary bards in the region. Having stated this, it is interesting to note that Ibbetson then also describes them as tumblers, a distinction usually reserved for bhands and nats in North India. This observation has so far remauned uncorroborated in other available sources, which does not mean that this was not the case but again points to the care needed in firstly, dealing with the subject of mirasis and secondly, in approaching source material.

Ethnographic information suggests that the musical functions of sarodis were the singing of ballads and panegyrics of heroes, accompanying their patrons to war and possibly, keeping genealogies. Despite a lack of documentation that would connect sarodis with the last of these functions, the role of these musicians as accompanists to Pathan war parties is relatively well known.[14] Mukhopadhyay (1977:45) records the most widely-held belief about this role:

> When the Afghans would go into battle they were accompanied by the Kabuli rabab. These rababiyas were known as mirs, and they used

to hang the instrument around their necks and lead the forces into battle on foot. They arrived in India playing the instrument like that.

The association between the sarod and the military activity of the Pathans is clearly articulated by Keramatullah Khan, a descendant of a family of musicians who migrated to India in the early eighteenth century:

> One thousand years ago the sarod was being used in Afghanistan and was considered both a popular and a worthy instrument because its sound was reputed to invoke valour and bravery. Consequently it became the official instrument of the military forces. It came to India about two hundred and fifty years back; but it has always undergone many and varied innovations. Therefore the present day product is the result of hundreds of such changes (Keramatullah Khan 1908:2–4).

Amjad Ali Khan, the well-known contemporary descendant of another lineage of Pathan sarodiyas, has frequently stated that his forefathers not only played the rabab but were also soldiers of fortune and horse breeders. They belonged to the Bangash tribe of Pathans who inhabited an area in the east of the Pathan homelands, now in Pakistan. He specifically mentions that his principal ancestor, Ghulam Ali Bangash, was a risaldar or cavalryman (Malhotra 1973:17).

Illyas Khan (1920–89), a later relative of Keramatullah Khan (1851–1933), states that apart from being sarodiyas, two of his ancestors who were also from the Bangash community came to India as fauz ka zamadars (recruiters and commanders of a platoon of mercenaries).[15] Najaf Ali Khan (1705–60) came from the town of Jalalabad in the Kabul district. Karimullah Khan (n.d.) was a resident of Ghazni, a district south of Kabul. Another ancestor, Madar Khan (1704–52), is mentioned by Irfan Khan as being the brother or first cousin of Karimullah Khan but he is not sure about his place of origin in the Pathan homelands.[16]

Though this information is inadequate, some interesting points can be made about sarodis:

i) that they are described as playing the sarod or the rabab;

ii) that these musicians are identified as sarodis suggests the existence of the term 'sarod' among Pathans long before its use to describe a Hindustani instrument invented in the mid-nineteenth century;

iii) that the rabab, or one type of rabab, or the rabab used in a particular way, or the rabab belonging to a specific Pathan clan, may have been known as sarod before the invention of the modern Hindustani instrument;

iv) that sarodis were part of a larger community of mirasis that spread from their homelands right across North India and therefore were by no means unique in their range of musical as well as non-musical functions, identity or their participation in jajmani networks;

v) that the main source of their patronage appears to have emanated from the military culture and military leaders of the Pathans;

vi) that this association between sarodis and the Pathan military and the functions they performed was also shared by musicians in other cultures in the region.

Fortunately, some details of the military functions of musicians who played on short-necked bowed lutes in regions geographically and culturally contiguous to the Pathan homelands do exist. For example, at the turn of the eighteenth century, a Venetian traveller, Nicholas Manucci (1656–1717), observed Rajput musicians playing the sarinda around Baluchistan. Bor quotes:

> When they drew near to their enemy, their musicians began to sing songs in a loud voice, with a violin accompaniment in praise of their courage. These musicians are also on horseback and well armed, all drunk with opium, their eyes flaming and red . . . I have sometimes seen some of them so impatient that, on hearing the violins strike up, though the enemy was still far off, they rode out of their squadron, and, putting their horses to full speed, galloped like madmen into the middle of the foemen, and there sacrificed their lives (1987:61).

Bor relates another account of the English traveller Robert Coverte, who was met by a group of Baluchi musicians around the Pakthunistan and Baluchistan border in 1610:

> . . . earely in the morning, and about breake of day wee met with tenne or twelve men playing Fiddles, as if they had come in a friendly manner to welcome us, but indeed they were no better then Theeves that intended to rob and pillage us, for by the Sun rising we were

> beset round them and their companions, whose certaine number we could not discern nor know (1987:61).

The fiddle commonly played by Baluchi musicians is the surod. Therefore, it is reasonable to expect that the fiddle played by the musicians from Baluchistan in the above passage was this same instrument. Another bowed double-chested fiddle from the Sistan and Baluchistan region of Iran (west of Pakistani Baluchistan) is also known as surod. This instrument is morphologically identical to its cousin from further east. The same military function could be ascribed to the Persian bowed lute known as the saroz, but which is also referred to as geychak (Bor 1986:10). Also in Baluchistan is a long-necked plucked lute resembling a larger version of a Persian setar which too is known as sarod. While documented accounts by travellers of Pathan sarodis playing the rabab or sarod in such a situation are not as yet forthcoming, stories and other oral accounts tend to project a similar imagery associated with these musicians.

The listing of non-musical occupations of mirasis also adds another level to our understanding of the complexities of the jajmani system. It seems common for sarodis to have also had non-musical occupations, but it is not possible to say how time was divided between various pursuits. Amjad Ali Khan says his forefather played on the rabab in his 'spare time'. Be that as it may, these non-musical roles were still in some ways connected with service provision to the military, either directly as soldiers or indirectly, as breeders or suppliers of horses. For many sarodis, it appears that the performance of music was not their full-time or only profession.

The Rabab

According to some accounts, the rabab played by Pathans is the direct antecedent of the Hindustani sarod. Without wishing to engage this claim at this point in the discussion, it must be noted that physical similarities exist between the two instruments out of which the sympathetic strings and the cut-away sections, or waisting, between the resonator and the neck are the most striking. There are many other features that organologically distinguish the two instruments. However, before contemplating any historical connection between them, it would be worthwhile to consider a closer look at the Pathan instrument. As will be evident from later discussion, the Kabuli rabab is distinct both from the larger rabab played in Punjab and that played by seniyas in the Mughal court.[17]

The overall shape of the rabab somewhat resembles a club used in battle. The resonator forms the widest part of the instrument from which its body tapers off gradually along the neck towards the pegbox. By contrast, the taper that connects the underside of the resonator to the back of the neck is quite pronounced, with the resulting distinctive shape sometimes being called the 'camel's hump'. This rabab is normally crafted out of a single piece of wood, mulberry or walnut, which is hollowed out by hand from the resonating chamber to the upper nut. A piece of goat's skin is stretched over the resonating chamber, which makes a drum-like sound when lightly tapped with the fingers. The main bridge, made of camel bone or deer horn, is positioned on top of this skin. A wooden fingerboard, sometimes inlaid with intricate designs fashioned from mother-of-pearl, is fitted on top of the carved neck. There are either three or four movable gut frets attached to the fingerboard. The pegbox, which curls back from the end of the fingerboard, is often carved out in the shape of a bird's head.

The number of strings on the instrument varies from twelve to eighteen, of which six are main playing strings. These are made from animal gut and are tied at one end to the tailpiece, passed over the top of the bridge and threaded through small holes in each of the six tuning pegs which run laterally through the pegbox. According to Day (1974:128) and Kukertz (1976:20), the main strings of this rabab were tuned C, F, G-G, c-c, that is, the strings tuned to the two highest pitches being doubled. Notwithstanding this description, the rabab is currently tuned C, G, c-c, f-f, which suggests that the tuning given by Day may be unreliable. The instrument has a potential melodic range of between one and a half and two and a half octaves, depending upon the construction of the instrument and the technique of the performer.

The other seven to eleven strings, known as taraf or sympathetic strings, were earlier made of copper or brass, although steel strings are now used. They are also fixed to the tailpiece but run through small holes drilled through the bridge and so, are positioned underneath the main strings. They are then threaded through small holes made in a row in the upper fingerboard and attached to pegs that are positioned in holes drilled along the upper length of the neck with the lowest-tuned string closest to the pegbox. The positioning of these strings under the main gut strings means that they are normally not struck directly. On some rababs there is also a drone string positioned closest to the plucking hand of the performer. The sympathetic strings are tuned diatonically (involving the tones of a scale without chromatic alteration) according to the basic scale of the music to be played. There are, therefore, two tiers of strings on this type of rabab—the main gut strings and the metallic sympathetic strings—with each tier clearly demarcated by its positioning and its acoustic properties.

One distinguishing characteristic of the Pathan rabab is the markedly indented waist, variations upon which occur on lutes found in the local regions of Sind, Baluchistan and Sistan, where such an indentation facilitates bowing. However, the overall size and shape of the Pathan rabab with its double courses of strings, makes it unlikely that such an instrument would have been bowed despite occasional allusions to this practice.[18] Instead, the main strings are plucked with a triangular plectrum made from wood or bone. When played, the rabab was generally held at an angle across the body of a seated musician, with the resonator in the lap and the pegbox close to the left shoulder.

It was previously mentioned that there are a number of rababs or rabab-like instruments from the subcontinent that can be compared with the Pathan rabab. Thus the rabab played in Kashmir is identical to that played by Pathans. Surprisingly, however, the existence of this Kashmiri rabab has been generally ignored in the retelling of the histories of the sarod. We do not know whether this instrument was introduced into Kashmir by the Pathans or vice versa or if both developed independently of each other. We do know, however, that many different designs and types of plucked short-necked lutes are played across the region from Afghanistan to Assam (cf. Plates 2-1 and 2-2) and that the Pathan rabab is one among these many.

The overall shape of the instrument, the skin-covered resonator and wooden fingerboard, places the Pathan rabab among a widespread pool of similar short-necked plucked lutes evident throughout the north and north-west of the subcontinent. On the other hand, the taraf and the indented waist of the instrument positions the Pathan rabab within a more localized area—the north-west of the subcontinent—where its features are shared by bowed instruments such as the sarinda, known in Baluchistan as surod and in Sistan as sorud.[19] While other instruments with sympathetic strings in the region are all bowed, the Pathan rabab, and the Kashmiri rabab for that matter, are the only plucked lutes with sympathetic strings. The design and specific characteristics of the Pathan rabab are also found to exist in different configurations not only in the north-west of the subcontinent but right across North India.

Etymological Origins of Sarod

On the subcontinent, attempts to trace the genesis of the instrument have become inextricably entangled with the etymology of sarod. Alongside the ploy of linking the name of this instrument to a particular language, be it Greek, Persian or Sanskrit, lurks a tacit implication that also stakes a claim on the origins of the instrument in the culture of that language. Thus, Keramatullah Khan asserts that sarod is a Greek word, while Dick contends that the word comes from the Persian verb sarodan, meaning 'to sing' (*NGDMI* 1984, vol. 3:298). Amjad Ali Khan has stated that sarod is a Persian word meaning 'melody' but he has also said that it is a Persian/Farsi word meaning 'mausiqi' (music).[20] Others have mentioned that the term came from the Farsi word shahrud ('the king of lutes'), which was supposedly an instrument invented around 913 CE in the Abn-At-Abbas region of Samarkand (*SRA 1* 1991:9). Another etymology, espoused by Sourindra Mohun Tagore in his book on Indian musical instruments, *Yantrakosha*, traces sarod to the Sanskrit word sharad, which means 'autumn' (1976:28). Although Tagore's explanation now has few believers, his attempt is evidence of the proclivity of sections of the Bengali bourgeoisie towards the end of the nineteenth century to 'Sanskritize' North Indian culture, a process which sought to filter out of its purview non-Hindu participation in the development of Indian music.

It is therefore helpful at this stage to assume a position at a little distance from these speculations and approach the issue of etymology from a different perspective. To begin with, it is often implied in the above accounts that sarod was first introduced as a musical term in India during the mid-nineteenth century when the Kabuli rabab was supposedly modified to become the Hindustani sarod. Despite this proximity in time, it is not known who actually gave the Indian instrument this name, or in doing so, the reasons for choosing the word 'sarod' for it. It is therefore worthwhile considering the following points:

i) the term sarod has been a part of musical nomenclature in Persia for centuries where it has a general meaning derived from the old Farsi verb sarodan ('to sing') and a specific one which refers to a genre of music, thus:

> Contemporary national, institutional and instructional anthems are called soruds . . . The sorud, unlike tasnif and tarane is meant to be sung by a group, not just by an individual (Caton 1982:26).

ii) documented descriptions of a double-chested fiddle in Baluchistan called surod and in Sistan, sorud, date back to the seventeenth century.[21] While the design of these bowed instruments clearly differs from the Pathan rabab, information indicates that these bowed lutes also had military applications.

iii) statements by Mukhopadhyay ('the name Kabuli rabab only came into vogue in India, in Afghanistan it was known as surud' [1977:46]), Keramatullah Khan (1908), Imam (1959:24), Gangopadhyay (*SRA 1* 1991:50)[22] and Hasan (1983:114) suggest that a Kabuli rabab or a type of rabab was referred to as surud or sarod long before the invention of the modern instrument.

iv) in premodern times, the mirasis of the Pathans were known as sarodis who, we are told, 'played the rabab or sarod.'

It may be possible to read various different meanings into this material, but it does reasonably point to the term having currency and meaning in at least some part of Pathan culture before the invention of the Hindustani sarod. Hence, its choice as a name for the

Hindustani instrument, in whose invention these Pathan musicians played a significant role, was perhaps not as arbitrary as is often implied in the accounts of the origins of the term but was something that appeared to be already grounded in the musical practice of the region.

However, additional questions need to be addressed before this line of reasoning can be properly substantiated. In particular, it is important to know why Baluchi and Sistani short-necked bowed lutes are called sorud and surod.[23] Can this sharing of a common term be imputed to these instruments sharing similar functions in their respective militias? Could it be because they engaged in similar military functions and the military-based music they played was analogous to the Persian musical genre described as patriotic group singing by Caton?

Alternately, could it have something to do with the fact that of the many Pathan clans, the development of the Hindustani sarod has been, as later chapters establish, most commonly connected with the Bangash? Within the Pathan homelands, it was the area inhabited by the Bangash that lay closest to Baluchistan and Sistan and the cultural influence of Persia. This geographical and cultural proximity may account for why the instruments of this region shared this term. At the same time it may also account for the instrument being more commonly known as rabab elsewhere in the homelands. Whether bowed or not, the rabab was certainly referred to by that name and not as sarod in the Lodi and Mughal courts in India.[24] Is it possible that its subsequent use in India may have been derived from the greater representation of Bangash centres of power in the Indo-Afghan empire of the eighteenth century than had previously occurred during Pathan rule in India?[25]

These questions warrant a separate study. In the meantime, perhaps the most concrete position that can be put forward is that the naming of the sarod was not an arbitrary decision but one derived from nomenclature already existing in at least some part of Pathan culture before the invention of the Hindustani instrument. Therefore, even though the etymology of the term can quite easily be traced to Persia, its use as a Hindustani musical term was directly derived from the way it was earlier found and practised in the Pathan homelands.

Accounting for Terminology

From both the earlier and ensuing discussion it will be evident that a problem exists in the consistent use of musical terminology to describe Pathan musicians and their instrument. Like many terms in Hindustani music, the meaning and significance of a term can vary according to the cultural context and historical period in which it is found. Thus, in the eighteenth century, the terms rabab and sarod were used both within Pashtun communities in their homelands and in India to describe what is nowadays most commonly known in India as the Kabul rabab or Afghan rabab. The qualifier 'Kabuli' or 'Afghani' has been added in India to differentiate this instrument from the Indian or seniya rabab.

In Pashtun, the players of this 'Afghani' instrument were known as rababis or sarodis. However, once these musicians became part of descriptions of Hindustani music, they became known as rababiyas or sarodiyas in this new linguistic and cultural environment. Further, it is often assumed that the use of the term sarod was first formulated by Pathans in India to mark the invention of a new instrument some time in the mid-nineteenth century. However, as later discussion shows, the term sarod was already in use, for example by Imam (1959), in accounts of Hindustani music in Lucknow to describe the Kabul rabab before the invention of the Hindustani sarod occurred and further, the musicians that played this instrument were referred to as sarodiyas.

After the invention of the Hindustani sarod, the terms sarodiya and sarodi in India exclusively came to refer to the players of the Hindustani instrument. The terms Kabuli or Afghani rabab have been more uniformly used to describe the rabab/sarod played by Pashtuns and to differentiate it from the modern Hindustani sarod. This is the way the terms are generally understood today. Yet in the early history of the sarod tradition in India the use of these terms were obviously not so clearly defined. In order to avoid the confusion of having to qualify a particular term every time it appears in ensuing discussions, the following convention has been adopted in this study. The rabab/sarod played by Pathans prior to the invention of the Hindustani sarod will be referred to in this text as the Afghani rabab and its musicians as Afghani rababiyas. The term sarod and sarodiya will be used in this text, outside of specific quotes from other sources, to describe the modern Hindustani instrument and its players.

Sound Sources

It is one thing to describe the Afghani rabab based on what we can see of the instrument and how it is played, but it is a different matter altogether to write about the qualities of the sound that can be produced on it. How is the sound we hear now different or similar to what Pathan musicians heard two hundred years ago? On the basis of comparison of contemporary rababs and those in museums or private collections that have survived over the last couple of centuries, the instrument appears to have changed little in design or material culture. It seems to have retained the fundamental characteristics of its sound over this period.

It is true to say that sound is given expression through musical style and genre. It is also the case that style and genre can be historicized, i.e. in a particular period, a particular genre of music was played and was later followed by another genre. However, it is not so easy to say this about sound. This may be because sound is located within, and tends to respond to, its own matrix—the instrument, the musician and the wider culture of sound and its aesthetic conventions. The qualities of musical sound depend upon the quality of each of these separate parts—the quality of the instrument, the quality of the musicianship, the quality of internalization of the aesthetic conventions of musical sound, along with the quality of the intuition and understanding of the interaction that takes place between them.

Each of these parts on its own may be subject to historical change. Advances in technology may bring about changes in the material culture or design of the instrument. Changes in performance practice or the functions of musicians may have an effect on musicianship. Changes in the cultural ideology of sound may occur due to the influence of new patron groups or perhaps even because of changes in performance criteria. The nature of the above matrix is such that if change occurs in any one part, the effects are likely to be felt in the other two. For example, new influences and experiences in the wider culture of sound might be expressed in the modification of an instrument or changes in the technique of the musician. Or alternately, if an instrument is introduced into an unfamiliar soundscape, then over time it is likely that the instrument becomes adapted to, or 'indigenized' within, that new environment and musical techniques developed for playing it.[26] Yet, due to the indeterminate numbers of musicians, instruments and countless interpretations of sound involved, any changes, adaptations or modifications that do take place are neither uniform nor able to be plotted in a linear manner.

As this study is not concerned with documenting the history of the Afghani rabab beyond what has already been provided, the following section focuses on those components and sound properties of the instrument relevant to a later investigation of the origins of, and influences on, the sound of the Hindustani sarod. Out of these, the resonant properties of the rabab figure prominently in the discussion because it is a defining characteristic of both the rabab and the sarod and also because, in this instance, it gives a unique depth to their respective sounds.

Resonance and Sustain

The components of the instrument which act on or contribute to its overall sound and characteristic resonance are many—the strings, the skin-covered resonator, the bridges, frets, the wood and so on. Leaving the rest aside for the moment, and just focusing on the strings, it is evident that there are two tiers of sound derived from the main strings on the one hand and the sympathetic strings on the other. The main strings, made of gut, are pressed over gut frets with the fingers of the left hand against a wooden fingerboard. Most of the notes produced on the instrument use these frets; other notes, particularly those in the upper octave of the rabab, can also be produced by pressing these strings directly onto the fingerboard. Plucked with a wooden or bone plectrum and utilizing the other materials already mentioned, the gut strings on their own produce a note which has little sustain or resonance due to the combination of the acoustic properties of wood, gut strings, frets and the flesh of the fingertips. If the shape of the note's attack and decay can be described visually, it could be said to resemble a teardrop. That is, after the initial excitement of the strings that comes with the strike of the plectrum, there is a fairly rapid and uniform decay of sound. However, when the notes produced on the main strings are coupled with the effect of the copper or bronze sympathetic strings, two things begin to happen. One, the overall volume of the instrument becomes louder and its sound can carry over a greater distance. Two, on a very subtle level, the shape of the note or its envelope of sound is altered. This is to say that if a single note on the main string is struck, a sympathetic string tuned to an equivalent pitch, and sometimes others tuned to its related harmonic series, begin to resonate in response. Being made of metal, the sympathetic strings sound for a longer period than the plucked main strings even though they are themselves not plucked directly. Because of the slight delay between these two events, the decay of the note produced on the main string is slightly affected. This is because the two sounds merge, causing the period of decay or the sustain of the note to be extended, and the above teardrop shape of the note then tends to becomes elongated. So that even while the actual decay of the note on the main string fades away quickly, the memory of it passes through to the sympathetic strings. In this way the sympathetic strings capture the surplus sound energy of the main strings and convert them into partials and harmonics which in turn modify the note transients.

While this may be the case for an isolated note, when a sequence of notes is played on the main strings, waves of resonance flow out of the sympathetic strings with undulations created by the strings in various states of excitement and decay. Given all the right performance conditions, the overall effect produced by these two tiers of sound and their subtle interaction is perhaps the most defining characteristic of the rabab. The backdrop of sound created as the sympathetic strings go through cycles of excitement, resonance and then decay, is capable of producing complex and shifting textures of sound. The ebb and flow of these cycles on numbers of strings in different permutations and combinations follow the melodic contours of the notes produced on the main strings. The waves of sound produce a type of shimmering effect further enriched by the swirling of harmonics and partials thrown up by the waves, thus giving a distinctive 'flavour' to the sound. Against the sustained resonance of this sonic backdrop, the notes of the main string appear in consonance, dissonance or assonance—but always contrasted in some way.

A musician will directly and significantly contribute to the quality and flavour of this sound in a number of ways. This may be done through their 'touch' on the main strings with their left hand and the control over the subtleties of the right-hand plectrum technique. These properties are in turn also enormously reliant on the timing and co-ordination between the hands of the musician in striking the instrument. The sound quality of the instrument can be further enhanced through the accuracy applied in tuning and, most importantly, the mood that a musician brings to an occasion. Musicians also contribute to this process of sound production indirectly and more subtly by their sensitivity, aural skills and the degree of internalization of a wider soundscape. All these attributes, in other words, constitute the conditions and contingencies of a performance practice.

Generally speaking, it is not possible to account for all the situations and circumstances in which the rabab was played, be it solo, in small or large groups of other rababiyas, as accompanists for ballad singers or community martial dancing such as the Pathan katthak dance. It comes across clearly that the Pathan military musicians described in oral histories of the sarod therefore could be counted as only one group within a larger fraternity of Afghani rababiyas. Out of all the performance situations in which the rabab was found, theirs could hardly be counted as the most ideal. Though it could be argued that, under the right conditions, the sympathetic strings of the rabab helped to raise the volume of sound of the instrument in outdoor situations but, given the din of the battlefield, one would expect this effect to have been negligible. Notwithstanding this situation, Quddus (1987:92) has captured the most commonly-held popular imagery of these musicians in this rather romantic description:

> And then around the campfires, on the furrowed fields and in the hujras,[27] they sing of their bloody battles, of their golden crops, of their unexcelled hospitality, of their unending blood feuds, of their outlaws, of their weapons, and of their love and sorrows and suffering.

On the limited basis of available oral accounts, it can be tentatively suggested that on the whole they would have performed outdoors, not as soloists but in accompaniment to other activities—processions, ballads or leading the troops—and the locations would include the battlefield and military camps. The comparison of sarodis with kalawants, if true, suggests that these musicians did exhibit music skills that would afford them some status within the larger fraternity of mirasi musicians—a prospect which may suggest that there were also soloists among sarodis.[28] Generally speaking, the range and depth of the aesthetic conventions informing the musical practice of sarodis would have been grounded fundamentally in their participatory role within a community in which their jajmans also resided, and defined by a specific range of cultural functions. Perhaps the most valued among these was the function of invoking valour among the troops, although how this may have been achieved is not known. In fact, at the end of the day, we do not have a clear impression of the performance practice of these musicians or even of their precise roles in playing martial music.

Conclusion

Musicians of Pathan background have played fundamental and pivotal roles in the development of the sarod tradition in India. We are, however, left only with an impression of their past and their functions as mirasis within their own communities before their migration to India. We know that Pathans had musicians known as sarodis who were mirasis and that they accompanied their armies into battle as soldiers or musicians or at least received patronage from the military through other non-musical services that they provided, such as supplying horses or as troops themselves. The roles played by these musicians do not seem to have been unique but were shared by musicians in culturally contiguous regions.

The legacy of this music culture in the development of the Hindustani sarod tradition can be linked to at least three areas—the name of the instrument, some specific design features of the Kabuli rabab and the contribution of the descendants of Pathan musicians in India—that have a direct bearing on the process of the invention and popularization of the sarod. However, the rabab played by the Pathans was not entirely unique in conception or design and many of its defining features could be found in different configurations in other instruments. It shared both of its names, rabab and sarod, and certain design and acoustic features such as the indented waist and sympathetic strings, with other instruments in contiguous regions. Specifically, the term rabab was used in Kashmir and Punjab, while the term sarod was used in Baluchistan and Sistan. It also shares a more general affinity in overall structure and design with a host of other short-necked plucked lutes from right across the north of the subcontinent, some of which, like the chitra vina, date back for almost two millennia.

Notes

1 According to the 1891 Census of India, there were more than 700,000 Pathans in India, out of which the Yusufzai, numbering 114,692, were the single largest group (Crooke 1974, vol. 4:170–71).

2 Stephens (1955:230) stresses the broad cultural affinity between Persia and the Durranis, 'The Afghan royal house, largely Persian by culture, is Pathan by race.'

3 The three aspects of Pathan interaction that Pakhtunwali prevails over, which are invariably interconnected, are badal: revenge through retaliation regardless of cost or consequence; melmastia: open hospitality and protection to all who may demand it; nanawati: essentially an extension of melmastia which has earlier been thought of as asylum but is defined as a supplicant asking for sanctuary from an aggrieved party for a past indiscretion rather than the supplicant merely surrendering themselves (Crooke 1974, vol. 4:168).

4 Some members of the Bangash and Orakzai clans are known to be Shias but they are in the minority relative to the Sunni. Even rarer

are the pockets of Pathans in more inaccessible areas who have remained with beliefs which pre-date Islam (Spain 1963:85–86).

5 Personal communication with Illyas Khan, 1982 and Irfan Khan, 1998. Also recounted by Gangopadhyay in *SRA 1* 1991:50.

6 This dance apparently takes its name from the Katthak tribe or division of Pathans; for a brief description, see Quddus (1987:93). This particular dance bears no relation to the kathak dance of North India.

7 Hereditary social and occupational categories of musicians such as dom, dhadhi, qawwal, kalawant, bhand, and charan, among many others, originated and functioned within the jajmani system. The status of each group and its members varied substantially across region and time depending upon the social standing of their patrons. With the effective marginalization of the jajmani system in the nineteenth century, our understanding of the meaning, practices and terminology of this way of organizing musical activity has similarly receded over time. See Neuman (1980:124ff.).

8 Sarod, in this context, refers not to the Hindustani instrument, but as later discussion speculates, was a name that some Pathans used to refer to what is more commonly known outside that region as the Afghani rabab.

9 See Neuman 1975, and also his *An Ethnographic Atlas of Music Traditions in West Rajastan* edited jointly with Shubha Chaudhuri and Komal Kothari (forthcoming from Seagull Books, Calcutta).

10 In this instance 'sarodi' is misprinted as 'sardoi' in Ibbetson. On more than one instance on the following page in Ibbetson, however, these musicians are correctly identified as 'sarodis'.

11 The most common use of the word koum denotes 'a people' or 'a community', but used in this context, it refers to a specific endogamous, hereditary caste.

12 See Erdman (1985:81).

13 Punjabi dhadhis still perform musical functions in the gurudwaras of some Sikh communities but these days seem to be more generally grouped together within the larger and more inclusive group of Sikh ragi musicians.

14 Also see Malhotra (1973:17) and Buddhadev Dasgupta, interviewed by Dipali Nag for Calcutta Doordarshan, 1982.

15 Personal communication: 1982. Also documented in Mukhopadhyay (1977:47).

16 Personal communication: 1998.

17 In other parts of the world, notably South East Asia, rabab exclusively refers to a family of bowed instruments.

18 For example, Day (1974) makes particular reference to the sarod sometimes being bowed in his description of the instrument.

19 On this point the sarod can be linked with the more ubiquitous sarangi, which is generally associated with the west and the northwest of the subcontinent.

20 Personal communication: 1986.

21 The listing of the singer called Sarod Khan by Abul Fazl among the most famous musicians in the court of Akbar also suggests that the term was known in India long before this time.

22 Gangopadhyay states: 'In Kabul this instrument was known as Sharudh. The Sharudh was a little bit smaller than the original rabab and was made [from] the wood of walnut.'

23 In addition to these bowed lutes, I have also come across a long-necked plucked lute from Baluchistan resembling the Persian tambur but which is also called sarod.

24 For example, see Fazl (1973 vol. 3:269), and Kuppuswamy and Hariharan (1984:62–63).

25 According to Gommans, a separate tribe or sub-tribe called Bangash did not exist before the sixteenth century (1999:172).

26 The indigenization of the guitar in Hawaiian and Hindustani music is a good example of this situation. See McNeil (1995).

27 A hujra is a section of a farmyard including the verandah, a special guest room and the open ground immediately in front.

28 This detail is further explored in the next chapter.

Sarodis, Migration and Mohullas

SUCCESSIVE WAVES OF PATHAN MIGRATION to India have occurred since the end of the tenth century AD. By the beginning of the thirteenth century this migration '. . . began on a sizeable scale in the whole of northern India from the Indus to the Brahmaputra' (Quddus 1987:32). The Lodi dynasty (thirteenth to fifteenth century) was the most notable outcome of such migrations. It was from at least this time that the Afghani rabab could be found in India. 'During the Lodi Pathan rule of Delhi by Sultan Zainulabidin (1416–67) . . . some new musical instruments like the Rabab from Persia and Turkestan [were introduced].' (Kuppuswamy and Hariharan 1984:62–63) Umar Khan, from a line of Pashtun musicians who had settled in India, mentions that Afghani rababis and daf (frame drum) players,

> . . . . singing and playing battle and heroic tunes (jang aur bahadur nagmen gate-bajate) led the forces of the Mughal emperor Babar when he arrived in India in the late fifteenth century and that these musicians, who were known as mirs, were looked upon with respect. After the defeat of the Mughal Humayun in the early sixteenth century some of these musicians went to Iran and others remained in India (Umar Khan 1976:95).

A member of a different branch of the same musical lineage, Sakhawat Hussain Khan, claimed that his ancestors were among these musicians in Babar's army. Later descriptions of musical instruments in the *Ain-i-Akbari* mention that a rabab with twelve to eighteen strings, matching that played by Pathans, was evident at the court of the Mughal emperor Akbar.

Despite this long history of Pathan settlement in India, the search for the origins of the Hindustani sarod tradition is confined to the migration that took place in the late seventeenth and eighteenth centuries. Why this should be so is not entirely clear. No doubt a number of reasons may have been responsible for this connection among which the political decentralization following the decline of Mughal paramountcy, the potential opportunities for successor states such as Rohilkhand and the lucrative economic trade in horses with Central Asia are not the least significant. Even as speculation on this question remains open, two things are certain: that the Afghani rabab was known in India long before this period, and that the settlements in which Pathan power had earlier been concentrated in India had disappeared by this time (Gupta 1977:133).

Migration

Not many studies have so far focused on Pathan migration and settlement in India in the eighteenth century. Consequently, the notable aspects and consequences of the political, military, economic, social and cultural dynamics of this historical event have not been reasonably documented.[1] Out of those that have, Gommans has provided the most comprehensive and compelling account of this migration in the eighteenth century and the subsequent establishment of an Indo-Afghan empire. Through extensive documentation, Gommans has alerted us to the historical richness and political importance of this episode in India's past and has provided a vital glimpse of a dynamic experience whose significance in the shaping of modern Indian history is often underestimated. It is also a history in which the lives of sarodiyas and the early development of the sarod tradition were inextricably tied.

We know in general that there were many dimensions to, and consequences of, Pathan migration to India. Along the significant trade routes, regular links were maintained with traders, markets and fairs in the Pathan homelands and deep into Central Asia (Gommans 1999:175). These links carried alongside them religious and political movements and organizations between the north-west cultural orbit and

Pathan settlements in India. Of the many outcomes of the Pathan migration of this period, those relevant to this study are: the establishment of the Rohilla province/state in North India and the linking of Pathan settlements established in India with Central Asian markets. Consequently, these settlements developed, at least for a while, enough political strength and resources to permit Pathan principalities to entertain pretensions as successors to the Mughal state; the melange of clans, tribes, allies and other recruits of the Pathans tended to gravitate around two social and ethnic poles—the Rohilla and the Bangash.

This phase in Indo-Afghan history began in the late seventeenth century when a few Pathan military leaders were granted positions of authority in the Mughal imperial administration in return for their services on the battlefield. The reward also took the form of a grant of a jagir (a defined estate and a control over the revenue it generates). *The Imperial Gazetteer* reports that around this time Muhammad Khan, belonging to the Kaghzai line of the Karlani tribe of Bangash, brought twelve thousand mercenaries to the Mughal emperor Farrukh Siyar and fought on his side, for which he was rewarded with a grant of land in Bundelkhand. In 1714 he obtained a grant nearer his home and founded the city of Farrukhabad (Hunter 1881, vol. 12:64).[2]

The province of Rohilkhand—politically dominated by Rohilla Pathans—which had been forged east of Delhi was considerably expanded after 1739 (Schwartzberg 1978:54). The formation of the province was initiated by Daud Khan, an Afghan soldier of fortune, who had arrived in India from the Kandahar province south of Kabul and settled in a village situated at the south-west corner of the Bareilly district (Hunter 1881, vol. 3:121). At first the Rohillas cohabited peacefully, albeit uneasily, with the Hindu Rajputs who had long been established in this area. However, in a matter of three or four decades, the Pathan forces had gained effective military control of the area and all but expelled these previous occupants.

> By 1742 Ali Muhammad Rohilla [son of Da'ud Khan] had gathered a force of thirty to forty thousand horsemen, besides many others

permanently settled in Rohilkhand (Hunter 1881, vol. 3:121).

Besides this large-scale settlement, Pathan presence in India also appears to have taken the form of small-scale mobile parties of mercenaries or banditti, known as lashkar (irregular army, encampment of an army). Although lashkars were not directly enlisted by a major court, they were either employed by landlords or other such patrons in an ad hoc manner as mercenaries or retainers. Some of these lashkars grew sufficiently in strength and organization to become independent private armies. These militias often seized tracts of land when the Mughals or the local overlords did not have sufficient strength to restrain them from doing so (Gupta 1977:134). Thus various groups of Pathans consolidated their authority over large tracts of land in a continuous block between Delhi and Agra in the west, and between Awadh and Allahabad in the east.

According to census figures in *The Imperial Gazetteer*, the bulk of Pathan settlement in Rohilkhand was in the districts of Shahjahanpur, Bulandshahr, Farrukhabad, Rampur, Muzaffarnagar, Bareilly, Moradabad and Najibabad (Hunter 1881, vol. 12:64–65).[3] Other areas of North India, such as the province of Bundelkhand (a region that now falls in eastern Uttar Pradesh and parts of Bihar), the central Indian states of Tonk and Palanpur, the province of Junagadh in the Kuchh region and an area in South India roughly between Kurnool and Vellore, also had significant Pathan settlements (Gommans 1999:19). Pathan forces in Rohilkhand were strengthened by the steady migration of their kinsfolk throughout the eighteenth century. By 1802 it was thought that there were as many as one hundred thousand mercenaries and banditti in that province alone (Bayly 1983:219).

Rohilkhand took its name from the disparate collection of Pathan clans settled in this area, collectively known in India as Rohillas—after a Pashtu adjective rohelah or rohelai, from rohu, meaning 'mountain' and therefore 'hill people'. According to Bayly (1983:120):

> . . . the Rohillas were a mixture of pedigree Pathan families who had

> fallen on hard times, converted Hindus, and soldier adventurers from the north-western mountains. They were in the process of developing a tribal identity which expressed real or fictive kinship and newly forged marriage alliances. Like other Afghans, they were full of the pride of ancestry, tracing their genealogies back to Abraham.

Rohilla itself is not a Pathan clan name. Whether this term was imposed from outside or not, it served as a means of uniting and identifying a people who, while hailing from various clans, nevertheless shared a cultural and social affinity as well as common financial and political objectives.[4] Gommans (1999:170) clarifies the rather fluid meaning of the term and its evolving function as an inclusive political and social concept.

> The equation of Rohilla with Afghan served to counter the view that Rohillas were merely Indo-Afghan renegades and slaves of mixed origin. Besides the extension of the term Roh opened up the Rohilla ranks for various new immigrants who claimed their origin from Roh. As such it created the idea of a new Afghan enclave which was entirely detached from the once adjacent territories of Hind, Sind, Iran and Turan. It shows . . . that terms like Rohilla or Afghan are not rigid ethnic categories but denote a fluid Indo-Afghan category open to repeated accommodation.

The term Rohilla implied clan neutrality. Any divisiveness based on clan lines would have been politically counterproductive to the establishment of a cohesive and militarily-effective Pathan presence. The various clans became united behind common aims and '. . . there arose the consciousness of the oneness of their race.' (Gupta 1977:135) In addition to the amalgam of Pathan clans labelled as Rohillas in India, other non-Pathan recruits were used to swell their ranks. The incorporation of non-Pathans into the Rohilla fold is suggested by Crooke (1973:58) who adds that under the Pathan 'constitution' it is possible for a number of alien groups to live under the shade of a tribe.

Besides the Rohillas, the Bangash played a significant role in the development of the Indo-Afghan domination. Like the term Rohilla, it seems that Bangash also had a similar connotation of heterogeneity in their homelands. According to Gommans, a separate tribe or sub-tribe called Bangash did not exist before the sixteenth century (1999:172) and Bangash was a collective name for the various tribes that inhabited the region in the Pathan homelands known as Bangash. Like Rohilla, Bangash were thus a mixed community of Pathans. But unlike Rohilla, which only came into use in India, Bangash initially identified a group of people belonging to a localized area in Afghanistan although its definition later became wider and more diffused within the greater cultural mosaic of India.

> The Bangash label served as an external marking vis-à-vis other Hindustani or Afghan groups like Rajputs, Rohillas or Afridis and at the same time could appeal to all sorts of ethnic sub-groups from within the Bangash area (Gommans 1999:173).

It is worth noting that the Bangash Pathans of Farrukhabad considered themselves superior in nasab (ancestry) to the Rohillas.[5]

Engineer (1995:12–13) stresses that markings such as Rohilla and Bangash can denote ethnicity as primordial identity and can also be utilized for negotiating inter-group power and status. The meaning of such terms in any given context was contingent upon the location specified, the period in history and the particular political circumstances in which they were embedded. Gommans' study alerts us to the political, cultural and social complexity of this period which then explains why attempts to reconstruct the formation of the sarod tradition encounters enormous difficulties.

The Indo-Afghan Empire in the Eighteenth Century

Aided by a mild climate and fertile lands, the Rohilla and Bangash nawabs shaped an important province that rivalled its eastern neighbour, Awadh. The increase in land-based revenue and rise in the overall prosperity during this time added to their military authority which was effectively exercised through the region tò add to their collective. Even though Rohilkhand emerged as one of the country's most prosperous agricultural regions in the eighteenth century, it endured a brief, if not eventful, existence of seven decades or so. Opinions of the political achievements of the Rohilla nawabs during this period are generally mixed, ranging from the usual colonial bombast that the rulers exhibited the worst kind of despotism (Barton 1983:222) to rather more salutatory remarks about the efficacy of Pathan administration (Brodkin 1973:131).

The rapid demise of the Indo-Afghan empire in the late eighteenth century can be narrowed down to three primary factors: the wars against them by the British; the sudden disenfranchisement of Pathan military organizations; the demise of the open military market economy of Hindustan and its replacement with a British monopoly over military resources. Having gained military ascendancy over Rohilkhand, the British then retreated and left the administration of the province to Awadh. Within a matter of only twenty years the agricultural economy of Rohilkhand, with the exception of the tiny state of Rampur, was reduced to a state of desolation (Brennan 1970:444–45). Exacerbated by a keen disinterest in the upkeep of the province by the Awadhi administration, this sudden downturn was no doubt further amplified by growing British ambition in the area. The justification the British formulated for finally seizing the area from Awadh for themselves, as Brodkin (1973:138) suggests, struggles to hide the real motive for attacking Rohilkhand in the first place. Rohilkhand was incorporated into the British Raj in 1801, it being the 'duty of the Company . . . to rescue the numerous inhabitants of the country from the grievous and increasing oppression which they suffer under the administrations of a Prince whom the power of the company had placed over them . . .'. The primary British concern following the cession of Rohilkhand was to secure land revenue.

However, any British concerns over the alleged oppression by the 'prince' of Awadh were quickly forgotten in the early 1800s as those remaining in Rohilkhand reeled under the new land-based revenue assessments by their colonial administration (Brennan 1970: 443–465). The colonial revenue assessments precipitated a significant decline in the population during this time and much of the land that had been brought under cultivation by the Rohillas was simply abandoned and left fallow (Brodkin 1973:137).

Faizullah Khan, the last remaining Pathan nawab of the Rohillas, was allowed Rampur as an independent kingdom from the British. The reason behind this act of colonial benevolence is not entirely clear although it is generally assumed that it was because of assistance given to the British during their takeover of the province. The descendants of Faizullah continued to control this area until Indian independence in 1947. The remaining Pathan strongholds in Rohilkhand, and in other areas such as Farrukhabad, were forced by the East India Company to surrender their sovereign rights in the initial decades of the nineteenth century.

Rohilkhand had been the largest of these Pathan states and its demise, the bloodiest. Even after its downfall, rebellions against the British by Pathan soldiers continued, like in Bareilly in 1816. Rohilla mercenaries participated actively in the rebel cause in 1857. At the same time, Pathan mercenaries hired themselves out not only to other Muslim states but also to the Marathas (Kolff 1990:188). The direct takeover of Rohilkhand cleared the way for the British East India Company to turn on their erstwhile allies and orchestrate the annexation of Awadh within decades.

From 1900 onwards, political, religious and trade links between Afghan settlements in India and the north-west and through to Central Asia were severely strained. Significantly, this also meant that the Pathan settlements in inner-India were cut off from the north-west cultural orbit. In the face of this isolation, those Pathans who migrated to India were to be eventually absorbed into the broader syncretic social and cultural fabric of North India.

Pathans, Horse Traders and Musicians

Besides being mercenaries and soldiers, Pathans in India also raised and traded horses. Apart from being one of the most important and expensive items of military equipment at the time, the supply of good quality horses to regional courts and armies amounted to a huge and lucrative market. Indigenous Indian horses were much inferior to those of Central Asia and the subcontinent, with a few exceptions, did not provide suitable pastures for grazing horses (Gommans 1999: 79ff.).

Pathans had long traded in horses with Central Asia and so their migration into India provided them with an ideal opportunity to extend this market to North India. According to Gommans, Pathan traders would buy horses in Afghanistan brought from Central Asia, fatten them up in the lush grazing areas of the hills and then bring them down to India for sale (1999:16). There was an effective open market in this trade at the time, an enterprise aided by there being no shortage of buyers of war horses in India among local Hindu and Muslim rulers, and even the British East India Company. As the alluvial region of Rohilkhand was the best area in North India to graze horses, Pathan settlements tended to concentrate in areas such as Shahjahanpur, Saharanpur, Najibabad, Muzaffarnagar and so on. The nearby town of Haridwar was the main horse market of the north.

This military-commercial enterprise provided the patron classes, resources and networks of patronage with which Afghani rababis were able to make a living in India. In fact, some of these Afghani rababis appear to have been well ensconced in this military trade setting, doubling up as militia leaders, mercenaries, horse breeders and traders. The parts of Rohilkhand where these musicians settled, particularly Shahjahanpur, Muzaffarnagar, Saharanpur and Bulandshahr, were also important horse breeding and trading districts.

While census figures collected by British and other historical sources indicate the significant numbers of Pathan militia who migrated to India in the seventeenth and eighteenth centuries and the extent of their formidable presence in the region east of Delhi, it is not so easy to ascertain the number of musicians who may have been among them. Nonetheless, some indication of their population in India can be gauged by the number of Afghani rababis who once populated the Pathan stronghold of Shahjahanpur. According to Kolff, there were fifty-five mohullas (neighbourhoods, quarters) of Pathan troops in this district in the eighteenth century (1990:13). As a social phenomenon, the mohulla was characteristic of Islamic towns and cities throughout West Asia.[6] Bayly mentions that Shahjahanpur '. . . nearer the heart of Rohilla power, was an example of tribal elders (malika) founding mohullas around them' (1983:487). Once formed, it was occupied by a homogenous population with respect to religion, national origin, clan, occupation and income. A close settlement such as this provided physical and moral protection for immigrants of a similar ethnicity and social status. The social dynamics of the mohulla provided security for such groups and also ensured the continuity of the social and cultural conventions of its inhabitants. In this way it was a thriving refuge for newcomers who needed only to seek out the appropriate quarter to find acceptance and sustenance.

Out of these fifty-five mohullas, there were reputed to be eleven of sarod players alone (Mukhopadhyay 1977:109). If this information is correct, and there appears to be no reason to dispute it, then it appears that sarodis comprised a surprising proportion of the Pathan military in Shahjahanpur. That there was a sufficient number of sarodis to constitute even one mohulla, let alone eleven in the one area, suggests that the total number of these Pathan mirasis in India could quite conceivably have been in the hundreds, if not thousands, at the height of Pathan influence in the middle of the eighteenth century.

Irfan Khan, a contemporary sarodiya directly descended from a Pathan musician family, holds that within the eleven mohullas there were thirty-two households of sarodiyas in Shahjahanpur and that these families all claimed Bangash identity. He has mentioned the names of two of these households, sarodiyon ka bangla and sanjai, the latter of these belonging to Murad Ali Khan's extended family.[7]

The social dynamics within mohullas of sarodis, in particular, would have maintained a connection between sarodis and their own community and, at the same time, would have contributed to the continuation of the transmission of their musical knowledge and practice. While interest here is on the musical role of sarodis, the fact that they came to India as mercenaries, horse traders, horse breeders and musicians cannot be so readily overlooked. This holding of multiple occupational roles appears to have been a widespread practice shared by other mirasis in North India.[8] The requirements of a patron would have determined the extent to which any one of these occupations was to be followed at any given time.

Therefore any attempt to ascertain the size of sarodi migration to India encounters a blurring of demarcation between the musical and non-musical roles of military musicians. Nevertheless, the dynamics of this situation hints at a fluidity within the occupational and social contracts maintained through jajmani transactions and perhaps suggests that there may have been different types of Afghani rababis, of varying degrees of musicianship, who fulfilled a range of functions within their communities in India.

The Disenfranchisement of Pathan Sarodis

The rapid disintegration of the Indo-Afghan empire held an important consequence for sarodiyas. The absence of military pursuits meant that the primary network of patronage through which musicians had supported themselves was severely curtailed. Despite this, the social setting of the mohulla continued for some time and appears to have provided limited opportunities for sarodis to continue to earn a livelihood from music. But as these old jajmani networks were steadily diminished, new opportunities and alternate sources of patronage also began to materialize. The remaining princely courts and urban elites of expanding cities and towns such as Lucknow, Farrukhabad and Rampur that had benefited in the wake of post-Mughal political decentralization, began to offer new opportunities for mirasi musicians from different communities in North India. Like the mirasi singers, sarangi and tabla players known in Lucknow as bhands, doms, and dharis, sarodis from the second and third generation of Pathan migrants also gravitated to these centres. Granted that their numbers were probably in the hundreds, it is not possible to consider all the options that disenfranchised musician soldiers could have pursued.

The transition from the mohulla to urban centres took place over a number of decades as individuals adapted to this change of setting in many different ways. Some travelled periodically between the mohulla and Lucknow, while others eventually managed to shift permanently to urban centres. As the oral histories examined later in this chapter show, some others had established an association with Rewa and Gwalior courts through military service or trade. Some musicians obtained seasonal or permanent employment in smaller courts in far-flung areas of Pathan influence such as Tonk or Palanpur, while others ended up as accompanists to tawaifs in less salubrious urban settings (Plate 4-1). Interestingly, a few enlisted in the British army and ended up in places like Myanmar.[9] Although it is recorded that the British were initially suspicious of these tough cavalry soldiers, they nevertheless eventually recruited Pathans into the Rohilla Horse, Gardner's Horse and other irregular units in the north-western provinces called Provincial Battalions (Bayly 1990:171).

Despite these upheavals, little information concerning this period is directly mentioned in the stories or other recollections by members of Hindustani sarod lineages. There are probably a number of reasons for this, but it is primarily because of a general reluctance on the part of musicians to highlight such social or musical backgrounds when recalling their family history.[10]

Ethnographic Material on Sarodis and Sarodiyas

The following information on the lives of immigrant Pathan sarodis and their descendants in the eighteenth and early nineteenth centuries is largely drawn from personal accounts and orally-transmitted family histories which have been passed down through successive generations of sarodiyas in India. In the last three decades or so, some of this information has also been documented in various publications, of which D. K. Mukhopadhyay's study in Bengali (1977) of various gharanas is the most comprehensive. Based on this material, three separate family histories of sarodiyas, each with contemporary representatives

Descendants
Najaf Ali Khan (1705–60) Shahjahanpur
Khaler Khan (1730–82) Shahjahanpur
Hussain Ali (1752–1801) Lucknow

Table 3-1: Descendants of Najaf Ali Khan

in Hindustani music, are examined below. In addition, other sarodiyas from the early 1800s, whose lineages are unrepresented in contemporary Hindustani music, are also discussed.

Najaf Ali Khan and His Descendants

Illyas Khan (1908–89) was, until a few years ago, the most senior representative of this family lineage and for a long time, the Principal of the Bhatkhande Music College in Lucknow. He chose to play the sitar and not the sarod. He recalls many details of his family's early history in India. He provides further information on Najaf Ali Khan (1705–60) who was previously mentioned to have been the first of his ancestors to migrate to India. Najaf Ali Khan left the town of Jalalabad, in the Kabul district, in the early 1700s and settled in Delhi.[11] Illyas Khan describes him as a risaldar with the Pathan forces. His decision to go to Delhi on arrival in India suggests that Najaf Ali Khan was initially a mercenary and a musician with a Pathan militia enlisted by the Mughal army.[12] After some time, Najaf Ali moved permanently to one of the eleven mohullas of sarodis in the Shahjahanpur district. Najaf Ali Khan's move from Delhi to Shahjahanpur coincided with the declining fortunes of the Mughals in the early 1700s as well as the opportunities created by the political and geographical expansion of Rohilkhand for Pathan mercenaries and the musicians who accompanied them.

Towards the end of the eighteenth century, some of Najaf Ali's descendants migrated to Lucknow after the banning of Pathan armies by the British. His grandson, Hussain Ali Khan (1752–1801), was the first in the family to move permanently from Shahjahanpur to Lucknow. His migration was probably an outcome of the fact that the Awadhi capital was now the sole centre of power and wealth in the region. *The Imperial Gazetteer* states that Shahjahanpur cultivated a more amenable relationship with the Awadhis than other parts of the Rohilla province.

Shahjahanpur, indeed, lying on the border between Awadh and Rohilkhand, formed a sort of debatable land between the two provinces but the sympathies and connections of the Shahjahanpur Pathans lay always with Awadh rather than the Rohillas (Hunter 1881, vol. 8:254).

The amiability of this political relationship therefore possibly made it easier for sarodis to move between Shahjahanpur and Lucknow than would have been possible for sarodis from other areas. Any connection that had previously existed between Shahjahanpur and Lucknow was further consolidated when, in 1774, Rohilkhand was incorporated into the territory of Awadh.

Hussain Ali Khan was 'the first person in the family to start playing the Indian raag system' and was also supposed to have learnt briefly from the seniya rababiya Pyar Khan (Mukhopadhyay 1977:111).[13] As Tables A-1 and A-2 indicate, however, there existed two seniya musicians by the name of Pyar Khan in the late 1700s. Irfan Khan, the nephew of Illyas Khan, states that it was Pyar Khan, descendant of Tansen's son Bilas Khan (n.d.) and elder brother of Basat Khan (1787–1887), who provided some musical instruction to Hussain Ali.[14] While the association of Hussain Ali Khan's name with that of a seniya is no doubt a valuable detail, no further information is noted by Mukhopadhyay or any other source which describes in what context, and to what extent, this training took place. Nevertheless, an obvious inference can be made that sarodis from Shahjahanpur were able to make a living by playing the Kabuli rabab in Lucknow from at least the end of the eighteenth century. One can also infer that it was not until the third generation of these mirasis in India that we come across sarodis starting to play Hindustani music in expanding urban centres such as Lucknow. The early genealogy of this lineage is represented in Table 3-1.

Karimullah Khan, Madar Khan and Their Descendants

Karimullah Khan and his younger brother or cousin, Madar Khan, migrated to India some time in the first half of the eighteenth century (Illyas Khan, personal communication: 1982 and Irfan Khan, personal communication: 1998). They left the Ghazni district, south of Kabul, to settle in the village of Bugrasi in the Bulandshahr district

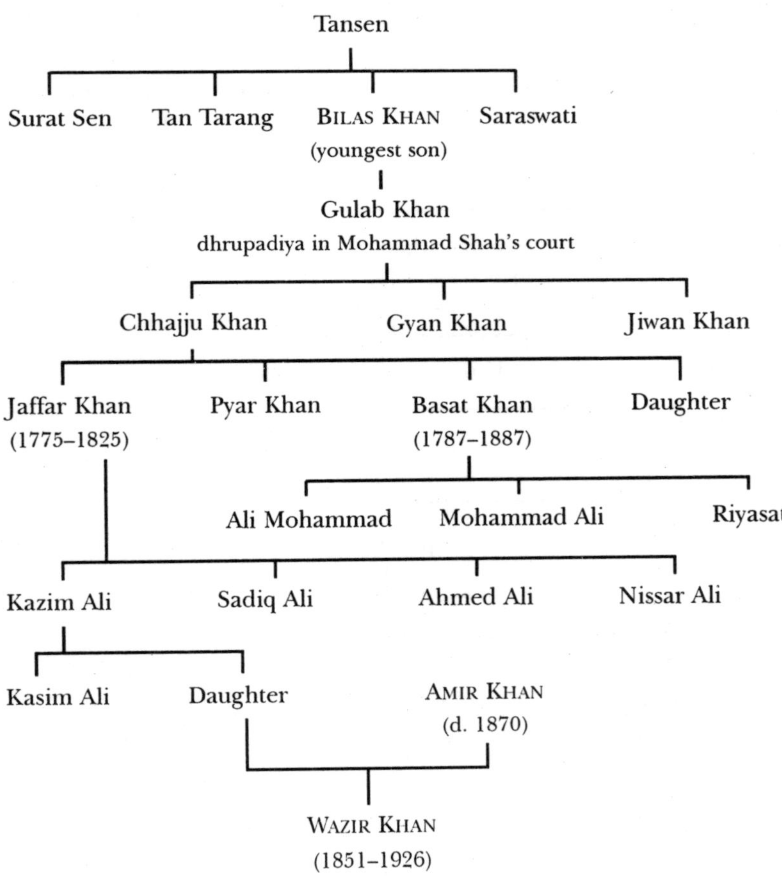

Table A-1: The rababiya lineage descended from Tansen's youngest son, Bilas Khan

in Rohilkhand, approximately 150 kilometres east of Shahjahanpur. According to Mukhopadhyay,

> By profession Karimullah was a fauj ka zama'dar [a recruiter and commander of an army of mercenaries]. His son Rahimullah used to live in the Kunjpura sector in Baragaon village of Muzaffarnagar. Rahimullah's son Haqdadullah went from Muzaffarnagar to Bulandshahr. Haqdadullah Khan married a relative of Karam Khan [Karam Khan himself was a close relative of Haqdadullah Khan].

Later, at the invitation of Karam Khan, Haqdadullah Khan settled permanently in the corner of a house in Bugrasi village in Bulandshahr district . . . . Haqdadullah Khan was a horse trader as

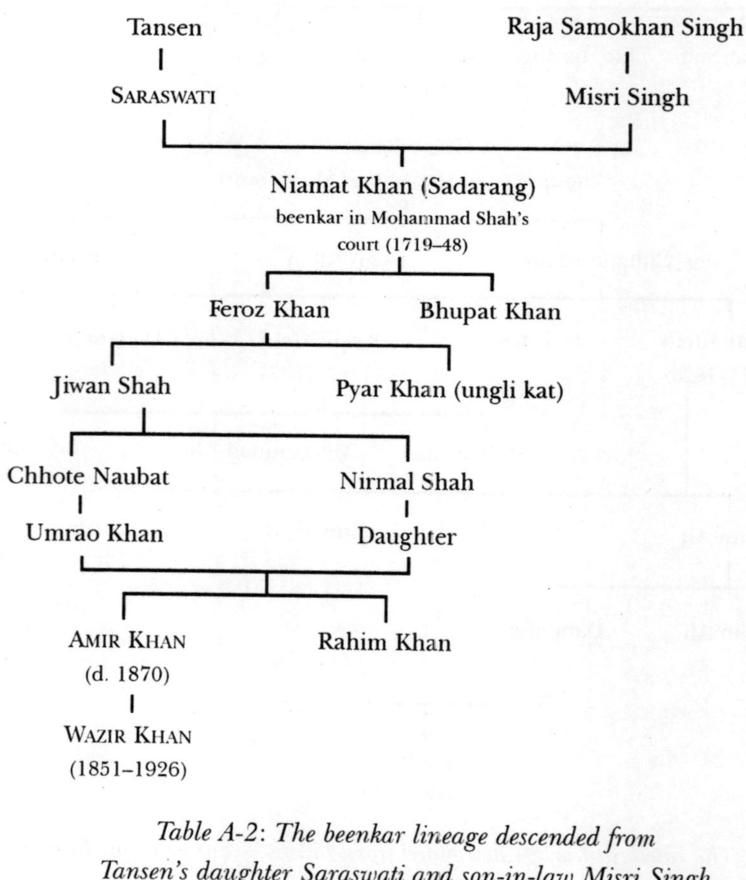

Table A-2: The beenkar lineage descended from Tansen's daughter Saraswati and son-in-law Misri Singh

well as a musician. One part of the house was used only to practise music where Karam Khan used to play his Kabuli rabab. He used to make frequent trips to perform at the court of the Nawab of Lucknow (Mukhopadhyay 1977: 47).

We can infer from the marriage mentioned here that social contacts existed across these two districts and over long distances. Although the marriage occurred between individuals from mohullas of different districts, the families involved nevertheless both belonged to the Bangash tribe of Pathans. This marriage possibly suggests that these village-based musicians, in India at least, were part of larger endogamous social entities organized over large distances.

Karimullah was a musician and a commander with the Pathan forces, a position with high social status among Pathans and other military groups. But there is no mention whether his son Rahimullah had another military or trading occupation. Rahimullah's son, Haqdadullah Khan, apart from playing the Kabuli rabab also engaged in horse trading. Trips made by Karam Khan (1787–1850) in the early nineteenth century to perform in Lucknow are an interesting phenomenon. The timing of his trips, incidentally, would have coincided with the period when Najaf Ali Khan's grandson, Hussain Ali Khan, was supposed to have moved to Lucknow in search of work. Mukhopadhyay says that Karam Khan did not follow any other profession besides music, therefore indirectly implying that his musical status and the amount of patronage he received was sufficient for him and, unlike other sarodis, he had no need to pursue any other occupation (1977:48). But we do not know what he actually played in the court of Lucknow and in what musical context and whether he performed as an accompanist or as a soloist.[15]

Mukhopadhyay states that in his old age Karam Khan received some training from the seniya rababiya Basat Khan. The extent of this training is open to question but it could have taken place around or not long after Hussain Ali's training from Pyar Khan. Haqdadullah Khan's son, Niamatullah Khan (1827–1903), left the mohulla in Shahjahanpur along with his family and migrated to Lucknow around the middle of the nineteenth century. Three sets of genealogical details for the family are listed below. The first (Table 3-2) was provided in an interview with Illyas Khan in 1982, the second (Table 3-3) is taken from Mukhopadhyay (1977:56) and the third (Table 3-4) was supplied by Irfan Khan (personal communication: 1998).

While discrepancies do exist between the details supplied in the above tables, the three accounts need not necessarily be considered contradictory. There is no dispute, for instance, between the accounts about the main musical personalities in this family and from whom they learnt. In his version, Illyas Khan appears to have chosen to highlight the genealogical details of his family in terms of musical pedigree, i.e. as a line of transmission of musical knowledge. Mukhopadhyay appears to have concentrated on the kinship relations of the lineage. Irfan Khan's account follows

Mukhopadhyay's in all details except in naming Karimullah's younger brother, Madar Khan. The main differences in these details can therefore be attributed to Mukhopadhyay highlighting descent based on kinship as opposed to Illyas Khan who emphasizes a line of descent, albeit slightly incomplete, based on musical transmission.[16] Irfan Khan further clarifies this by providing full kinship details.

Ghulam Ali Khan and His Descendants

Amjad Ali Khan is among the best-known sarodiyas in contemporary Hindustani music. Along with his two elder brothers, Mubarak Ali

Madar Khan (1704–52)
|
Rahimullah Khan (1728–79)
|
Haqdadullah Khan (1775–1806)
|
Karam Khan (1787–1850)
periodic visits to Lucknow

Table 3-2: Descendants of Karimullah Khan (according to Illyas Khan)

Khan and Rehmat Ali Khan, also sarodiyas, he traces his ancestry to a lineage of Pathan musicians who migrated to India some time in the eighteenth century. The details of this ancestry have been cited in newspapers, magazines and record covers. Nearly all of these sources follow the version outlined in the passage below, which is drawn from an interview with Amjad Ali Khan published in the journal *Sangeet Natak*:

> My forefathers came to India from Afghanistan, and they were soldiers and horse breeders. The first ancestor that I recall was Ghulam Bandegi Khan Bangash. He left Afghanistan around the time of the great revolt and came to the court of Maharaja Vishwanath Singh or Rewa, where he was appointed Risaldar in the state cavalry. Ghulam Bandegi brought with him a rabab on which he used to play during his leisure hours (Malhotra 1973:17).[17]

We do not know the district or town in the Pathan homelands that Ghulam Bandegi Khan originally came from, but we do know that he belonged to the Bangash koum. The son of Ghulam Bandegi, Ghulam Ali Khan, was born in Rewa, which is situated near the northern border of the modern state of Madhya Pradesh, approximately 140 kilometres south of Allahabad. Rewa, earlier known as Bhata, also lay just outside

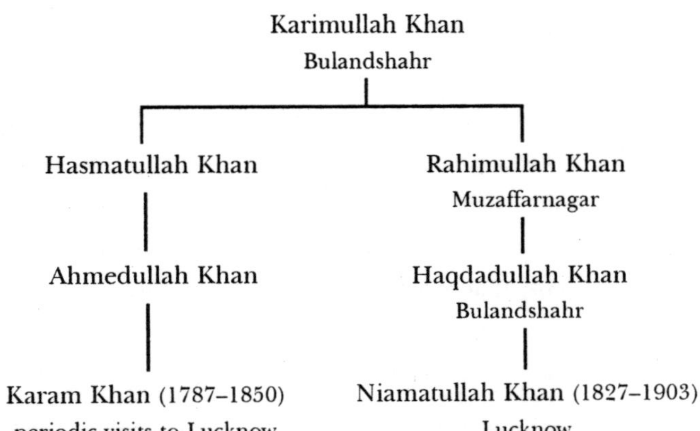

Table 3-3: Descendants of Karimullah Khan
(according to Mukhopadhyay)

the southern border of Rohilkhand and was often known to give refuge to Pathan soldiers (Kolff 1990:48). Amjad Ali Khan's statement that the primary professions of his ancestors were soldiering and horse breeding, and that they played the rabab in their spare time, reinforces earlier comments about the difficulty in determining a demarcation between the musical and non-musical roles of mirasis.

Amjad Ali Khan continues that when Ghulam Ali was about ten years old, his father began to train him in 'the art of playing rabab':

Karimullah Khan Bulandshahr	Madar Khan (1704–52) Bulandshahr
|	|
Hasmatullah Khan	Rahimullah Khan (1728–79) Muzaffarnagar
|	|
Ahmedullah Khan	Haqdadullah Khan (1765–1836) Bulandshahr
|	|
Karam Khan (1787–1850) periodic visits to Lucknow	Niamatullah Khan (1827–1903) Lucknow/Bengal/Nepal

Table 3-4: Descendants of Karimullah and Madar Khan
(according to Irfan Khan)

> When the Maharaja [of Rewa] learnt of their interest in music he sent for . . . Ghulam Bandegi Khan and [asked him] to entrust his son to him so that he could teach him how to play classical music on the rabab . . . [after fifteen years] the Maharaja complimented him [Ghulam Ali] by saying that now he had taught him to play his rabab like a been he should embark upon a tour of the country to play to music loving audiences in all the big towns (Malhotra 1973:18).

Some minor variations in this ancestry are occasionally cited. For example, it is sometimes stated that Mohammad Haashmi Khan was the father of Ghulam Bandegi Khan, and it was the former musician who was the first ancestor of his family to arrive in India.[18] This migration took place in the first half of the eighteenth century. Another version contends that Ghulam Bandegi Khan migrated to India from Afghanistan and that Ghulam Ali was his grandson (Mukhopadhyay 1977:130).[19]

Other Sarodiyas

The early history of the three principal families of sarodiyas examined above can be recalled today because they have contemporary representatives in Hindustani music who are able to ensure the continuation of their family occupation. The question remains, however, as to what happened to the other musicians from mohullas in Shahjahanpur, and the towns and villages of Bareilly, Bulandshahr and Muzaffarnagar districts. Elder members of the Bugrasi village, 38

Mohammad Haashmi Khan
|
Ghulam Bandegi Khan
Rewa
|
Ghulam Ali Khan (?–1870)
Rewa, Gwalior/Farrukhabad

Table 3-5: Descendants of Mohammad Haashmi Khan

kilometres from Bulandshahr, were able to remember the names of a number of sarodis who resided there in the first half of the nineteenth century but said that most if not all of these musicians eventually moved to Lucknow. Apart from these elders, however, most people in the village seemed surprised to hear that Bugrasi could have had such a heritage. At present there is little remaining in such towns that suggests a past connection with Pathan culture or the sarod in particular.[20]

Even though Afghani rababis either migrated to, or made periodic visits to Lucknow, there is little mention of them in the descriptions of the musical life and musicians of Lucknow in the mid-nineteenth century by Imam (1959) and Sharar (1975), two of the most important sources of this period.[21] This suggests that these Pathan musicians, barring rare exceptions, did not have sufficient social or musical status to warrant inclusion in such chronicles.

Besides Lucknow, the Pathan court of Rampur was apparently well known for its contingent of sarod players, as is suggested by the oft-quoted observation by the British Captain, T. French, in the mid-nineteenth century: 'the Pathans are remarkably fond of this instrument which is very common in Rampur' (Tagore 1965:264).[22] This reference to the sarod being common in Rampur is supported by ethnographic material from the turn of the twentieth century. While information about the lives of sarodiyas in Rampur before this time is scant, it appears from oral history that the Pathan nawabs continued to provide a form of jajmani patronage for Pathan mirasis after the demise of Rohilkhand even as they attracted some of the best Hindustani musicians to their court. However, the descriptions of the musical life of Rampur invariably highlight the latter and the musical roles of Afghani rababis, whose presence there is not disputed, is generally overshadowed. For this reason, information on their lives, except for the handful of the most renowned individuals, is not readily available.[23]

A matter worthy of comment is that the Pathan musicians mentioned in Tables 3-1 to 3-4, all belong to the Bangash clan. This observation is supported by the sarodiya Mukhtar Ahmed (1945?–96), also of Bangash Pathan descent: 'The instrument came to India with Pathan soldiers and horse traders belonging to the Bangash clan.' (*SRA 1* 1991:58) Bangash power during this period centred on Farrukhabad which became an important financial centre in the eighteenth century, complete with the most important mint in the subcontinent at the time (Gommans 1999:130). Yet there is only scant mention of any connection between sarodiyas and this court in their family histories. While Farrukhabad may have featured prominently in the tabla tradition and still lends its name to perhaps the largest contemporary tabla gharana, no similar connections exist between it and sarodiyas.

Of the many Pathan clans that had settled in Rohilkhand, the Bangash were among the smallest in population. According to the

Census of 1891, the population of Pathans in this area was around 700,000. According to this source, the greatest number among them was the Yusufzai (around 1,15,000) while the Bangash, estimated at around 10,000, was one of the smallest (Crooke, 1974, vol. 4:170–71). The question arises therefore as to why the Bangash koum has such a strong presence in the Hindustani sarod tradition. It may be due to the fact that the patron groups of Pathans such as the nawabs of Farrukhabad were themselves Bangash. Very likely, the Bangash became a prominent community through the wealth they accrued, the powerful nawab they established and the sphere of political influence they exerted. It may also be that the social and musical status of Bangash mirasis was favoured over Rohilla rababis. Bangash, of course, was an umbrella term describing a loose confederation of tribes, making it possible for previously non-Bangash musicians surviving under Bangash patronage to be also accommodated under, and identified with, Bangash. This led to musicians more widely identifying with the term Bangash than was actually the case. This speculation aside, the question of the prominence of Bangash in the development of the sarod is likely to remain unresolved for some time yet, as will the issue of non-Bangash Pathan involvement in the development of the sarod tradition.

Migrating Sounds

The sudden curtailment of Pathan influence in India along with the advent of new networks of cultural patronage in post-Mughal successor states such as Awadh, compelled many Afghani rababis to look for patronage outside of their communities. At the same time, this search also presented opportunities to access and assimilate new sounds, musical practice, instrumentation, musical knowledge and so on. From the beginning of the nineteenth century, sarodiyas arrived as migrants in new musical milieus and cultures of sound in the urban centres of post-Mughal India. In places like Lucknow and Rewa, Afghani rababis encountered a new range of instruments, genres and types of musicians. These musical milieus were dominated by musicians known as seniyas, acclaimed for their pre-eminent interpretation and performance of the musical genre dhrupad.

Through seniyas, some Afghani rababis became privy to new streams of musical knowledge and practice, but the nature of this association is not as straightforward as may be implied in oral accounts. There was a large gulf that separated these two groups of musicians both in musical status and social standing; sarodiyas were marginally positioned in the court, relative to the literally aristocratic status of seniyas. Further, sarodiyas also had to contend with the fact that seniyas were hardly renowned for teaching the core of their expertise and knowledge to outsiders. Their knowledge was a valuable inheritance because it had been cultivated and closely guarded within the family for generations. Statements concerning the training that sarodiyas received from seniyas at this time, and any implications attached to such associations, must therefore be considered in light of this fact. A few sarodiyas did receive musical training under seniyas in the early part of the nineteenth century but it would have been necessarily limited. Nevertheless, the reputation of sarodis as expert kalawants would have perhaps more readily facilitated their learning from seniyas, than from other mirasis.

Through contact with seniyas and other musicians, a handful of Afghani rababis were exposed to a new soundscape and musical practices. Even though the design and construction of their rabab did not change, the concepts of sound quality aesthetics, musical voice and conventions did. Comments, such as Ghulam Ali Khan learning to play his 'rabab like a been' and Hussain Ali Khan 'playing raag music on rabab', indicate that Afghani rababis soon began adapting their techniques and sound production to express their experience and exposure to this environment.

However, there were considerable limitations in the technical abilities of the Kabuli rabab compared to the been, especially in terms of the latter's ability to replicate the human voice. The quality and the musical forms of the 'raag music' played by Afghani rababis had to be positioned relative to that practised by others who had inherited training, and were highly skilled, in the genre of dhrupad.[24] Therefore, these statements hold more meaning if they are taken, not so much as literal accounts of what may have happened, but as indicative of a process whereby Afghani rababis internalized and experimented with Hindustani music practice and its prevailing notions of sound and musical aesthetics.

Conclusion

The political conditions which prompted the wave of Pathan migration in the early eighteenth century led to the significant penetration of the political and cultural orbit of the north-west into that of inner-India. For most of that century there was an overlapping of these two orbits, most noticeably in the Pathan state of Rohilkhand. By the end of the eighteenth century, the infiltration of British colonialism into Awadh and Rohilkhand forced Pathan settlements in India to be disconnected from their homelands and Central Asian trade routes. Concurrent with this, the rise of post-Mughal successor states created new networks of patronage and opportunities for musicians in courts and urban centres. By the late eighteenth and early nineteenth centuries, some Afghani rababis adapted to and were accepted within these networks. In such musical settings there was the opportunity for a few Afghani rababis to adopt new musical practices and receive training from seniyas. Having come into contact with this training, even from their marginal position in Hindustani music at the time, Pathan musicians entered into another musical soundscape and started to assimilate themselves, their music and the sounds produced on their instruments.

Notes

1 Studies by Baily (1988), Brennan (1970), Brodkin (1968, 1973) and Husain (1979) among others, combined with documentation in colonial records and regional languages, provide an overview of the formation of Rohilkhand.

2 Prior to this time he had been based in a village near Kaimganj, 70 kilometres south-west of Shahjahanpur. See Dayal (1975:101–05) for a detailed account of the rise of the Pathan 'adventurer', Mohammad Khan Bangash, within the ranks of the Mughal imperial service.

3 On Bulandshahr, 'One Rohilla subdivision remained known as the "Rohillas of the Twelve Towns", an indication of the close connection between urban and genealogical history'—K. L. Lachman Singh, *Historical and Statistical Memoir of Zillah Bulandshahar* (Allahabad 1874:118), quoted in Bayly (1983:122).

4 Crooke outlines details of the composition and population of the different Pathan groups in Rohilkhand and other provinces in India in the late nineteenth century (1974, vol. 2:155–171).

5 '. . . [Rohillas] were not allowed to marry Bangash daughters, they were offered Bangash khil'ats and had to accept Bangash precedence in protocol. The Rohillas were generally looked down upon as parvenu slaves and horse dealers, whereas, the Bangash seated on their elephants, regarded themselves as real Pathans, entrusted with high mansabs earned through their gallant service to the [Mughal] imperial throne.' (Gommans 1999:170)

6 Sylvia Vatuk (1972) has examined the phenomenon of the mohulla in terms of social organization and kinship in North India.

7 Personal communications: 1998, 1999.

8 See Nahata (1961), Taki (1993), Crooke (1974) and Ibbetson (1970), among others.

9 *Illustrated News of London*, 'New Regiment for Burma', January–June 1891, vol. 98, pp. 211–12.

10 When the gharana system began to dominate the mode of patronage in Hindustani music in the late nineteenth century, musicians were concerned with affirming their place in that system. Evoking a mirasi background and jajmani transactions would not have helped these efforts. This is so because by that time the term mirasi had become an oppositional marker to that of a gharana musician who derived status from being a soloist sustained by feudal networks of patronage and those emerging under the new urban elites; those musicians who accompanied courtesans occupied the marginal spaces of the musical culture and were from that time called mirasi. The term retains these negative connotations to this day.

11 Personal communication: 1982.

12 It had been common practice for the Mughals to use Pathan mercenaries in their armies during the reign of Emperor Aurangzeb (1658–1707). Within the Mughal administration, the musicians that accompanied armies 'were equated with accountants, writers and

trained soldiers as far as their pay and allowances were concerned, except the trumpeters who, because of their special importance, used to get double the salary.' (Majumdar 1960:203)

13 Seniya is a term that refers to the descendants of the famous court musician Tansen who was the principal musical figure in the Mughal court of Akbar.

14 Irfan Khan names Khaler Khan's son as Hasan Ali (not Hussain Ali) and provides slightly different years during which he is thought to have lived, viz. 1752–1809.

15 The only reference to Karam Khan's playing is in relation to his manner of holding the instrument. Mukhopadhyay writes, 'Karam Khan used to play the Kabul rabab in his lap. At that time the seniya rabab was played over the shoulder. Karam Khan did not play like that.' (1977:47–48)

16 Karam Khan's father and uncle, Ahmedullah and Hasmatullah Khan, are both mentioned by Mukhopadhyay in his text. However, neither of them are described as musicians. In this familial setting first cousins are also called brothers.

17 The reference to the great revolt by Amjad Ali Khan in this interview is not clear. It seems that Pathans often rebelled against the Mughals such as the Yusufzai tribe in 1667 and the Afridi tribe in 1673. This event could be the more widespread general upheaval that occurred throughout the region during a couple of decades before and after the death of the Persian Emperor Nadir Shah in 1747.

18 Personal communication: 1985.

19 Mukhopadhyay (1977:130–31) makes the point of repeating this familial relationship between Ghulam Bandegi and Ghulam Ali Khan.

20 During the course of field trips between 1982 and 2000, I had travelled through towns in the one-time Rohilkhand province where sarodiyas were known to have lived, such as Najibabad, Muzaffarnagar, Saharanpur, Shahjahanpur and Bareilly. Like the terms sarodi, Pathan cultural markers have disappeared or been dominated by Hindustani forms.

21 This reference by Imam, which is considered fully in the following chapter, mentions only two sarod players, Dahajudaulah Dhari and Ghulam Ali Dome.

22 French is referring here to an instrument which he calls sarod but whose description otherwise resembles the Kabuli rabab, again suggesting that the Kabuli rabab was also sometimes called sarod, prior to the invention of the Hindustani sarod.

23 Biographical details of sarodiyas in Rampur are provided in the following chapter.

24 These distinctions are considered in detail in the following chapter.

Inventing the Sarod

THE ENCOUNTERS OF A HANDFUL of Afghani rababiyas with seniyas in the first half of the nineteenth century created a need for an instrument that could express the rababiyas' experience of this association. The eminent sarodiya Buddhadev Dasgupta describes this point in the history of the tradition as, 'these rababiyas looked at their own instruments and found them wanting' (Dasgupta, Calcutta Doordarshan: 1982). The timing of the invention of the sarod, therefore, seems to have been anticipated in the growing aspirations of a few Afghani rababiyas to try and create new musical voices inspired by their own experiences of Hindustani music.

While this reasoning may provide us with an entry point to understanding why the sarod was invented around this particular time, a significant problem arises when we turn our attention to the more contentious issue of exactly who may have invented it. Apart from there being more than one version of this event, there is little if any documentary evidence to categorically support any one claim. Over time, this situation has contributed to a climate of contestation between the numbers of claims in circulation and constitutes a fundamental, ongoing and often acrimonious point of disagreement within the tradition.

Before considering the details and implications that define the invention of the sarod, it is worthwhile taking stock of the conditions of Afghani rababiyas leading up to the event. In so doing it should be noted that around the middle of the nineteenth century there were possibly hundreds of rabab-playing Pashtuns engaged in a range of musical functions, spread across many parts of North India, connected to various types of social organization forms of patronage. It is possible to discern among these four broad areas of musical function in which Afghani rababiyas were involved. There were those:

i whose patronage depended upon aristocrats and other elites of North India;

ii whose patronage was derived principally from the Pathan community in India, both elite and community based;

iii whose patronage was derived from or connected to the courtesan culture, of which Lucknow was the most significant location;

iv who took up other professions or instruments, or who played non-professionally.

To locate these categories geographically, it can be said that Lucknow was the most significant site of 1 and 3; other North Indian courts such as Gwalior and Darbhanga were also sites for 1; the province of Rohilkhand in general was the primary site of 2; the court at Rampur was the site of 1, 3 and probably also 2; and there were no specific locations for 4. The musical and social status derived from each site generally decreases down the list. Musicians belonging to 1 were soloists; those connected with 2 could be soloists or accompanists; those in 3 were almost exclusively accompanists. The invention of the sarod can be linked to the first two of these categories, i.e. the places where there were soloists, out of which Rampur and Lucknow were the most significant locations. The following section considers the networks of patronage of music provided in these two places and the musical activity that took place there.

Rampur

The political history of Rampur can be traced to the early 1740s when the Mughal emperor made the Pathan, Ali Muhammad Khan, Nawab of Aonla, a small district situated midway between Bareilly and Rampur, near the geographical centre of Rohilkhand. Within a short period of time he had also gained control over the neighbouring districts of Moradabad, Sambhal and Shahjahanpur and the land-based revenue that they attracted. After his death in 1748, Ali Muhammad's uncle, Hafiz Rehmat Khan, oversaw the consolidation of his family rule over the region (Table A-3). Finally, after the annexation of Rohilkhand to Awadh in 1775, one of Ali Muhammad's sons, Faizullah Khan was left with the small fertile province of Rampur (Bayly 1983:121). Any pretensions of political autonomy were lost after the Nawab of Awadh signed Rohilkhand over to the British in 1801. From this time onward, the Pathan nawabs of Rampur, like many other indigenous rulers in the wake of British colonialism, effectively became functional sovereigns within the colonial system, or 'princes' as they were known in the colonial discourse of the British Raj.

Shah Alam (n.d.) and Hussain Khan (n.d.)
(Afghan brothers settled in India)
Daud Khan (n.d.)
Ali Mohammad (n.d.)
(adopted son and the first nawab, d. 1748)
Hafiz Rehmat (n.d.)
Faizullah Khan (1767–98)
Ghulam Mohammad (1798–1822)
Ahmed Ali (1822–40)
Yusuf Ali (1840–64)

Table A-3: Genealogy of the Rampur Nawabs upto the mid-nineteenth century

Available descriptions of Rampur court during this time are therefore quite sketchy. It is not known for certain how many sarodiyas received patronage in Rampur and what musical roles they had performed there. Whether the patronage offered by the court before the rebellion of 1857 extended beyond a courtesan culture is also not yet clear. It is worth noting that while it is certain that sarodiyas were resident in Rampur before this time and perhaps in quite significant numbers, there is no mention of seniyas, kalawants, qawwal-bachche (another hereditary occupational community of musicians), or any other North Indian musicians of renown in descriptions of Rampur prior to 1857.[1]

The Pathan heritage of the nawabs, and the overall Pathan identity of Rampur State probably contributed to the survival of sarodiyas in India after other centres of Pathan concentration had been dissolved in the wake of colonial ascendancy. To illustrate this point, it is known that at least six families of sarodiyas trace their musical ancestry in India to Rampur. There is mention of a Dahajudaulah Dhari and Ghulam Ali Dom, the lineages of Abid Ali Khan, Mudru Khan, Ahmed Ali Khan and Asghar Ali Khan—all of whom were connected with Rampur in the first half of the nineteenth century. Others, such as Fida Hussain Khan, shifted from Shahjahanpur to Rampur during this time. Even though Fida Hussain was commonly known, and is still sometimes referred to, as Fida Hussain Khan of Shahjahanpur, he first established his career as a sarodiya in Rampur.[2] Apart from this musician, it is possible that a number of other sarodiyas continued to live in, or migrated to, this last remaining Pathan state in India.

Lucknow

Out of the many competing regional powers that emerged during the period of political decentralization following the demise of the Mughal empire (1730–75), Awadh developed both economically and politically into the singlemost dominant political power in North India. The beginning of the post-Mughal state of Awadh can be traced to the early 1700s when Saadat Khan, his family and retainers, arrived in Delhi from Nishapur, in Khorasan, southern Persia. Like many other aristocratic fortune seekers before him, Saadat Khan was attracted to India by the liberal patronage extended to Muslim notables and their retainers by the Mughals. In return for successful and loyal service, he was appointed the subadar (governor) of the province of Awadh in 1722.[3]

As Delhi waned, Awadh benefited substantially, doubling its geographic area during the period of decentralization. The extension of Awadh's boundaries meant that the amount of revenue that Saadat Khan's administration was able to collect also increased considerably. The extra financial resources were redirected initially into the growth of the local power base, manifested in the expansion of its military forces and administrative bureaucracy.

While ostensibly maintaining allegiance to the emperor, in a short span of time, Saadat Khan had concentrated sufficient military strength in Awadh to entertain ambitions of spurning the Mughal authority. At the time of his death in 1739, instead of his position being relinquished in accordance with Mughal ordinances, control of the area was passed on to his son-in-law, Safdar Jang (1739–54). By this stage the authority of the Mughals had weakened to the point that the emperor was unable to effectively retaliate against this act of defiance. The Mughals made various attempts to undermine Saadat Khan's political successors (Fisher 1987:27) but the latter retained control of the province until its annexation by the British in 1856 (a list of Awadhi nawabs is provided in Table A-4).

When Asafud-Dawlah became the fourth Nawab of Awadh in 1775, he assumed control of the largest state in North India. It was at this time that he relocated the capital of the province from Faizabad to Lucknow. In order to protect the material gains the Awadhi elite had acquired over the previous decades, including those from plundering Rohilkhand, they set about promoting the legitimacy of their own claims to sovereignty over the province, with the intent to transcend any previous claims on the area by the Mughals. Drawing upon their Safavi Persian heritage, and specifically their Shia religious beliefs, the Nishapuri elite under Nawab Asafud-Dawlah promoted their ethnic, cultural and religious background as a means of differentiating their rule from the Sunni orthodox doctrine of the later Mughal regime.

The details of the history and development of Awadh is well documented in many studies.[4] From these it is clear that the culture of Lucknow was impregnated with Persian overtones but the reality of its location in Hindustani and the diversity of its population meant that, overall, it was a highly syncretic culture. The aspects of Lucknow that are of greatest importance to this study are the elaborate and highly-refined court culture that became synonymous with Lucknow and the courtesan culture of Lucknow which became emblematic of the cultural life of the city.[5]

From the late eighteenth century the Awadhi nawabs were successful in attracting the best artists and musicians in North India who in turn received lavish patronage at the court. Details of the court culture have been documented in the middle of the nineteenth century most notably by Sharar and Imam, with further descriptions of the period appearing in *Tarikh-e-Lakhnau* (Mahdi n.d.), *Qadeem Lakhnau ki Twaifen* (Hussain 1977) and Hasan (1983). From these sources we know that seniyas, and to some extent qawwals, dominated the court due to their high musical status. While the court was the singlemost important patron of music in Lucknow, there were diverse music making activities that also existed outside the court in its eight thousand imambaras (places of Shia congregational worship) and countless brothels.

Of all its musical activities, however, nineteenth-century Lucknow is most popularly remembered for the refined and extensive courtesan culture that, some say, developed because of the lavish patronage of an indulgent elite but which more likely flourished due to the widespread participation of individuals from almost every quarter of that society. This scene is often portrayed in colonial discourse as one of unsalvageable moral decadence and proof of the effeminacy of Awadh's rulers. It is not surprising then that, until quite recently, this historical setting had been either largely ignored or even filtered out of musical histories. For whatever reasons, this moral sensibility resounded among the western-educated, metropolis-based Indian bhadralok (lit. 'the respectable') who also championed the austerity of Victorian morality and sensibility (Hasan 1983:146).[6] Ironically, it was from among these same classes that patronage for the tawaif would, to no small extent, later continue in the metropolises well into the twentieth century. Whatever the reasons for ignoring this aspect of musical history, the significance of the contribution of courtesan culture, or tawaif-bazi, on the development of modern Hindustani music is becomingly increasingly appreciated and, as this interest grows, there appear to be more serious attempts aimed at the documentation and study of this setting.

One theme that does emerge from the small amount of documentation that exists is that the courtesan culture of Lucknow was characterized by a diversity of ethnicities, a complex range of intersections of social and cultural worlds and sensibilities as well as a degree of fluidity for determining the social ranking of its participants. Accordingly, courtesans were classified as belonging to a number of categories like tawaif, domni, kanchani, takiya, allah-bandi and najjin, depending upon their ethnicity and social background. Differences in status between these classes of courtesans was most apparent in the location of their performance and their clientele. For example, takiyas were relegated to the less salubrious parts of Lucknow, such as the chowk (marketplace), Akbari Gate and Chawal Wali Gali, and catered to the needs of the commoner (Hasan 1983:118). At the same time, some courtesans from other classes such as domnis were afforded more privileged positions and lived within the confines of the court:

> It has, however, to be emphasised that despite large scale patronage to courtesans by the royalty and nobility, [the] majority of them had to be content with clients belonging to the shurafa (gentry) and lower classes (Hasan 1983:116).

The distinctions made on the basis of location appear to be one of the primary considerations for determining the social status of a courtesan and her troupe. Top-ranking courtesans performed in the palaces and mansions of the elite closer to the centre of the city,[7] while those with less status performed in kothas and inns in other parts of the city. Those with the least status performed in makeshift premises such as tents pitched on the margins of the city. Musicians derived their own social status from the prestige afforded the courtesan whom they accompanied.

However, the classification of courtesans solely on the basis of where they were employed belies the ethnic, caste and functional diversity that seems to have existed in their community in Awadh. For instance, a primary distinction was acknowledged between courtesans known as tawaif or domni. The difference between these two categories was not merely limited to the former being a Persian term and the latter Hindu. Qureshi differentiates these two types of courtesans on the grounds of performance practice; tawaifs were known to sing and dance in front of both men and women, domnis performed only for women (1981:46). Sharar also supports this performance practice of domnis, which

> . . . became the most important feature of all wedding celebrations and so fascinated the ladies of wealthy families that there was no household that did not employ a troupe of domnis . . . the domnis themselves were averse to dancing and singing before a male audience (1975:145).

It should be noted that despite the clear demarcation between tawaif and domni suggested by the above definitions of performance practice, it does not always appear to have been consistently observed.

In addition to these characteristics, courtesans were also categorized according to caste. Sharar, for example, further describes courtesans whom he refers to as the 'queens of the bazaar', viz. kanchani, chuna wali and nagarant (1975:146). From his account it appears that these three castes, employed in the urban kothas, were equally renowned for prostitution as for any musical or dance prowess.

The variety in their performance location contributed to a great range in social status among courtesans. While historical references to the tawaif often contribute quite disparaging remarks about these performers, other descriptions clearly counter the universality of such comments. For instance, some courtesans enjoyed sufficient social status for the wealthy to send their sons to them for 'grooming' and etiquette, just as it was usual for the house of the chief courtesan or chaudhrayan to be the chief meeting place for the most important musicians in the city (Sharar 1975:139). Further, in rural areas, tawaifs were often so valued by their zamindar patrons that they were assigned their own lands (Cole 1988:88).[8]

With respect to religion, Cole is of the opinion that tawaifs were originally Hindus of a low caste who often came from the ranks of widows. Apparently up to 85% of tawaifs in Lucknow were Shia by birth or conversion and it appears that most of these low-caste Hindus converted to Islam (1988:87). This last point is also supported by Hasan.

Even the courtesans mostly recruited from low Hindu castes, including Naiks of Kumaon Hills, embraced the religion of the rulers and completely merged into Shia culture (Hasan 1983:8). The incentive for such a high incidence of conversion could possibly be attributed to the greater protection provided for Shia tawaifs under Awadhi law due to the recognition of 'temporary marriage' or muta between a courtesan and her 'patron' at the time of 'extra-musical pursuits'.

There appears to be some kind of connection between the increase in both the activity and reputation of Lucknow's kothas and courtesan culture in general in the early nineteenth century and the migration of disenfranchised mirasis to Lucknow from surrounding areas around this time. As previously mentioned, this migration was largely prompted by the assumption of military control of Awadh and Rohilkhand by British forces in 1801 which in turn was accompanied by the disenfranchisement of the formidable state army as well as other local mercenary forces (Marshall 1975:467). Apart from causing the disenfranchisement of personnel who depended on the military for their livelihoods, it also resulted in the demilitarization of regional politics (Kolff 1990:187). The number and types of musicians who were ancillaries to the various military forces in the region and who were touched by this social upheaval is unlikely to be known for sure, but their numbers appear to have been in tens, if not hundreds of thousands. For example, Kolff writes that before the demilitarization of Awadh, the forces of the regional districts of Unnao and Rai Bareilly alone numbered 50,000 troops (1990:187–88). If this was the case, it is not unreasonable to assume that the total number of troops in the region, including Rohilkhand, affected by this act would have been substantially higher. The general displacement caused by this act is perhaps reflected in the rapid increase in the population of Lucknow that in 1799 was estimated at half a million and by 1858 had doubled to one million (Habib 1985:365).

As a result of regional demilitarization, mirasis such as Afghani rababiyas who had previously relied on the patronage of their own communities, now looked towards centres such as Lucknow for patronage. Once in Lucknow these mirasis were more commonly known as doms and dharis. In a chapter entitled 'Light Entertainment', Sharar mentions that

> from the earliest days . . . some of the doms and dharis in Lucknow came from there [Bareilly, an important centre of Rohilla power]. From this it would appear that the Khans [Pathan leaders] of Rohilkhand had an appreciation for music and that, because of their generosity musicians were able to prosper at Bareilly and Moradabad. From there too the most expert doms and dharis came to Lucknow and made the city their home (1975:78).

Neuman (1977:133) more specifically states that on arrival in such places as Lucknow, the brothels and courtesan salons were probably the primary location in which immigrant rural mirasis found employment:

> It would seem a reasonable hypothesis that the brothel has in effect served as a transitional institution in the urbanization of rural musicians, a function similar to that serving the courtesans . . . For folk musicians migrating to urban centers, the brothel was the one institution where there would be regular performance opportunities, perhaps for folk music and almost certainly for folk derived music. Consequently, the brothel would be the institution most amenable for the beginning of a folk musician's career in the city (Neuman 1977:607).

This may also give some clues regarding the increase in the prevalence and influence of regional genres that contributed to the music of this setting which was dominated by thumri (Shukla 1983:277–81). The dynamic and dramatic rise in the prevalence of thumri in Lucknow could perhaps have been fuelled, to some extent, by the migration to Lucknow of disenfranchised military musicians and the expansion of courtesan culture (Plate 4-1). While the relevance of this setting in the development of instrumental music is still in need of investigation, snippets of oral information are available which connect the sarod with courtesan culture and which also tend to support Neuman's hypothesis.

Apart from the salons and brothels, there was another location that appears to have provided significant patronage to migrant musicians from the countryside and this was the imambara. The imambara was perhaps the most portentous representation of the dominant Shia ideology promoted by the ruling elite of Awadh. The most outstanding of these constructions was the Bara Imambara, commissioned by Asafud-Dawlah and completed in 1791. People of influence also demonstrated their allegiance to the dominant religious and political convictions of the time by personally financing the construction of many other imambaras:

> Asafu'd-Dawlah's courtiers emulated his construction program in their own areas, so that in every neighbourhood they put up new mansions, imambaras and mosques . . . Most of Lucknow's Shi'a grandees . . . built imambaras in this period as did many Sunnis and Hindus. In the early 1800s some 2,000 large imambaras and 6,000 smaller [ones] embellished Lucknow (Cole 1988:96).

It logically follows that the proliferation of imambaras in the first half of the nineteenth century initiated, or even was the result of, a corresponding rise in Shia religious activity. Central to this activity were the dirges and elegies recited or sung during religious assemblies, known as majlis.

The five principal musical forms in majlis—soz, salam, marsiya, nauha and matam, are referred to as 'chants' but were commonly sung with accompaniment. These forms are unified by their context and basic religious theme (Qureshi 1981:41).[9] In addition to these 'chants', elegies could also be presented as a straightforward reading in the manner of taht al-lafz khwani, similar to that practised by poets in secular poetry readings (Cole 1988:107; Sharar 1975:82–87). Considering the number of imambaras that existed in Lucknow during this time, it is therefore understandable why the popularity of the majlis permeated across many levels of Awadhi society:

> The Majlises have had a very marked influence on Lucknow society and because of them culture and etiquette became a part of life for a large number of people. The taste for marsiyas and soz gave new life to poetry and music and the love for these two arts spread not only

among men but reached as far as the noble ladies in purdah (Sharar 1975:217).

By the same token, the large percentage of Shia adherents among tawaifs in Lucknow could also have been due to the employment prospects presented to these performers by the 8,000 imambaras in the city. Qureshi has written that, apart from male gawaye ('classical' singers), the professional performers employed to 'chant' majlis at congregational gatherings were tawaifs and domnis (1981:46). Sharar also describes how,

> . . . at Muharram, thousands of enthusiasts came to Lucknow from other places and sat hopefully in Haidar's Imambara waiting for the courtesan Lady Haidar to commence her song of lament [soz] (1975:139).

When this specific musical function of courtesans is considered, a tantalizing connection occurs between the timing in the growth of courtesan culture in the early nineteenth century and that of the massive imambara construction programme which began during the late 1700s.

Therefore, in addition to Neuman's observation that the brothel provided a point of access to urban patronage for regional musicians, it also appears that, in the case of Lucknow, the potential for employment provided by imambaras may have also been a significant contributing factor leading to the expansion of courtesan culture and the creation of performance opportunities for musicians migrating from regional centres, such as Afghani rababiyas.

The East India Company and the Demise of Awadh

As the nawabs of Awadh were in the process of politically and culturally consolidating an immanent basis for their rule, they also had to contend with the expansion of British colonialism out of Bengal into North India. British interference in the running of the State began as early as the 1760s under the auspices of the East India Company. From this time Company representatives started to politically engineer a series of agreements which effectively saw the military control of the province progressively wrested from the hands of the Awadhi administration. The nawabs were compelled under these agreements to increasingly rely on British forces to defend the province. In return, Awadh was obliged to remit a large annual fee. As the size of the British military presence in Awadh increased, so did the company's demands for remittance (Marshall 1975:466–67). By 1801, the financial pressure brought to bear on the local administration opened up the way for the British to annex a string of districts from Gorakhpur to Rohilkhand (Fisher 1987:17). The loss of these districts led to Awadh being surrounded on three sides by British territory.

At first, the colonial military presence contributed to a stability within the province. It acted as a deterrent to traditional rivals from staging incursions into the region, of whom the Marathas had historically presented the greatest threat. The temporal authority that

Saadat Ali Khan 'Burhan-ul-Mulk' (1720–39)
Mansur Ali Khan (1739–56)
Shuja-ud-Dawlah (1756–75)
Asafud-Dawlah (1775–97)
Wazir Ali (1797–98)
Saadat Ali (1798–1814)
Ghaziyud-din Haidar (1814–27)
Nasirud-din Haidar (1827–37)
Muhammad Ali Shah (1832–47)
Amjad Ali Shah (1842–47)
Wajid Ali Shah (1847–56)

Table A-4: The Nawabs of Awadh

the British now wielded in Awadh, however, was far from an altruistic gesture towards the nawab. Rather, it was used by the British for their own advantage in order to raise revenue and to serve as a platform from which they could influence regional politics. Barnett succinctly sums up these effects:

> The British had indeed altered Awadh's internal power structure by

> replacing its military aristocracy, guaranteeing the security of its borders, and trying to siphon off 53% of its net assessed revenue by treaty (1980:250).

The assumption of the military control of Awadh by the British was accompanied by the disenfranchisement of the formidable state army as well as other local mercenary forces in the region (Marshall 1975:467). Apart from causing the disenfranchisement of personnel who depended on these forces for their livelihoods, the ascendancy of British temporal authority also resulted in '. . . . the demilitarization of regional politics.' (Kolff 1990:187)

With the temporal authority of Awadh effectively in the hands of the British, the basis of the regime's immanent authority not only remained intact but was actually consolidated. This rather untenable political situation, however, was not destined to survive for any length of time. The steady erosion of the Awadhi power base finally exposed the province to the real designs of the British who had gained the upper hand in 1856 when they annexed the province. This occurred during the reign of Nawab Wajid Ali Shah, who was deposed by the British and subsequently exiled in Calcutta.

Sarodiyas in Lucknow

Accounts given by descendants of sarodiyas still resident in Bugrasi village and Shahjahanpur, both in the state of Uttar Pradesh, recall that substantial numbers of their Afghani rabab-playing menfolk migrated to or visited Lucknow during the nineteenth century in search of work.[10] However, there is little written documentation which specifically mentions these musicians or the types of employment they found. In fact, there is a lack of commentary on sarodiyas in general in the musical descriptions of Lucknow as recorded by Imam and Sharar. If substantial numbers of sarodiyas had migrated to Lucknow in the early nineteenth century, as suggested in the oral accounts, they may not have been mentioned because the people that they played for, and the types of places they played in, did not have sufficient social or musical status to rate a mention in these now important historical documents. Nevertheless, Imam does record two brief descriptions of sarodiyas in Lucknow before the invention of the sarod. Writing in 1856 he notes:

> . . . among the instrumentalists [in Lucknow], Dahajudaulah Dhari and Ghulam Ali Dome of Rampur, both sarodiyas, were masters of their time. But both are dead now (1959:24).[11]

It is sometimes thought that the Ghulam Ali described in this passage is the same as the Ghulam Ali Khan credited with the invention of the sarod.[12] There are, however, some reasons to think that this was not the case. While Ghulam Ali Khan may have visited Rampur at some stage of his life, he was not generally known as a sarod player of Rampur. Further, at the time of the rebellion, when Imam wrote his chronicle and by which time Ghulam Ali Dome had passed away, Ghulam Ali Khan was in the process of shifting to Gwalior where he eventually passed away in 1870 (Malhotra 1973:18). Such chronological, ethnographic and geographical discrepancies make it clear that these were two separate individuals. This does not mean that Ghulam Ali Khan was never in Lucknow or that he never performed at the Lucknow court. Rather, it means that Imam's reference to Ghulam Ali Dome should not be mistaken as proof that Ghulam Ali Khan was a court musician of Wajid Ali Shah. Considering that Pathans settled in Lucknow constituted approximately one sixth of the entire population of the city (Hasan 1983:8), and that many sarod players had migrated to or visited Lucknow from Rohilkhand over six or seven decades, it is perhaps not unexpected that there should be more than one sarod player by the name of Ghulam Ali.

This also raises two important issues. First, that these two musicians who were both dead by 1856 are named as sarodiyas before the sarod was supposedly invented, a point that reaffirms the contention that the term sarod was most probably in circulation among some sections of Pathans to describe the Kabuli rabab, or at least a variant of it, before the invention of the modern Hindustani sarod. As Miner has also noted, the sarod is described by Imam as having gut strings and originating from the rabab but being one and a half times the size of the former in length (Khan 1925:58). It may be the case, as Miner contends, that in 'Karam Imam's Lucknow, the sarod was a larger version of the Afghani rabab, presumably with gut strings, wooden fingerboard and sympathetic strings.' (1993:67)

Second, that these sarodiyas have been given the appellation of occupational labels dhari and dom which are terms used in other places by Imam to describe the musicians who accompanied courtesans (1959:15). The placement of the above two sarodiyas in a list of sarangi players suggests that these sarodiyas were also engaged to accompany courtesans. That a sarodiya with the title dhari performed this task seemingly indicates that the hereditary occupational category of dhari changed in orientation from describing military musicians in the Mughal setting to describing instrumental accompanists to courtesans in Lucknow.[13] Whereas hereditary occupational groups of Pathan rababiyas and sarodis were known generically as mirasis when they functioned and received jajmani patronage from within their own community, they became doms and dharis when recast into the eclectic mix of ethnicities and musicians found in Lucknow.[14] This use of these appellations to describe Afghani rababiyas indicates something of the social level of the entry point that these Pathan musicians passed through on their way to their eventual social and cultural assimilation into Hindustani music.

As was the case with other immigrant rural musicians, also referred to as dharis and doms by Imam and Sharar, it seems that courtesan culture provided the most immediate and accessible means for immigrant sarodiyas to make a living in Lucknow in the early nineteenth century.[15] It would certainly have been more likely than the exclusive aristocratic world of seniya and qawwal-bachche court musicians who specialized in rabab, been and sursringar which would have appeared socially and culturally formidable and, for this reason, very difficult to access.

While there is strong reason to suspect that courtesan culture provided an entry point for sarodiyas in Hindustani music in the first half of the nineteenth century, there is a definite need for further documentation of this connection both in Lucknow and Rampur. In the mean time, a tantalizing hint of this connection appears in a reference to a female sarod player. The last nawab of Awadh, Wajid Ali Shah is quoted as having written:

> The Darogha of Department of Entertainers whose name was Mahdi and who was posted as such during the reign of Jannat Makan (Amjad Ali Shah [1842–47]), persuaded a courtesan, Mahboob Jan, who was famed far and wide for playing sarod and dancing to come to me under a pretext . . . When he had found that I had passed a general order to fetch singing girls and admit them in my harem, he thought it was in his interest and conducive to his promotion to bring someone forcibly or under a false plea to me (Hasan 1983:114).

This passage, apart from briefly disclosing something of the gross exploitation that was also inherent in this setting, again uses the term sarod before the invention of the modern instrument. Corroborating evidence linking the sarod with the courtesan culture of Lucknow during this time is still rather meagre and this connection must remain as reasonable conjecture until further information comes to light.

Other Places

Outside Rampur and Lucknow, some Afghani rababiyas were also known to have been employed in other courts around the country. Besides Ghulam Ali Khan who had been in Rewa and Gwalior, Garg has mentioned the name of Saadat Khan whom he says was a sarodiya employed in Gwalior around the middle of the nineteenth century (1978:568). This was probably around the same time that Ghulam Ali Khan was there. Garg states that this musician was employed by the court of Maharaja Jayaji Ray and that 'he had no equal as a sarodiya.' (1978:568) The musical function for which Saadat Khan was employed by this court, however, is again not specified. Further, no details are given of his family background except to say that he was known to have taught some students out of whom none are still remembered.

Other Pathan strongholds, such as Farrukhabad, Moradabad and Bareilly, which were also ceded by the British around the turn of the nineteenth century, may have provided some sort of opportunities to

Afghani rababiyas to make a living. These places do not, however, figure in surviving oral or written accounts connected with the sarod.[16] The same can be said of other smaller and more obscure Pathan courts such as Tonk and Palanpur in the western regions of present-day Rajasthan. While sarod players may have spread out in search of work after the demilitarization of the region by the British, their families, relatives and connections with their 'home' towns of Shahjahanpur, Muzzafarnagar and so on, continued. Long after he had permanently left the area, Niamatullah Khan for example, is said to have built a shrine in Bugrasi village and a large tract of land in Shahjahanpur is still in the hands of family members.[17]

While significant numbers of sarodiyas spread across North India and were engaged in a variety of activities, it was only those with some contact with seniya musicians who made the most successful adaptation to Hindustani music. The invention of the sarod is connected to these particular sarodiyas and, further, the history of the sarod in India is primarily the history of these sarodiyas. Outside of this narrative, however, the imagination is fired to ask, 'What of those sarodiyas who did not belong to this milieu?' Given that there is some indication that the overall numbers of sarodiyas in India (as provided in descriptions of Rampur and Shahjahanpur) over time far outweighed those few individuals endowed with seniya or some other substantial form of 'classical' training, a significant historical dialectic becomes apparent between 'classical' and 'regional' sarodiyas. It is unlikely that our knowledge of the latter group will ever really go beyond a somewhat vague impression but it is important to bear in mind that such a history does also belong to the sarod tradition.

Leaving aside this historical absence and its compelling silence for the time being, it is necessary to first outline why seniyas assumed so much importance in the professional lives of sarodiyas before considering the details of individual accounts. In approaching this issue two things need to be considered: one, the notable disparity in musical and social status between Afghani rababiyas and seniyas which largely determined the social mode of contact between the two groups and two, the invention of the sursringar in the first part of the nineteenth century which to a large extent mediated the musical contact Afghani rababiyas had with seniyas at the time.

Seniyas and the Sursringar

The seniya Jaffar Khan (1775–1825) set out to improve the resonance and tonal quality of the seniya rabab in Awadh in the 1820s (Plate 4-3). The innovations which he effected to his instrument resulted in the invention of the sursringar (Plate 4-4). In contrast to most instruments in Indian music, the origin of the sursringar is relatively clearly defined and its history uncontested. Its invention is important to this study because the physical changes made to the seniya rabab were to later significantly influence the way sarodiyas were to think about, and eventually construct, their own instruments.

Credit for the invention of the sursringar is commonly attributed to the seniya Jaffar Khan who, like his equally renowned father Chhajju Khan, was an expert rababiya. Gosvami relates the most commonly-held account of the way, and the reason why, this instrument came into being.

> Once he [Jaffar Khan] and his cousin Nirmal Shah, had to demonstrate their skill on the [seniya] rabab and the veena [been] respectively at the court of Benaras. After Nirmal Shah had done so, it was Jaffar Khan's turn to play. It being the rainy season, he found his instrument, covered in hide and played mostly on catgut, being damp, would not emit good tones. His position became awkward in the soiree as Nirmal Shah and he had always been competitors . . . He took a month's time from the Maharaja of Benaras, promising to demonstrate his art at the end of it. During this period he came and stayed with an instrument maker of the city, and evolved a new instrument on the basis of the rabab (1957:302–03).[18]

The sursringar therefore, came about through a number of fundamental physical changes being made to the seniya rabab. Specifically, these were the fixing of a metal plate to the whole surface of the fingerboard, the use of wire strings as distinct from gut strings, and the replacement of the heavy wooden resonator with gourd. In this last instance, the resonator of the sursringar came to resemble the main resonator of the surbahar and the sitar. The sursringar also notably continued to make use of the flat jawari bridge found on the rabab and been (Plate 4-2). Apart from these major structural changes, some of the ornamental features of the seniya rabab were also transferred to the sursringar. For example, the characteristic 'lips' which appear on the rabab, between the underside of the neck and the resonator and the underside of the neck and the pegbox, were also quite common on the latter instrument. The function of the lip adjacent to the pegbox helped the performer position the instrument on his left shoulder while playing. Unlike the rabab, which was played with a bamboo plectrum called jawa, the strings of the sursringar were plucked with steel wire plectrums like the mizrab of the sitar.[19]

Important physical differences also existed between the sursringar and the rabab in the design of their pegboxes. For example, the nine pegs of the sursringar were generally arranged in a straight line on each side of the solid pegbox, with four on one side and five on the other. This arrangement more closely followed the shape of the pegbox of the been, and was quite distinct from the open design of the pegbox of the seniya rabab. The tuning of the sursringar approximated that of the seniya rabab. The sursringar was, however, fitted with three extra playing strings not found on the rabab, along with two chikari and one drone string. Chikari strings are usually tuned to the upper tonic and are used to rhythmically punctuate phrases. The inspiration for fitting these strings probably came from the been. The main strings of the sursringar varied in number between five and six. Further, the tuning of these strings could vary according to the raag chosen. Nevertheless a common tuning for the five main strings of the instrument is as follows: sa, pa [mandra (low) octave], sa, re, pa [madhyam (middle) octave]; with sa, pa or ma or ga, and sa as the rhythm strings (Mukherjee 1986:10).[20]

In addition to the main gourd resonator, the sursringar was generally constructed with a smaller detachable upper resonator made of gourd as well. This extra resonator also appeared on the surbahar, with both of these designs probably being inspired by, if not based on, that of the been. In performance practice, the forte of the sursringar was alap with 'both techniques of rabab and veena [been] playing . . . being used on this instrument' (Gosvami 1957:20). This mixture in playing technique therefore also expressed the physical design of this instrument which combined the features of the rabab with the been. Out of the innovations made to the seniya rabab which resulted in the invention of the sursringar, the most significant were those made to the actual sound-producing components of the instrument, viz. the resonator, fingerboard and strings. According to Mukherjee, 'Naubat Khan (Junior) "Nirmal Shah" told Jaffar Khan and [his younger brother] Piar Khan that an instrument with better tonal qualities than the been had been invented' (1986:10).

The innovations in sound production which gave the sursringar its voice, and which distinguished it from the seniya rabab, were generated through the pressing of wire strings onto a metal fingerboard by the performer, using the hard surface of the fingernails and the right hand to pluck the strings with a wire plectrum.

The methods devised by seniyas for teaching musicians outside their family were designed to ensure that access to direct or 'authentic' musical training remained within their own bloodline. While seniyas taught their own offspring dhrupad, it was previously mentioned how other vocal forms, such as khyal, were used as a medium to instruct other disciples. Restrictions in the transmission of vocal music were also mirrored in their practice of teaching instrumental music where instruction on the been, rabab and sursringar was confined to immediate family members. Imam provides an indication of how rigidly this practice was adhered to: 'The trouble is, the rules of been are taught by the Ustads to their sons only and not even to their daughter's children' (Imam 1959:23).

In order to circumvent the teaching of been or rabab to musicians proscribed by their self-imposed regulation, seniyas instead gave instruction to other disciples through, at the time, newly-created instruments such as the sitar and surbahar. Through this practice, seniyas zealously protected their musical status. An instance which illustrates the seriousness with which this practice was adhered to concerns Pyar Khan, one of the sons of Chhajju Khan, who did not have any sons. For this reason he decided to unreservedly pass his art onto Bahadur Hussain, the son of his sister. In doing so, Pyar Khan is alleged to have so angered his other brothers that he caused a rift in this branch of the seniya lineage.[21]

When sarodiyas sought to learn from seniyas, they also had to negotiate these same practices of restricting musical transmission. They too were not privy at that time to direct instruction on been, seniya rabab or sursringar, but received training initially via the Kabuli rabab and then the Hindustani sarod. At the same time, the amount of material received and type of training that each sarodiya who studied with a seniya received, varied according to the context of the exchange and talent of the student.

Accounting for the Invention

Three separate accounts concerning the invention of the sarod are detailed below. Each account focuses on a particular sarodiya, viz. Niamatullah Khan, Ghulam Ali Khan and Abid Ali Khan who, in each case, is claimed to be the first person to have invented the instrument. Another very different version as argued by Ali Akbar Khan, Sharan Rani and Lalmani Mishra, does not dwell on the inventor of the instrument per se, preferring instead to argue that the sarod is the latest in the line of development of Indian musical instruments which can be traced back two thousand years. Their argument is considered more fully at a later stage.

Out of the three versions connected to Pathans, it is the second that is most commonly heard. As the lineage descended from this sarodiya has perhaps produced the greatest number of descendants in contemporary Hindustani music, this claim has had the greatest number of voices to carry it and hence has gained the greatest currency. By comparison, the first claim is less well known but better supported through documentation. The third claim is quite obscure and reference to this has not appeared in any other source.

a) Niamatullah Khan

Niamatullah Khan (1827–1903) was previously mentioned as the grandson of the Pathan, Karimullah Khan. When Nawab Wajid Ali

Shah was deposed by the British in 1857 and exiled to Matiyaburj in Calcutta, Niamatullah Khan (Plate 4-5) was one of the musicians of that entourage (Illyas Khan, personal communication: 1982). The fact that he was part of the exiled monarch's darbar in Calcutta for around eleven years tends to support claims by later family members that Niamatullah was also employed by, if not well known to, the Lucknow court prior to the annexation of Awadh. During his time in Lucknow he was apparently given land in Ramnagar, in what is now the old part of Lucknow, by Wajid Ali Shah (Irfan Khan, personal communication: 1998). It was while he was in the service of that nawab that Niamatullah Khan is credited by his descendants with having invented the sarod. This took place some time in the 1850s. However, it is not clear whether it occurred in Lucknow or after the nawab's exile to Calcutta in 1857.

This claim is reiterated in the previously-quoted source *Israr-i-karamat urf naghmat-i-n'amat*, published in 1908. In this short book, Niamatullah Khan's son, Keramatullah, writes that the sarod was 'invented' around fifty years ago, which would place this event some time in the late 1850s, an assertion that is reiterated by later descendants (Solis 1970:26). This view is also mentioned by Mukhopadhyay (1977:48) and Mishra (1985:34). Mohammad Irfan Khan (b. 1956), the great-great grandson of Niamatullah Khan, is of the opinion that it was on the suggestion of the seniya Basat Khan that Niamatullah Khansahib changed the wooden plate of the sarod to the metal one (Plates 4-6 and 4-7) and did away with the gut strings and switched over to metal strings (*SRA 1* 1991:44).[22] A contemporary descendant, Ghulfam Ahmed Khan, provides the following account:

> He joined the court of Nawab Wajid Ali Khan and became a disciple of Basat Khan who was a grandson of Tansen. Niyamat-ullah Khan offered one lakh [one hundred thousand] silver coins to his guru and started learning Hindustani raags. He was an ardent and devoted disciple. During his training he took his guru's permission to alter the design of sarod because it was not possible to do 'soot' and 'meend' work on sarod. His guru Basat Khan gave him permission to change the existing form of sarod. Niyamat-ullah Khan took his

> sarod to an ironsmith and asked him to change the centre wooden main body and put an iron plate in its place. Besides he got iron, brass and bronze strings attached to his sarod. This fully changed the sound and lent depth to the music. He practiced intensely on the new sarod. His guru was greatly pleased and asked Niyamat-ullah Khan to play sarod in a function organized in the court of Wajid Ali Shah. Nawab was extremely impressed by his sarod playing and conferred upon him the title of 'sarkar'.[23]

Besides the innovation of the metal fingerboard and steel strings, Niamatullah Khan also considered the suitability of the four gut frets used on the rabab and their usefulness on the metal fingerboard of the sarod. Niamatullah Khan's son, Keramatullah Khan, states that, 'In its initial stages there were also four frets attached to the neck which he removed. Many people copied this new improved instrument, still maintaining the gut frets, which were not effective on the metal fingerboard, although some people thought it was easier to play with the frets. My father did not agree' (Keramatullah Khan 1908: n.p.).

Irfan Khan is of the opinion that the sarod could only be given its present state some time around the middle of the nineteenth century, a view that is also shared by a distant family member, sarodiya Mukhtar Ahmed (*SRA1* 1991:58). After Niamatullah Khan had settled in Calcutta, he is said to have come into sustained social and musical contact with the seniya Basat Khan (1787–1887), who had also previously been with Wajid Ali Shah in Lucknow. According to Mukhopadhyay, '. . . right from Lucknow, Basat Khan was very impressed with Niamatullah's talent and in Matiyaburj he agreed to give him training on his new instrument' (1977:49).

While this training did take place in Calcutta, it would nonetheless appear to have been somewhat limited, as Garg records that Basat Khan remained in Matiyaburj for only one and a half years (1978:264). The matter of Basat Khan's brief stay in Calcutta is supported by Roy Choudhury who records that after 1857, Basat Khan spent most of his life in Benaras and Bihar (Roy Choudhury n.d.1:22–23).

Apart from Basat Khan, Niamatullah Khan is also said to have learnt from another seniya, Kasim Ali Khan, who was a beenkar and rababiya. This seniya was the grandson of Jaffar Khan—a relationship that also made him the grandnephew of Basat Khan—from whom he learnt as well (Garg 1978:264). Mukhopadhyay has noted that 'Niamatullah Khan was living with Kasim Ali in Matiyaburj, and Kasim Ali used to practice in front of him for hours on end. Therefore the talented and hardworking Niamatullah had the opportunity to really develop his raag system' (1977:49).

According to another family member, Illyas Khan, the most essential feature which Niamatullah Khan received from this seniya training was an understanding of the complicated bol patterns which had been developed on the seniya rabab, the purity of which, he is at pains to add, has been maintained by successive generations (1982).[24] At that time the seniya rabab was unsurpassed for the playing of jod and tarparan. These two stylistic terms also denote sections of an instrumental performance in dhrupad, both of which concentrate on complex rhythmic variations based on strings of bol patterns and their variations.

After spending eleven years in Nawab Wajid Ali Shah's court in Calcutta, Niamatullah Khan went to Nepal in 1873 and was employed in the royal court in Kathmandu for a further thirty years. In 1903 he went to Delhi, where he passed away shortly afterwards.

b) *Ghulam Ali Khan*

The name of Ghulam Ali Khan figures strongly in any discussion on the history of the sarod and, specifically, the invention of the instrument. However, as is also the case with Niamatullah Khan, we do not know exactly when or where this event took place. While there can be no real doubt about the importance of the contribution Ghulam Ali Khan made to the development of the modern sarod, differences in accounts of his musical life sometimes generate confusion over some crucial details.

It is not known for sure when Ghulam Ali Khan was born, but it is known that he was the son of the previously-mentioned Ghulam Bandegi Khan, the Bangash risaldar who was in the service of Maharaja Viswanath Singh of Rewa.[25] *The Imperial Gazetteer* records that Bisnath Sinh [Viswanath Singh] became the ruler of Rewa some time after 1813 and remained there until succeeded by his son Raghuraj [Singh] in 1834 (Hunter 1881, vol. 8:57). Amjad Ali Khan, the well-known contemporary descendant of this lineage, states that from the age of ten, Ghulam Ali Khan received musical training in Hindustani music in Rewa from the Maharaja. By the age of twenty-five, Ghulam Ali Khan had embarked on a tour of the country during which time he is thought to have visited many courts. When the rebellion occurred in 1857, Amjad Ali Khan states that Ghulam Ali Khan 'moved north-westwards to yet another state, that of the Scindias of Gwalior, and was soon appointed court musician to the Maharaj' (Malhotra 1973:18).

In another version Mukhopadhyay records that, after leaving Rewa, Ghulam Ali Khan was employed for a substantial period by the Nawabs of Farrukhabad, a strong Bangash Pathan state situated in Bundelkhand and surrounded on three sides by Rohilkhand (1977:131). In contrast to this claim, Amjad Ali Khan does not mention that Ghulam Ali Khan ever lived in Farrukhabad, but rather implies that after leaving Rewa, his forefathers shifted to Gwalior where he was employed as a court musician. The Maharaja of Gwalior presented Ghulam Ali Khan with a house in Jivaji Ganj where he lived for some years before he passed away in 1870. Mukhopadhyay, nevertheless, maintains that Ghulam Ali Khan spent most of his playing life in Farrukhabad where he came into contact with Pyar Khan seniya (the same seniya who had also taught Karam Khan) and only moved to Gwalior later in life (1977:131).

Even though there may have been a number of discrepancies concerning the biographical information of Ghulam Ali Khan, the connection between this sarodiya and the invention of the sarod is widely and strongly held. The innovations that Ghulam Ali made to his instrument amounted to substituting the wooden fingerboard of his rabab with a metal plate, removing the frets and replacing its gut strings with wire strings drawn from steel. Although these are the same modifications that Niamatullah Khan had also made to his rabab, the results were noticeably different.

c) Abid Ali Khan

Mukhopadhyay has written that Abid Ali and Mudru Khan were said to have been the most well-known sarodiyas in Rampur during the period 1870–90 (1977:80). However, very little is known of their biographical details other than that they were of Pathan descent and that their ancestors had been in the military service of the Mughal Emperor Bahadur Shah in Delhi at the beginning of the eighteenth century. In an interview when he was in his late eighties, in 1986, Mohammad Ali Khan (b. 1908), the grandson of Abid Ali Khan, recounted: 'Abid Ali Khan played both the Kabul rabab and the sarod. He and Mudru Khan, his cousin brother [first cousin], are believed to have been the best artists before the two contemporaries Alauddin Khan and Hafiz Ali Khan.'[26]

Mukhopadhyay also claims that both had learnt from the seniya Bahadur Hussain Khan in Rampur: 'Abid Ali Khan was famous in gat-toda on sarod. He also learnt tarana from Bahadur Hussain.' (1977:80)[27]

Mohammad Ali Khan also contends that it was his grandfather, Abid Ali Khan who was really the first sarodiya to have modified his instrument by adding a metal fingerboard and steel strings (personal communication: 1986). He was unable to specify when this was supposed to have taken place except to say it was 'maybe sometime in the 1860s'. He nevertheless continued to stress that he and his family believed that Abid Ali Khan was the inventor of the sarod and that other sarodiyas merely copied his innovations. Abid Ali Khan's son was the well-known sarodiya Ahmed Ali Khan of Rampur and later, Calcutta. Mohammad Ali Khan did not follow music as a profession but rather became a tailor.

Inventing the Sarod

We know that the invention of the sarod comprised more than one event and a single outcome. Inherent in the process was the mixing and matching of components from two sources of Hindustani music, the first being the dominant musical gene pool of the seniyas and the second being the much smaller and relatively more 'limited' pool of sarodiyas. 'Limited' is used here in the sense of a limited access to resources, i.e. patronage, transmission and material culture, the limited scope of sarodiyas' social and musical status in Hindustani music at the time as well as the musical and technical limitations of their own rabab to play Hindustani music.

The modifications made to the instrument by Ghulam Ali Khan, Niamatullah Khan and Abid Ali Khan on the surface share the common addition of a metal fingerboard with steel and brass strings. The metal fingerboard was apparently most commonly fashioned from discarded large double-ended hand-operated saws used for felling trees. According to Barlow, these flat plates were simply screwed onto the wooden fingerboard without any flanges.[28] The steel strings that were used at that time were individually handmade (Barlow, personal communication: 1998). Steel was used for the taraf, chikari and the pa, sa and ma strings; brass was used for the lowest of the main playing strings—kharaj sa—due to its particular tensile and tonal qualities.

However, besides similarities in the use of these components, marked differences existed between the sarods of Niamatullah and Murad Ali Khan, son of Ghulam Ali Khan. This dissimilarity is most evident in the design of their pegboxes. For example, in Plate 4-7 the pegbox of the sarod played by Keramatullah Khan, son of Niamatullah, maintains the open design of the Pathan sarod which is also found on the seniya rabab. According to Illyas Khan (personal communication: 1982), Keramatullah Khan inherited the same design of instrument as that played by his father, Niamatullah Khan. In Plate 6-1, the pegbox of the sarod built by Abdullah Khan and later also played by his son Amir Khan is a straight, closed design, which follows that characteristic of the sursringar and the been (Plates 4-4 and 4-2). These designs are consistent with the pegboxes found on the instruments played by the seniyas from whom Niamatullah Khan and Murad Ali Khan received their training. For example, Niamatullah had learnt from the seniya rababiyas, Basat Khan and Kasim Ali Khan; consequently, the design of the pegbox on his sarod can be said to be consistent with that of the seniya rabab. As Murad Ali Khan was trained by the sursringar player Bahadur Hussain Khan, this musical relationship was also expressed in the design of the pegbox of his sarod. The difference in the constructions of each of these pegboxes would obviously not have affected the sound qualities of the instrument. However, it could be argued that by adopting such designs for their pegboxes, sarodiyas expressed a socio-musical bonding between themselves, their instruments and their interaction with the seniya tradition.

Besides the contrasts in the shape of pegboxes, there was also another feature which differentiated the been-shaped pegbox of the Rampur sarodiyas and the seniya rabab-shaped pegbox of the Niamatullah Khan/Keramatullah Khan sarod. When the gut strings of the Pathan sarod were replaced, the two double courses which had been the highest playing strings were reduced to single courses. Previously there had been six main playing strings on the Pathan sarod, including the two which had been doubled, whereas on both the Ghulam Ali and Niamatullah types of Hindustani sarod there were only four. In both cases, two extra drone strings were added to utilize the remaining two pegs in the pegbox. However, the sarod of Murad Ali shows an additional two chikari (rhythm/drone) strings whose pegs were fixed in between the pegs of the taraf (sympathetic strings) and the nut. By way of comparison, Niamatullah Khan added only one of these chikari strings to the sarod he played. The main strings were tuned in order of ascent to the pitch sa, pa, sa, ma. This tuning was identical to that which Dick states seniya beenkars had previously adopted for their instruments earlier in the nineteenth century (*NGDMI* 1984, vol. 3:732).

Overall, the use of frets on the metal fingerboard of the sarod never really seemed to have caught on. Apart from some early experimentation alluded to in the above passage, there was only one major sarod player, Fida Hussain—'The Holy Terror of Rampur'—who is popularly accredited with having maintained two frets on his instrument. However, a photograph of Fida Hussain and his instrument at the Lucknow Music Conference in 1925 does not show these frets.

Inventing Sounds

The substitution of the rabab's wooden fingerboard with a metal plate and the replacement of its gut strings with wire strings drawn from steel is generally regarded as the defining moment in the birth of the Hindustani sarod. This at least is the common understanding of the invention of the sarod, one which dwells on change to physical components, the design of the instrument and the materials used in its construction. However, it can often be overlooked that for Afghani rababiyas the motivation for the invention of the sarod would more likely have been inspired by, and most immediately evident in, the fundamental change in the tonal quality and resonance of their new instruments.

Not only did they now have a substantially different and wider panorama of potential sounds at their disposal, there was the possibility for developing new playing techniques and realizing subtle melodic nuances. In short, they had a new musical voice to explore. For this reason the invention of the instrument can be argued to be as much about these considerations as about the mechanics of modifying and rearranging material components. It should perhaps also be acknowledged that physical acts of invention by Afghani rababiyas were preceded by the desire to craft a new variety of voice that would more successfully express their experience of the sound culture of dhrupad as practised by seniyas than they had so far been able to achieve on their rababs.[29] Therefore, the creation of a new variety of musical voice assumes as much, if not more, importance in defining the point of invention of the sarod as any physical modification.

Musicians

Though direct access to the seniya tradition is now passed, we are still able to access the sounds and styles of dhrupad through contemporary performances of this genre and high quality sound recordings.[30] Accordingly, due to the continuity of the fundamental principles of aesthetics and performance practice, we are still able to experience the sound culture of dhrupad in a way that is not entirely dissimilar to how Afghani rababiyas may have heard it in the nineteenth century. In this way, sound can sometimes resist historicization and, in doing so, can create an audible link with the past in a manner that puts it at odds with historical views of events arranged in a chronological sequence.[31]

Having been introduced to something of the specialized domain of the sound culture of seniyas, a handful of Afghani rababiyas found themselves, like new immigrants elsewhere, marginal figures on the fringes of a dominant music culture. This musical and social domain of the vocal and instrumental lineages of seniyas would no doubt have simultaneously appeared daunting, challenging and inspiring to those Afghani rababiyas who came into contact with it at that time.

The musical voice, instrument design and materials that each Afghani rababiya developed varied according to the nature of the relationship with seniyas. Those sarodiyas who learnt from seniya rababiyas had a different experience of dhrupad sound culture than those who learnt from seniya beenkars. As noted above, this distinction was not only reflected in the early designs of sarod in the nineteenth century but also in the musical styles of the early sarod lineages.

The restrictions in the lines of transmission of knowledge that seniyas observed meant that the finer techniques, structures, compositions and sensibilities of dhrupad remained confined within seniya bloodlines. Nonetheless, it is true that a few Afghani rababiyas did come into sustained contact with seniyas and the former did start to become acquainted with something of the sound and aesthetics of dhrupad as practised by seniyas. This fertile association provided the catalyst for the invention of the sarod at this particular point in history and the different circumstances under which this contact occurred explains why there were so many different types of Hindustani sarod in circulation in the nineteenth century.

Instrument

The action of pressing wire strings against a metal fingerboard with the fingernails gave sarodiyas a greater potential inventory of sound qualities than was previously possible with gut strings held against guts frets on a wooden fingerboard by the pads of the fingertips. It was because the ensuing change in the fundamentals of sound production was so significant that it seems difficult to ignore this dimension when considering the invention of the sarod.

The change in sound production also meant that sarodiyas were able to realize some of the basic and fundamental techniques of the dhrupad instrumental genres on their new instruments. For example, the most immediate outcome of this innovation was the scope for meend and the exploitation of overtones and partials that it provided on a string instrument. In its simplest form, meend can be described as the glide or slide between two notes. In dhrupad there are, however, more indirect and elusive effects of meend and these relate to the ability to endow musical sound with a chant-like quality known in Indian aesthetics by the Sanskrit term 'aas'. Attaining this sound quality in performance creates the potential to accurately and effectively express srutis or microtonal deflections. These are the basic components in the enormously complex melodic conception of dhrupad. The subtle incorporation and accenting of srutis in the melody is achieved on a primary level through the use of meend. This facility, along with the judicious use of ornamental devices such as murki and other alankars, enabled a competent performer to develop his own voice on the instrument, one that sought to imitate something of the quality and richness of the voices cultivated within the sound culture of dhrupad. The experiences of the Afghani rababiyas with their new instrument in some ways would have mirrored those previously encountered by seniya rababiyas when they invented the voice of the sursringar. A point also worth noting is that concurrent with the invention of the sarod, the dhrupad genre was in the process of being given a voice and adopted by musicians from other communities onto non-seniya instruments such as the surbahar and sitar.

In practice, though, the dhrupad that had inspired Afghani rababiyas to invent the sarod remained a distant and idealized model for them at the time and one that individual artists would struggle with for the following few decades. There were no doubt many reasons why this was so, including the fact that the Hindustani sarod with its taraf meant that the basic sonic setting of this new variety of instrument fundamentally differed from that of the been, sursringar and seniya rabab. Attempts by sarodiyas to reconcile and combine their understanding of the stylistic elements of dhrupad with the effect of the taraf strings must have also been an important factor influencing the outcomes that sarodiyas sought to attain through the further modifications and innovations of their instruments over the ensuing decades.

The Music

For sarodiyas, the musical potential of dhrupad must have seemed enormous but, having arrived at its fringes and with only restricted exposure to its performance practice, repertoire and transmission, their ability to engage with dhrupad content, structure, form and style was in reality limited. We do not know for sure what sarodiyas actually played on their newly-invented instruments. While the sarodiyas mentioned in the above accounts had received some training in raag sangeet from seniyas, which also occasionally included learning a genre known as tarana, oral history tells us that their performance was mostly arranged around gats (compositions), taans and todas.

As discussed further in the next chapter, gats were pre-composed pieces set to a time cycle. There were basically three different types of gats that had been developed in instrumental music at that time, the Feroz Khani, Masit Khani and Reza Khani gat.[32] The playing of a gat or a series of gats was apparently interspersed with taans, melodic or scalar passages of varying complexity and speed, and todas, melodic variations of the raag built on rhythmic compositions adapted from the pakhawaj repertoire. Further, it seems not to have been that common for vilambit alap to be played extensively on the instrument at this time. Instead, it is commonly recalled in oral history that performers played a short introduction in which it was usual for the main shape of the raag to be outlined in a medium tempo before the introduction of a medium or fast tempo gat section.

Although oral accounts go to some length to stress the connection between early figures in the sarod tradition and seniyas, it could perhaps be said that the nature of this association is reflected in what we know of the repertoire of sarodiyas around this time, which in terms of structure and basic melodic conception boasted a simpler architecture of content, structure, form and sound in comparison to dhrupad. In a way, discrepancies in performance models expressed and made audible the marginality of the social and musical positions of sarodiyas, vis-à-vis seniyas, at that time in Hindustani music.

Conclusion

While it is unlikely that we will ever know for certain who first invented the sarod and exactly when this took place, we can, however, make a number of assumptions about the invention of the instrument itself. First, the inventors of the instrument were second or third generation immigrant musicians from the Bangash clan of Pathans; second, the process of invention was heavily reliant on seniya musicians, either via their innovations that created the sursringar or by their suggestion to individual sarodiyas that they adopt the salient features of the sursringar on their Afghani rababs; third, there was a huge difference in the musical status of seniyas and sarodiyas which framed and controlled the nature of interaction between the two groups of musicians; fourth, sarodiyas were already on their way to becoming Hindustani musicians before the invention of the sarod, they just needed to find a suitable voice on their instruments; fifth, sarodiyas set about emulating the voices which seniyas had developed on the sursringar and the seniya rabab on their own instruments; sixth, the voices that sarodiyas ultimately developed combined the approximation of the sounds of sursringar and seniya rabab within the sonic setting of the sympathetic strings of the Kabuli rabab.

Those sarodiyas who successfully adapted to post-1857 conditions were the ones who i) were soloists, ii) were patronized either by Pathan or non-Pathan elites, iii) had some seniya training and iv) had made the transition to the new instrument. The rest, an indeterminate number perhaps in the hundreds, were marginalized over the ensuing decades and little if anything remains of their legacy in contemporary Hindustan. It can be said therefore that the transition from Pathan to Hindustani sarod was not so much a reaction as an adaptation to a set of external factors which had begun to effect sarodiyas from at least the end of the eighteenth century.

Notes

1 See Roy Choudhury (1973:5–6) for discussion on this point.

2 Further information on the social and musical details of these families is examined in the following chapter.

3 The political and religious formation of post-Mughal Awadh has attracted the attention of a number of eminent scholars in the last few years who have added considerable depth to the standard colonial representation of Awadh as a decadent and oppressive regime. For example, see Barnett (1980), Bayly (1975; 1983), Cole (1988), Fisher (1985, 1987), Oldenberg (1984) and Pearson ed. (1985).

4 For example, see Cole (1988) for a detailed history of Lucknow and an extensive account of its Shia roots; Shrivastava (1983) for the establishment of the Awadh nawabs; Fisher (1985, 1987) for an in-depth study of Awadh's history, politics and eventual defeat; Irwin (1973) for a British colonial perspective on Awadh and also Llewellyn-Jones (1980), Marshall (1975), Oldenberg (1984) for general historical and political information.

5 For an overview of the cultural life of Lucknow, see Hasan (1983), Hussain (1977), Imam (1959), Kippen (1988), Sharar (1975) and Taki (1993).

6 This is, of course, not to ignore the capacity for the exploitation of women and the poor that was also part of the conditions of such a setting.

7 Some courtesans obtained recognition in society as sozkhwans and naukakhans, the performers of genres of music connected with Shia religious events (Hasan 1983:123).

8 Bor provides other valuable examples of the performance practice and social status of courtesans from around this period (1986:81–89).

9 Qureshi has written extensively on Islamic religious music in India. In one article, the author (1981:41) defines majlis chant as,

> not as music but as recitation or chant in which musical features are subordinated to a religious text and function. Along with other vernacular chanting traditions, majlis chant falls into the category of *nashid* (hymns based on vernacular poetry) as against *tahlin* (cantillation of the Qur'an in the original Arabic).

10 Based on information collected during fieldwork in western Uttar Pradesh, Najibabad, Shahjahanpur, Bulandshahr and Rampur during 1982 and 1986.

11 The word Ḍome in this passage refers to the occupational caste 'dom', which in this instance has been transliterated with an additional 'e'.

12 For example, see Solis (1970:6), Manuel (1985:345), Miner (1993:124) among others.

13 In the *Ain-i-Akbari*, dharis are described as those musicians who '. . . chiefly chant the praises of the heroes on the battlefield and who lend fresh spirit to the fight.' (Fazl 1965:276) See also McNeil (1992:58–62).

14 The use, and particularly the meaning, of these occupational terms appear to be heavily contingent upon the patronage setting and historical period in which they appear and this might explain why there is so much variation in the way they are used. For example, compare Crooke (1974:276–77), Neuman (1980), Nahata (1961), Imam (1959:19–25) and McNeil (1992:87). For more information on the link between these occupational categories and courtesans, see Sharar (1975:144), Shukla (1983:146) and in particular Hasan (1983:8ff.).

15 There are no doubt many reasons for such a subdued acknowledgment of the link between sarodis/sarodiyas and courtesans. Perhaps any lack of corroborating evidence could be imputed to a couple of reasons. Firstly, the memories of such musicians who were part of this scene in regional centres like Lucknow faded as the courtesan tradition was effectively marginalized and the patronage for this activity generally dried up. Secondly, it could be that any contemporary sarodiya lineage who may have had an association with this milieu would not be keen to acknowledge it in their own personal recollections because of the social disdain in which it was held within networks of patronage in colonial metropolises such as Calcutta.

16 However, a few decades later Farrukhabad had become a major centre of tabla playing and now lends its name to one of the principal gharanas of that instrument.

17 Irfan Khan, personal communication: 1998.

18 Benaras (Varanasi) was part of the province of Awadh during this period.

19 Personal communication with Somjit Dasgupta, 1998 and Anindya Banerjee, 1998. Anindya Banerjee plays both the sarod and the sursringar. Also see *NGDMI* 1984, vol. 3:478.

20 The notes used in Hindustani music: sa, re, ga, ma, pa, dha, ni, have their equivalents in the western solfege system: do, ray, mi, fah, so, lah, ti.

21 Stanley Pereira, personal communication: 1986.

22 This statement was also confirmed through a personal communication in June 1998.

23 Taken from http:\\www.sarodrabab.com/history.html

24 Personal communication: 1982. The topic of bol patterns requires some explanation. Bol (literally 'syllable', 'word') refers to the mnemonics which describe the rhythmic patterns created with the plectrum on the strings of an instrument by the performer's right hand. On the seniya rabab and the sarod, a downward stroke of the plectrum on the strings is known by the syllable da and an upward stroke as ra. A quick alternation of da and ra strokes produces dire. More complicated rhythmic permutations occur when these basic units are collapsed into each other to produce the units drar and dirda. Strings of bols are then created such as da drar da, dirda ra, da ra dire da, ra da ra da. Combinations of these strings of bols are exploited in todas which in the past were, along with taans, the primary forms of variation in the gat section of an instrumental performance. Todas themselves were based on compositions and figures drawn from the pakhawaj. The various ways these patterns are used in different sarod gharanas is a complex topic and one that warrants its own separate study.

25 It will be recalled that the Rewa court was known for its patronage of Pathan militia in India around that time.

26 This information comes by way of a personal communication in March 1986 with Mohammad Ali Khan who lived in an outer suburb of Delhi and was the son of Ahmed Ali Khan, the first sarod teacher of Alauddin Khan. Hafiz Ali and Alauddin Khan were important figures in the musical life of the Rampur court during the early twentieth century.

27 Bahadur Hussain was a famous seniya musician at the Rampur court at that time. 'To' means a 'bouquet' of rhythmic and melodic variations. In the above context, gat-toda probably refers to the

playing of medium and fast tempo gats with improvised variations based on the structure of the composition. See Solis for a detailed description of this term and the playing styles of sarodiyas descendant from Murad Ali Khan (1970:90–96).

28 Unpublished paper prepared for the conference *Indian Music and the West* organized by the Sangeet Research Academy, Mumbai, November 1996.

29 How dhrupad practised by seniyas differed from the performance practice of the genre in other locations and among other communities is a subject worthy of separate study.

30 There are a few sound recordings (both instrumental and vocal) of the last recognized seniya Dabir Khan (d. 1967) in circulation that provide us with some direct experience of their tradition.

31 Applied creatively the study of sound in history can therefore be exploited as a useful way of approaching the past, that is by hearing it. Perhaps the same could also be said of the other senses, viz. taste, touch and smell. For a discussion of the senses in anthropology, see Stoller (1989).

32 See Miner (1993) and Sanyal (1959) among others for further discusssion of these gats in instrumental music.

Sarodiyas and Seniyas

THE ANNEXATION OF AWADH IN 1856 led to the almost overnight destruction of one of the most important centres of musical patronage in North India in the nineteenth century. The stark change that descended upon Lucknow was to affect countless musicians, including sarodiyas, who were now faced with the choice of looking for work in other regional courts or finding sources of patronage in colonial metropolises such as Calcutta. Out of the regional centres, it was the nearby state of Rampur that ended up employing the greatest numbers of sarodiyas. Other courts such as Gwalior, Palanpur and Tonk were also known to have provided support.

While regional feudal networks of patronage began to be slowly marginalized, newly-emerging ones in colonial urban centres gradually started to expand. However, in the late nineteenth and early twentieth centuries, both of them operated alongside each other and it seems that a number of sarodiyas were able to move backwards and forwards between them for a while. In so doing, there were opportunities to not only earn a reasonable livelihood, but also a variety of musical ways in which to do so. At the same time that this was happening, two other important developments in North Indian music were also under way, and it is tempting to think that there may have been some sort of link between all of these things. One of these was that instrumental music and instrumentalists in general were experiencing a general upward mobility in their musical and social status, and the other was that seniya musical knowledge began to circulate more widely. This was also to be of some benefit to sarodiyas.

Patronage of Music in the Rampur Court

While some of the musicians who had been employed in the Lucknow court before annexation accompanied the exiled Wajid Ali Shah to Calcutta, a larger number appear to have remained behind in North India to look for other sources of patronage.[1] Having survived the rebellion relatively unscathed, the Rampur Nawab Yusuf Ali Khan (1848–68) was in a position to recruit many musicians who had become famous in Lucknow.[2] Accordingly, Yusuf Ali appointed two seniyas, Bahadur Hussain (d. 1873) and Amir Khan (d. 1870), as the chief musicians of his court.

Before this appointment, these seniyas had spent most of their life in Awadh, alternating between the Lucknow court and their family home in Benaras. By the middle of the century, Bahadur Hussain had acquired a considerable reputation for his sursringar playing. According to Roy Choudhury, Bahadur Hussain had 'such a charming style that people used to say that his fingers were made of diamonds.' He adds that Bahadur Hussain introduced many new alankars and variations on jhala to the seniya instrumental style on the sursringar (Roy Choudhury n.d.1:31). It will be recalled that his uncle Jaffar Khan had invented this instrument about thirty years ago (c. 1820). Bahadur Hussain received his musical training from another uncle, Pyar Khan, the younger brother of Jaffar Khan (Garg 1978:499). In addition to playing the sursringar, Bahadur Hussain was an exponent of the seniya rabab. He was also reputed to have had a high musical status as a vocalist of dhrupad and dhamar.

Amir Khan, the other seniya at Rampur, was the eldest son of the beenkar Umrao Khan. Both of these seniyas traced their lineage to Tansen's son Bilas Khan. Amir Khan received his musical training from his father and also gained a reputation for his been playing. However, according to Mukhopadhyay (1977:78), he never played this instrument in the Rampur court after a sursringar recital by Bahadur Hussain: a comment that implies that Bahadur Hussain was a better sursringar player than Amir Khan was a beenkar. Amir Khan therefore concentrated mostly on singing dhrupad and dhamar and it was for this vocal expertise that he is mostly remembered today. The charismatic musical influence of Bahadur Hussain Khan and Amir Khan was such that the musical reputation of the Rampur court was essentially built on the musical and social status of these two seniyas.[3]

Though seniyas may have dominated the leading places in the court, many other famous musicians were also employed alongside them at Rampur. Among the throng of famous musicians were the vocalist Enayat Hussain, son-in-law of Haddu Khan, the qawwal-bachche khyaliya of Gwalior who, along with his brother Hassu Khan, were seminal figures in the development of that genre. Other khyaliyas of the famous qawwal-bachche lineage, the brothers Ali and Fattu, were also resident in Rampur (Mukhopadhyay 1977:81). The thumri singer Sanada Piya, also from Lucknow, was employed there (Roy Choudhury n.d.1:32). Among the instrumentalists attached to the court were the renowned inventor of the surbahar, Ghulam Mohammad Khan and the famous sitariya Kutub-ud Dawlah, both of whom were originally from Awadh.

Apart from instrumental soloists, there were ranks of accompanists who played sarangi, tabla and pakhawaj. Added to this list of instrumentalists were, of course, an unspecified number of Pathan sarodiyas. All in all, there were literally hundreds of musicians said to have been employed by the Rampur court. In his memoirs, Alauddin Khan had put the figure at seven hundred in the early twentieth century, which also included those musicians employed to play in the Rampur State band (1982:30). In another account of the same period it is mentioned,

> Wazir Khan was the Ustad of the Nawab, and head of more than 500 musicians at the court of Rampur at least 50 of whom were amongst the most renowned instrumentalists and vocalists in the whole country (Sharar 1975:269, note 438).

This may have been the scenario in the early twentieth century at the height of the prestige of the Rampur court, but even in the last half of the nineteenth century the court had patronized hundreds of musicians out of whom at least two or three dozen musicians were known to be students of seniyas Amir Khan and Bahadur Hussain. As a result these two seniyas were responsible for providing instruction in the vocal forms khyal, tarana and thumri, as well as teaching many players the been, sitar, surbahar, sarod, sarangi and harmonium (Mukhopadhyay 1977:80–83). According to Roy Choudhury (n.d.1:33), Bahadur Hussain and Amir Khan influenced '. . . musicians of different styles of music [to adopt] the Raga system and the ways of execution of [the] Tansen gharana.' Mukhopadhyay contends that it was primarily the Nawab who was responsible for initiating a diversification in the lines of musical transmission across the different categories of musicians he employed (1977:83). This initiative by the Nawab, in fact, proved to be one of the distinguishing characteristics of all the activities connected with this court.

> It is important to note that at this time [mid-nineteenth century] no artist was permitted to teach, or even practise in front of, musicians from another gharana. It is the Nawab of Rampur who had sufficient influence and wealth to make this practice occur in his darbar (Mukhopadhyay 1977:79).[4]

Despite such categorical claims by Mukhopadhyay, previous discussion has shown that it was not completely prohibited for seniyas to teach musicians outside their family so long as they did not impart the khas taleem (special training/insider's knowledge) that constituted their family's musical inheritance. The self-regulatory restrictions that seniyas had imposed on musical transmission had been circumvented in the past by them adopting more indirect methods of training other musicians by modifying elements of the seniya vocal and instrumental style to accommodate instruction in other mediums such as khyal, tarana, surbahar and sitar. Another way was to instruct a range of musicians varying from qawwals to tawaifs on how to perform their own music better by extending the musical material that their disciples could draw upon in order to improve their own playing styles.

In the following material on the lives of sarodiyas, it becomes clear that the rather loose association between a small number of sarodiyas and seniyas strengthens after the mid-nineteenth century. The matter of how much seniya taleem these musicians incorporated into their playing, however, is still a contentious issue. If seniyas had earlier consistently avoided teaching dhrupad instrumental style to qawwals by only providing instruction on the surbahar, then it is unlikely that they would change their practice just to teach sarodiyas who, at the time, were of a lesser musical and social status. Therefore, the transmission of musical knowledge from seniyas to sarodiyas is also considered in the light of these past practices.

Sarodiyas in Rampur

After the rebellion, many sarodiyas spread out across North India and found patronage in various regional centres. Even so, it seems that Rampur accommodated the greatest concentration of these musicians. The following discussion considers the lives of three families of sarodiyas based in Rampur who came into contact with seniyas during the two or three decades following the rebellion. There were many sarodiyas in Rampur at the time other than those who belonged to these particular lineages. However, it is primarily due to their access to seniya training that these three lineages, and the sarodiyas that belonged to them, continue to be remembered through to the present.

The Descendants of Ghulam Ali Khan

While it does not appear that Ghulam Ali Khan had any direct or sustained professional contact with Rampur, two of his sons, Hussain Khan (n. d.) and Murad Ali Khan (d. 1910), were employed as sarodiyas there. The third son, Nanhe Khan (d. 1901), spent most of his life in Gwalior. Although Ghulam Ali Khan did not directly participate in the musical life of Rampur, he profoundly influenced the lives of his descendants through the modifications that he made to his instrument.

Out of Ghulam Ali Khan's three sons, Hussain Khan, the eldest, is said to have been the best sarod player at the time. His reputation as a player was probably due to a large extent to his training under the famous surbahar player of Lucknow, the previously-mentioned Ghulam Mohammad Khan (Mukhopadhyay 1977:132).[5] Hussain Khan had a son called Asghar Ali Khan (1842–1912), who is remembered for the innovations he introduced into his style of playing. Although it is not entirely clear what these innovations were, the contemporary sitariya and music critic, Subroto Roy Choudhury, is of the opinion that Asghar Ali was one of the first sarodiyas to have introduced extended meend in his playing, a technique facilitated by the modifications made by his grandfather Ghulam Ali Khan. The use of meend is indicated in his nickname 'Asghar Ali Khan and his singing sarod.' (Subroto Roy Choudhury, personal communication: 1986) Miner (1993:154) quotes Birendra Kishore Roy Choudhury as noting that Asghar Ali Khan 'is said to have had a sweet touch and could make the sarod sound like a flute.' There may, however, be another reason for these accolades. There is some mention in oral history that Asghar Ali had invented a new instrument called surchain or surchen that was a further modification of the sarod played by other members in his family. Reliable descriptions of this instrument are not forthcoming except for the indication that this instrument had a better facility for playing meend and vilambit alap than was possible on the sarod at that time. It was perhaps for this reason that Asghar Ali attracted such compliments for his playing style.

Ghulam Ali Khan (d. 1870)

Hussain Khan (n.d.)	Murad Ali Khan (d. 1910)	Nanhe Khan (d. 1901)
Asghar Ali Khan (1842–1912)	Amir Khan (1876–1934)	Hafiz Ali Khan (1888–1972)

Table 5-1: Descendants of Ghulam Ali Khan

At a latter stage in his life, Asghar Ali left Rampur and became a court musician at Darbhanga in Bihar. He eventually passed away there in 1912.[6] As Asghar Ali did not have a son, this branch of the family faded with his death. Even though his son-in-law, Aziz Baksh, played the sarod, Asghar Ali would not teach him at all. Mukhopadhyay relates how Aziz Baksh's father-in-law 'was so conscious about his position and so miserly with his knowledge that he did not want to teach Aziz. What Asghar Ali used to do was to close the doors and windows when he practiced. He used to teach his daughter who would then pass it on to Aziz.' (1977:134)

Another of Ghulam Ali's sons was Murad Ali Khan. Mukhopadhyay is of the opinion that he was the first sarodiya in this family to have received any significant musical training from a seniya. The second son of Ghulam Ali, Murad Ali, received his training in Rampur from Umrao Khan's eldest son and another great musician, Amir Khan. He also learnt from Ghulam Mohammad along with his own elder brother, Hussain Khan. Due to his extensive taleem and devotion, Murad Ali Khan established himself as a reputed sarod player and his speciality was the vilambit alap (1977:132).[7]

As seniya Amir Khan died in 1870, Murad Ali Khan's seniya training must have taken place during the 1860s. Because the date of birth of this sarodiya is not known, the period in which Murad Ali Khan would have been in contact with Amir Khan, is also unclear. Garg records that towards the end of the century, Murad Ali Khan moved from Rampur to Bihar. He was also employed by the Darbhanga court, along with his nephew Asghar Ali, from where Murad Ali would make periodical visits to perform in Calcutta (Garg 1978:53).

The Descendants of Najaf Ali Khan

It was earlier noted that descendants of Najaf Ali Khan had shifted from Shahjahanpur to Lucknow in the first half of the nineteenth century. After the annexation of Awadh, at least one of its members, Najaf Ali Khan's great grandson Enayat Ali Khan (1790–1883), travelled to Bengal and his biographical details are considered later in this chapter. However, Enayat Ali Khan's younger brother, Hasan Ali Khan, was employed by the Rampur court but again we do not know in what capacity. Even though the new steel-plated sarod came into existence during his lifetime, it is not known whether he adopted this instrument himself.

It was Hasan Ali's son, and Najaf Ali's great-grandson, Fida Hussain Khan (1855–1927), who achieved great renown for his playing and subsequently brought some attention to this side of Ghulam Ali Khan's descendants. While memories of the reputation of Fida Hussain Khan may have remained, few details of his life are still recalled besides a couple of anecdotes. For instance, Mukhopadhyay

(1977:113) has noted:

> Enayat Ali Khan's younger brother, Hasan Ali, had a son Fida Hussain who became a very popular sarod player. Apart from his training in his gharana, he also received talim from the seniya court musician of Rampur, Amir Khan. He spent all his life in the Rampur darbar and in musical circles he was known as a musician of Rampur. He died in his father's house in Shahjahanpur at an old age. He had an extraordinarily sweet hand and was considered to be the best sarod player of his time.

Najaf Ali Khan (1705–60)
Shahjahanpur
↓
Khaler Khan (1730–82)
↓
Hussain Ali Khan (1752–1801)
Lucknow
↓
- Enayat Ali Khan (1790–1883), Bengal
  → Shafayet Ali Khan (1848–1920)
- Hasan Ali Khan (n.d.)
  → Fida Hussain (1855–1927), Rampur
  → Taj Mohammad (n.d.)

Table 5-2: Descendants of Najaf Ali Khan

If, as Mukhopadhyay has written, Fida Hussain, was born in 1855 and had been a student of Amir Khan seniya, he could not have been more than eighteen years old when the latter died. Hence, the amount of direct seniya taleem he received can be brought into question. Illyas Khan is of the opinion that although Fida Hussain played the Hindustani sarod with its metal-plated fingerboard, he retained two of the original four gut frets of the Pathan sarod (personal communication: 1982). Even so, it is difficult to tell if these frets are attached to his instrument or not in a photograph taken in 1925 (Plate 5-1), although subsequent digital enlargements seem to suggest that there is an outline of two frets on the upper part of the neck. During his lifetime, Fida Hussain apparently became well known for the innovations he made in his playing technique and also for his subsequent virtuosity, particularly in the clarity of his fast taans. As a result he was sometimes referred to as 'Fida Hussain Khan, the Holy Terror of Rampur'. (Subroto Roy Choudhury, personal communication: 1986)

Fida Hussain was one of the first sarodiyas to have played the medium tempo gat set in teentaal known as Feroz Khani (Sanyal 1959:95).[8] Like his contemporary Asghar Ali Khan, Fida Hussain also used extended meend in his playing style (Ravi Shankar, personal communication: 1985). He is said to have travelled to different parts of the country and participated in a number of musical conferences, including the Lucknow Music Conference of 1925 organized by Bhatkhande (Plate 5-2). Irfan Khan recalls (personal communication: 1998) that his performance at this gathering, which featured some of the top Hindustani musicians of the time, was apparently well received as he was awarded twenty-six gold medals by the organizers and other patrons. Fida Hussain had a son, Taj Mohammad, about whom, apart from the fact that he was a sarodiya at the beginning of this century, little else is known.

The Descendants of Abid Ali and Mudru Khan

Abid Ali Khan's son was Ahmed Ali Khan (1856–1919).[9] Although he was primarily known as a Rampur sarodiya, from the 1880s onwards he spent a great deal of his career in Bengal. His biographical details are also discussed later in this chapter. Apart from Mohammad Ali Khan's assertion that Mudru Khan was a well-known sarodiya in Rampur in the late nineteenth century, details of his life are scarce. Umar Khan mentions that Mudru Khan's 'Chhote Ustad' was Chunnu Khan and that earlier, he was well known to the music listeners in Lucknow (1976:9). According to the discographer Michael Kinnear (1985), Chunnu Khan was the first sarodiya to have made a commercial recording. This record was produced in September 1906 on a single-sided ten inch 78rpm disc by the Gramophone Company with copies of the recording still in private circulation. The son of

Chunnu Khan was Aashiq Hussain Khan, who was apparently a very competent sarod player. He was also a disciple of the aristocrat and musician Chhaman Sahab of Rampur (Umar Khan 1976:9).

Abid Ali Khan (n.d.)
Rampur
|
Ahmed Ali Khan
(1856/7–1919)
Bengal

first cousins

Mudru Khan (d. 1895)
Rampur
|
Chunnu Khan (n.d.)
Rampur
|
Aashiq Hussain (n.d.)
Rampur

Asad Ali Khan (n.d.)
Rampur/Bengal
second cousin

Table 5-3: Descendants of Abid Ali Khan and Mudru Khan

In addition to these musicians there was another sarodiya in Rampur also related to Abid Ali and Mudru Khan. Asad Ali Khan was a 'family brother' (a second cousin of the same generation) of Abid Ali Khan. Asad Ali started his musical career as a vocalist and, according to Mukhopadhyay, learnt dhrupad, dhamar and tarana from Bahadur Hussain Khan. Later, when his vocal chords became damaged, he began to play sarod (1977:81). Umar Khan's recollection of Asad Ali differs and he cites him mainly for his playing of sursringar (1976:9). Asad Ali Khan was employed as a sarodiya at the estates of the wealthy Bengali zamindars of Dinajpur and Mukhtagachha. There are no contemporary descendants who musically represent this family.

Sarodiyas and Seniyas in Rampur

The ethnically-based client–patron relationship that once existed between sarodiyas and Pathan aristocratic jajmans can perhaps be cited as an important consideration in explaining why so many sarodiyas were able to become students of seniya musicians in Rampur. This relationship presumably favoured or privileged sarodiyas, both by providing patronage and by assigning these musicians a higher social status in the Rampur court than may have been possible at other courts in North India at the time. This community- and region-specific potential for improving social status made the contact between seniyas and sarodiyas possible and, for the latter, highly desirable.

In the above accounts at least one member from each of the three families of sarodiyas is claimed to have learnt directly from a seniya. Generally speaking, a sarodiya acquired musical status through a combination of three factors: one, becoming a disciple of a seniya; two, playing the new steel-plated sarod with its extended technical capacity and three, using this expertise to establish himself as a soloist while at the same time, distinguishing and distancing himself from a larger and a more general body of accompanists. This functional shift was expressed in the playing style of some sarodiyas who began to develop a solo repertoire which, importantly, was not associated with courtesans but with the medium tempo Feroz Khani gat, vilambit raag alap and other such inspirations based on the seniya practice of dhrupad.

One of the conditions which sarodiyas abided by in order to learn from a seniya was that they should not then pass on their knowledge to tawaifs or to their accompanists (Alauddin Khan 1982:45). It is not possible to determine on the basis of available information how many sarodiyas must have been employed in Rampur for the purpose of accompanying courtesans. This is so because descriptions of musicians at the Rampur court, as with the chronicles of other courts in North India, invariably focus on the best musicians at the court; those sarodiyas who did not become soloists lacked sufficient musical or social status to warrant a mention in such descriptions. Therefore those sarodiyas who did not learn from seniyas had little opportunity to acquire musical status themselves and hence this circumstance more likely meant that the most readily available employment would probably have been as accompanists to tawaifs.

Among those sarodiyas who had become established as soloists, some important developments occurred during this time. Firstly, it has been noted that some sarodiyas like Ghulam Ali Khan's eldest son, Hussain Khan, began learning from surbahar players whose speciality was raag alap. Secondly, sarodiyas like Chunnu Khan and others that were to follow, were among the first performers of Hindustani music to have had their music recorded by a record company. Thirdly, some sarodiyas, such as Fida Hussain, began performing in music conferences in North India alongside some of the best musicians of the time thus signifying, through their social and musical acceptance in this milieu, the end point in the cultural migration of sarodiyas from Pathan mirasi to Hindustani musician.

Patronage of Sarodiyas in Colonial Bengal[10]

During the last decades of the nineteenth century, the colonial centres Calcutta and Mumbai increasingly assumed importance as a source of patronage for Hindustani music. This diffusion of music culture to the metropolises was prompted by a series of political and cultural factors, among which the rise of a new class of patrons and resources from within the colonial state is most relevant to this study. G. P. Deshpande (1987:2170, note 3) observes, 'The dominance of landlords and absentee landlords in the sphere of arts and aesthetics is partly attributed to their being a leisure class of a kind. With colonialism, music entered the living room. In a caste society like India's, this had tremendous social significance.' This is not to discount the importance of other social and cultural factors which were to define and characterize the colonial metropolis such as Indian-European cultural syncretism, the imagined reclaiming of a golden Hindu past, the arrival of modernity and construction of an array of social and cultural institutions, the establishment of the Indian Civil Service and the formulation of new sensibilities and criteria through which social and political status could be pursued.[11] Many instrumentalists who were displaced from traditional sources of patronage in North India after the British annexed Awadh, migrated to Bengal in the last decades of the nineteenth century.[12] In employing Hindustani musicians, Bengali zamindars, by association, harnessed some of the prestige that could be derived from the Mughal and Awadhi traditions and in the process assumed the mantle of the legitimate successors, at least in terms of patronage (Mishra 1981:128).

A small number of sarodiyas also came to Bengal during this time. Perhaps due to their past associations with the courts of North India, they were also seemingly well patronized by Bengali zamindars. The social status which they were accorded by these patrons, conditions of music making in Calcutta and the huge zamindari estates in nearby areas, was significant enough to bring these sarodiyas into sustained contact with seniya musicians.

The Descendants of Karimullah Khan

Niamatullah Khan had two sons, Keramatullah Khan (1851–1933) and Asadullah 'Kaukab' Khan (1858–1915), both of whom became famous sarodiyas in their own right (Plate 5-4). These two musicians were stepbrothers as Niamatullah Khan had apparently married more than once. Earlier they had received their musical education from their father while he was attached to the royal court in Kathmandu, Nepal. Both of them were said to be well educated and both had published books on music. Asadullah Khan apparently, with the help of some students, wrote a book in Bengali called *Sangeet Parichay* (Mukhopadhyay 1977:53). Besides this, Sharar's account (1975:135) of the musical life of pre-rebellion Lucknow is much indebted to 'Professor Kaukab's writings'. Keramatullah Khan had published *Israr-i-karamat-urf naghmat-i-n'amat* under his name although, as he acknowledges, his father had earlier written the bulk of the text.

Besides learning from his father, Asadullah Kaukab Khan had also learnt sitar and surbahar from Sajjad Mohammad, the son of Ghulam Mohammad, who too was resident in Matiyaburj. He was also known to play surbahar and is said to have taught this instrument along with sitar to many students, out of whom Harendra Krishna Sheel was the most noted (Mukhopadhyay 1977:51). There are many recordings on 78rpm discs of 'Kaukab' Khan, and copies of these can still be found. Even though his brother survived him by more than eighteen years, there are no known recordings of Keramatullah Khan.

There is no ready explanation for Keramatullah Khan's reticence to record apart from the fact that he did not want others to copy what he had recorded. Apparently, Keramatullah Khan and Asadullah Khan would occasionally perform together (Sachindra Nath Roy, personal communication: 1998).[13]

- Karimullah Khan (Bulandshahr)
  - Hasmatullah Khan
    - Ahmedullah Khan
      - Karam Khan (1787–1850) (Bulandshahr/periodic visits to Lucknow)
        - Kifatullah Khan (Alwar)

- Madar Khan (1704–52) (Bulandshahr)
  - Rahimullah Khan (1728–79) (Muzaffarnagar)
    - Haqdadullah Khan (1765–1836) (Bulandshahr)
      - Niamatullah Khan (1827–1903) (Lucknow/Calcutta/Kathmandu)
        - Keramatullah Khan (1851–1933) (Kathmandu/Allahabad/Calcutta)
        - Asadullah Khan Kaukab (1858–1915) (Kathmandu/Calcutta)

Table 5-4: Descendants of Karimullah Khan and Madar Khan

After leaving Nepal, Keramatullah Khan eventually settled in Allahabad where he had established a music school. Asadullah Khan had apparently gone to western India for around four years after leaving Nepal following which he went to Benaras briefly and then, in 1907, finally settled in Calcutta where he established a music school called Sangeet Sangha. He also received patronage and support mainly from the Guha family of Masjidbari Street, besides which he was known to be in the occasional service of the extremely wealthy zamindars Jatindra Mohun Tagore and Sourindra Mohun Tagore [of Pathuriaghata]. In 1908, Motilal Nehru organized their performances in France and England. Family members recall that Asadullah Khan's sarod was broken before he arrived in Europe and, as an emergency step, he got hold of and modified a banjo by shaving off its frets and adding a metal fingerboard so that he could fulfil his playing obligations (Illyas Khan, personal communication: 1982). Later, he apparently became quite fond of this instrument and ended up making some recordings on 78rpm discs labelled 'Indian banjo', copies of which are still in circulation.

When Asadullah 'Kaukab' Khan passed away in 1915, Keramatullah Khan came from Allahabad and took over his brother's music school for a further fifteen years. He performed widely in many conferences and concerts across North India (Plate 5-5). He taught a number of students among whom can be named Birendra Kishore Roy Choudhury, Jogindranath Roy, Maharaja of Natore, Kishorechandra Dey, Kalidas Pal and Ananta Kumar Roy. These students were generally from aristocratic or otherwise wealthy families.

Kaukab Khan taught Dhirendranath Bose, the first Bengali to become a recognized performer of the sarod. This was an important development in the history of the tradition to date, as he was the first non-Pathan and non-hereditary musician to have systematically learnt sarod. Not that much is known about Bose other than that he did receive intensive training himself and in turn taught a number of students of whom Shyam Ganguly would later become most famous.

On the other side of the family, the son of Karam Khan was Kifatullah Khan, who also played sarod and was employed around the middle of the nineteenth century in the court at Alwar in Rajasthan (Illyas Khan, personal communication: 1982). Kifatullah Khan's son Shafiqullah Khan became a sitariya who earned a reputation for his technique of playing the instrument with two mizrabs. With his death, this musical lineage was effectively left unrepresented.

The Najaf Ali Khan Line

Enayat Ali Khan was the great grandson of Najaf Ali Khan and represented the fourth generation of this family of sarodiyas in India. While it is clear that Niamatullah Khan came to Calcutta as a member of Wajid Ali Shah's entourage, how and when Enayat Ali Khan migrated to Bengal is not known. Despite this lack of information, Mukhopadhyay (1977:112) is of the opinion that during the 1860s Enayat Ali Khan was employed in Matiyaburj, Calcutta, where he also came into 'close contact' with Kasim Ali Khan. This statement presumably implies that, like Niamatullah Khan, he was taught in the seniya style by Kasim Ali Khan. However, the amount of seniya training that Enayat Ali Khan could have had is again brought into question, because the period during which Kasim Ali Khan was meant to have taught Enayat Ali Khan, the latter would have been around seventy years old. Even so, according to Mukhopadhyay (1977:112), Enayat Ali Khan maintained a close relationship with Kasim Ali Khan during the remainder of his life. Niamatullah Khan is generally acknowledged to have had received a greater amount of seniya training than Enayat Ali, and to have been a better performer. For this reason, Enayat Ali became associated with, and musically influenced by, Niamatullah Khan during his time at Matiyaburj:[14]

> Initially he [Enayat Ali Khan] still played the Pathan sarod but after Niamatullah Khan had modified his instrument and included a steel plate, Enayat Ali accepted this instrument (Mukhopadhyay 1977:111).

Towards the end of the 1860s, Enayat Ali Khan left Calcutta and spent the rest of his musical career, which amounted to a decade or so, employed by different courts in greater Bengal, such as Panchokot and Tripura. In the early 1870s, supposedly at the request of Kasim Ali Khan, Enayat Ali Khan was employed by Rajendra Narayan Roy in Jaydevpur, now in Bangladesh. It was during this time that Enayat Ali Khan earned the distinction of being the first sarodiya, and possibly one of the first performers of Hindustani music, to travel to England. At the age of eighty-seven, he accompanied his patron Rajendra Narayan Roy to England in 1877 for the fortieth anniversary of the reign of the English monarch Victoria, where he performed on his sarod with the tabla player Atta Hussain. He died six years later at the age of ninety-three, still in the employ of Rajendra Narayan Roy (Illyas Khan, personal communication: 1982).

Enayat Ali Khan had a son Shafayet Ali Khan (1848–1920) who married Niamatullah Khan's daughter and thus formed a kinship between their respective families. Shafayet Ali Khan (Plate 5-6) received his training on the sarod from his father, and although he had married Niamatullah's daughter, this relationship did not endow him with any right to receive training from his father-in-law (Mukhopadhyay 1977:113). So, even though Shafayet Khan had become a part of Niamatullah's family in terms of kinship, this relationship was not sufficient to persuade his father-in-law to admit him to the line of musical transmission within his family. Instead, Niamatullah Khan reserved this knowledge for his own son Keramatullah Khan. Nevertheless, Shafayet Ali Khan was regarded as a good performer which enabled him to spend most of his career in the court of Nawab Rasul Khan in Junagarh, once a Pathan stronghold and now in Orissa, and Hjagara in Madhya Pradesh.

The Descendants of Abid Ali and Mudru Khan in Bengal

The most well-known descendant of these Rampur sarodiyas was the previously-mentioned Ahmed Ali Khan (?–1919). Ahmed Ali (Plate 5-3) had his initial musical training from his father Abid Ali Khan of Rampur, who had earlier received some training from the seniya Bahadur Hussain Khan (Mohammad Ali Khan, personal communication: 1986). Ahmed Ali left Rampur in the late 1870s and found employment with a number of patrons in Bengal in the late nineteenth and early twentieth centuries, such as the Tagores of Pathuriaghata, the Raja of Muktagachha and Seth Dulichand of Calcutta (Singh 1982:6).

Although he was based in Bengal, Ahmed Ali used to periodically return home to Rampur to perform. Besides the training he received from his father, it is possible that during the latter part of his career he also learnt from the seniya Wazir Khan (Solis 1970:40). A comment recorded about Ahmed Ali Khan is that he 'played tarana like a singer', an observation that Miner (1993:155) interprets as a trend by this standard of instrumentalists to imitate vocal genres directly.

Ahmed Ali Khan's name is most often recalled these days in connection with his role as Alauddin Khan's first ustad.[15] In his memoirs, Alauddin Khan recalled that he had travelled with his teacher to Patna and Gaya in Bihar, and in each place Ahmed Ali Khan supposedly collected four to five thousand rupees for his performances (1982:18). This was a substantial amount of money and also an indication of how lucrative some sources of patronage could be for Hindustani musicians at the time.

Ahmed Ali Khan's son, Mohammad Ali Khan, stated that in 1914 his father was employed by the Maharaja of Dinajpur (now in Pakistan) and that he occasionally performed at the court of the Maharaja of Indore as well. In 1919, Ahmed Ali returned to Calcutta and was invited to accompany a performance by Mubarak Jang, a celebrated dancer of those times. During the performance he fell ill and died shortly afterwards. None of his progeny were known musicians, including his son Mohammad Ali Khan who subsequently became a tailor.

Sarodiyas and Seniyas in Bengal

The above accounts describe how a few sarodiyas successfully engaged new networks of patronage in Bengal in the late nineteenth century. Some sarodiyas were able to find direct patronage from the landed elite, others from merchant classes and some others were able to establish their own music schools. Whatever the opportunity, the difference in these circumstances had a common thread in that they threw up new social conditions and contracts which needed to be negotiated by both patrons and musicians. Over a short period of time a new set of parameters for doing so was established that drew upon the sensibilities of past practices but was fashioned to suit the social and cultural proprieties and aspirations of the new elites. This process also created opportunities for some sarodiyas to move into different social domains which in some cases were quite lucrative, but which also required that their professional identity be defined according to a new set of parameters.

Previously, in North India, historical factors had determined that a sarodiya was Pathan by ethnicity whereas now, among their new patrons within colonial networks of patronage, their ethnicity was overshadowed by being more readily identified with a larger group usually referred to as 'Ustads from the North.' Accordingly, the conditions of patronage under colonialism meant that sarodiyas were no longer mirasis of the Pathans or doms or dharis to the Awadhis but grouped together in Bengal with other Hindustani musicians from the North including vocalists and instrumentalists of various ethnicities.

Besides this recasting of identity, the conditions within Bengal appeared to prompt other outcomes. As had happened with some of their cousins in Rampur, a few sarodiyas in Bengal were able to strengthen their relationship with seniyas and succeeded in securing further training from them. This had allowed Niamatullah Khan and Enayat Ali Khan to receive some form of seniya training with Basat Khan and Kasim Ali Khan during the 1860s. Similar to some sarodiyas in the North, Asadullah Khan Kaukab received musical training from a surbahar player. Also the music of some sarodiyas in Bengal, such as Kaukab Khan, were recorded onto 78rpm discs starting from the second decade of the twentieth century.

However, by establishing music schools, a common practice in colonial centres at that time,[16] sarodiyas began to teach students from outside their own family although the training provided in such schools produced few if any professional performers. Nevertheless, the institutionalization of music education in general did provide a number of positive outcomes for some sarodiyas. It was also during this time that Dhirendranath Bose became apprenticed to, and was given systematic musical training on sarod by, Asadullah Khan Kaukab. Through this direct, rather than institutionalized training, Dhirendranath Bose became the first non-Pathan to have received this training and to have become a recognized sarodiya. His success as a sarodiya is significant as it marks the beginning of a departure in the regulation of the lines of musical transmission practised by sarodiyas.[17]

Early Sarod Performance Practice and Playing Styles

Until now, discussion has attempted to show how the upward mobility in the social status of sarodiyas and the modifications made to the sarod expressed the unfolding of social and musical contacts between sarodiyas and seniyas. To document such contact through the developments that took place in the playing styles of sarodiyas, however, presents a much more difficult task. The intention here is therefore only to provide a general overview of the playing style and other details of music played by sarodiyas relevant to the current discussion.[18]

It is not possible either to be categorical or too general about what sarodiyas collectively or individually learnt from seniyas in the nineteenth century. This is especially so as some lineages of sarodiyas had learnt from seniyas who specialized in rabab and other lineages from seniyas who specialized in the been, while all lineages seemed to also have incorporated something of the playing style of sursringar. However, some general observations on this point can be made. Even in Bengal it appears that, like other musicians before them, sarodiyas did not receive direct training from seniyas in dhrupad performance during the nineteenth century. It seems that seniyas taught them to play a new type of performance genre such as the Feroz Khani gat that may have been invented for the purpose and was perhaps largely derived from dhrupad, or they taught sarodiyas existing genres such as tarana, or that they used their knowledge and technical expertise to teach sarodiyas how to play their own music with more proficiency. The general impression gained from both written and oral accounts of sarodiyas in the last half of the nineteenth century is that during this time a performance was typically structured around an aochar alap (a brief melodic introduction to the raag), followed by a gat and taans, todas and gatkari (variations).[19] This opinion is also given voice by Narendranath Dhar, a contemporary sarodiya:

> In the very beginning when bandishes [gats] began to be played on the sarod, they were considered to be the most important part of a recital. Artistes also used to meander around the most characteristic phrases of the raag rendered in the bandish. An artiste received wide acknowledgment from learned and renowned musicians and listeners of those days if he could play numerous gats in a single raag (*SRA1* 1991:29).

Buddhadev Dasgupta has stated that a well-composed gat displays a number of characteristics. He lists specifically that there should be notable excellence in:

a) phrasing, progression of notes and punctuation;
b) rhythmic patterns, to project its structural beauty;
c) prominent use of certain musical kriyas or elements of technique;
d) portraying some novel and uncommon features of the raag;
e) elements of surprise and beauty;
f) any other kind of movements off the beaten track (*SRA4*, 1997:158–59).

Over the last one hundred years or so, there have been many different and varied types of gats played by sarodiyas. Broadly speaking, until the mid-1800s, the predominant style played by sarodiyas was based on the compositions set to the sixteen-beat rhythmic cycle teentaal. These gat sections were mostly played to the accompaniment of tabla and sometimes pakhawaj. At this time it seems that the gats most commonly played by sarodiyas were either those set to a medium tempo, known as a Feroz Khani gat, or those set to the fast teentaal, called a Reza Khani gat. Feroz Khan was a seniya beenkar who apparently left Delhi some time around the turn of the nineteenth century and eventually settled in Rampur. Reza Khan developed the gat for the sitar in Lucknow from bandish ki thumri, a musical form played by instrumentalists to accompany courtesans (Shukla 1983:147; Miner 1993:26). Later that century, sarodiyas also started playing the Masit Khani gat which had originally been developed by seniyas specifically for the sitar.

While these three gats—Feroz Khani, Reza Khani and Masit Khani—became the most common forms for instrumental compositions, there are also a number of other gat types that have come to us through the sarod tradition. For instance, there are the genres of highly syncopated fast tempo gats based on tarana;[20] gats developed in Rampur which were variations of the Masit Khani type and which were known as Nawab Pasand;[21] slow tempo gats which incorporated and contrasted at least two different tempi known as tha-dhuni;[22] do-dhara gats in which individual phrases of the gat would be played and then immediately repeated before moving to the next phrase.[23]

The playing of the chosen gat would be interspersed with variations either composed or improvised. These variations were rendered in the forms of taans, todas and gatkari. Taans are fast melodic passages, and toda, rhythmically-based variations drawn from tabla and pakhawaj parans (patterns).[24] As a source of variation, gatkari, similar to the Reza Khani gat, seems to share much in common with the abhinaya in bandish ki thumri where the text of a melodic section of a thumri composition (sthayi) would be interpreted and re-interpreted by the performer using different mime expressions (abhinaya) at the same time that melodic and rhythmic variations were sung or played. For a sarodiya, this method of variation involved successively varying the gat through weaving rhythmic motifs into the composition itself. This technique is achieved on the sarod by the performer alternating the plucking of the right hand between the chikari and the main strings of the instrument.[25]

In terms of musical style, there appears to have been a difference between the sarodiyas who learnt from the seniyas Bahadur Hussain and Amir Khan in Rampur and those who were taught by the seniyas Basat Khan and Kasim Ali Khan in Bengal. The real speciality of the seniyas at the Rampur court was the dhrupad style of raag alap and they especially excelled in vilambit alap (Mukhopadhyay 1977:68).[26] The seniya instrumental style of raag alap on the sursringar and the been, as well as the vocal style of tarana, appear to have been a strong musical influence on sarodiyas in Rampur. The Feroz Khani type seems to have been preferred by sarodiyas in Rampur in the nineteenth century.

By contrast, sarodiyas in Bengal came under the influence of seniya rababiyas. The seniya rabab, with its gut strings and wooden fingerboard, did not have the necessary sustain (resonance) or tonal quality to carry the nuances on which vilambit alap is realized. Due to the technical limitations of this instrument, there was much less scope for the exploitation of meend in general and delicate microtonal material in particular, in the performance style of this rabab. The seniya rabab style differed from the sursringar and the been because it emphasized rhythmic development based on the vocabulary of stylized bol patterns that guide the performer's right hand. Therefore, the forte of this rabab was the use of bol patterns that were especially effective in the jod section of alap.

Illyas Khan has stated that the knowledge of seniya rabab bols and their grammar have been carefully preserved, and rigidly adhered to, by successive generations of his family (personal communication: 1982). The sarodiya Niamatullah Khan is reputed to have received training mostly from seniya rababiyas. As a result, 'Niamatullah established himself as a sarod player in Matiyaburj in Calcutta. He was responsible for introducing beautiful bandishes, taans and todas into the sarod playing style.' (Mukhopadhyay 1977:49)

Due to the emphasis Niamatullah Khan placed on the bol patterns in his playing, Dasgupta is of the opinion that this sarodiya was responsible for introducing the modern style of playing sarod like the seniya rabab (quoted in Solis 1970:40).[27] This style, however, placed a great deal of emphasis on drut gats and thus devoted much less attention to alap (Illyas Khan, personal communication: 1982). A number of Keramatullah Khan's gats were said to have been based on the bols of pakhawaj.[28]

Umar Khan (1916–82) was of the opinion that Ghulam Ali Khan, Shafayet Khan and Nanhe Khan, were noted for their fast gats and did not play many Masit Khani gats (quoted in Solis 1970:41). Other sources confirm that Ghulam Ali Khan played the Feroz Khani gat (Miner 1993:124). The previously-mentioned Fida Hussain Khan—'a master all-round'—has been described as the best exponent of this type of gat in the late 1800s (Sanyal 1959:96).

While sarodiyas were not known to have played the systematic unfolding of the full alap until the early part of this century (Perera 1994), nevertheless in the late nineteenth century, some sarodiyas, out of which Murad Ali Khan was the most famous, starting specializing in the first section of the dhrupad raag alap, i.e. the slow introductory vilambit alap (Mukhopadhyay 1977:133). Murad Ali's style was arguably influenced by the strong emphasis that Bahadur Hussain and Amir Khan placed on the sursringar and been.

Another point worth some attention concerns the playing position used by sarodiyas. Previously, it seems to have been common for sarodiyas performing in courts to either kneel on the floor while sitting on their heels in a pose known as the ardhabajrasana, or to stand while performing out of respect for their patron. However, this baithak (sitting) style changed when they started to play for patrons and audiences in the metropolises. In these places most sarodiyas adopted the ardhagomukhasana posture for performances (a sitting position in which the right leg is folded on top of the left leg), which has now become the standard playing position (Mukhtar Ahmed *SRA1* 1991:58).

Sound Experimentation

From the time of Akbar's rule, seniyas in essence had become the mirasis of the Mughals and like other mirasis, their fortunes eventually followed those of their jajmans. Their position began to wane around the same time that Mughal hegemony lost its own paramountcy at the beginning of the eighteenth century. Nevertheless, seniya performance practice, their musical knowledge and their treasured creativity in music continued to be a dominant influence on Hindustani music. Despite the decline in their social status, seniyas maintained their musical status through to the twentieth century particularly by virtue of their expertise in instrumental music at a time when the social and musical status of instrumental music itself was improving. Their musical expertise was in great demand by musicians outside their family and, through their indirect means of teaching non-related disciples, seniyas continued to stamp their impression on the development of music in North India.

Towards the end of the nineteenth century, khyal began to displace dhrupad as the preferred vocal genre.[29] It is difficult to resist pointing out the coincidence of this event with the marginalization of feudal patronage under colonization, the growth of modern networks of patronage in colonial metropolises and the decline in the social status of seniyas and pre-eminence of dhrupad. This is not to propose that there was necessarily a direct causal link in these events although it may be an argument worthy of further investigation. However, it can be inferred that the developments both in practice and patronage at that time were mutually beneficial to the emergence of khyal.

While khyal went on to become the dominant vocal genre in Hindustani music in the twentieth century, dhrupad continued to dominate the sensibilities and practice of instrumental music for most of that century. At the same time, the expansion in the breadth and depth of solo instrumental music in the last half of the nineteenth century resulted in the acceptance of new instruments for solo performances in Hindustani music. The been, rabab and sursringar were now joined by new recruits surbahar, sitar and sarod—a turn of events that led to an expansion of the number of instruments giving voice to

Hindustani solo instrumental music.

Underpinning this expansion was the diffusion of seniya musical knowledge and sensibility outside their traditional blood-based lines of transmission. An argument can, in fact, be reasonably formulated which would link the outcomes of this diffusion of knowledge with an increase in the numbers and types of instrumental soloists in the last half of the nineteenth century. The spread of seniya knowledge resulted in this particular conception of performance practice and aesthetics profoundly influencing many individual musicians who subsequently became principal figures in the development of Hindustani instrumental music. The fact that most, if not all, contemporary solo instrumentalists today claim to belong to the seniya tradition is testimony to the depth of this influence and a sign that this legacy is still somehow with us.

Musicians

The major performance and stylistic differences that had existed in the seniya instrumental tradition—apparent in the divide between been/sursringar on the one hand and seniya rabab on the other, and the bloodlines on which they were carried—also defined the basic areas of difference that existed between sarodiyas in the nineteenth century. But besides this overwhelming influence of the seniyas, some sarodiyas were also gaining musical knowledge from another emerging source, the qawwal-bachche and the surbahar.

In the latter half of the nineteenth century, a few sarodiyas started learning directly from two major performers of surbahar: Ghulam Ali Khan's sons, Hussain Khan and Murad Ali Khan learnt from Ghulam Mohammad; and Asadullah Khan Kaukab learnt from Ghulam Mohammad's son, Sajjad Mohammad.[30] These qawwal-bachche surbahar players had themselves learnt from seniya beenkars. Indeed, one of the supposed motivations for inventing the surbahar was that it enabled non-seniyas to learn the style and music of the been without compromising the regulations in the transmission of seniya taleem. The nature of this association had led to surbahar players emulating the structure and style of beenkar ang on their own instruments. For this reason it is generally understood that they had a better knowledge of vilambit raag alap than sarodiyas at that time although there is no definite indication that they were more amenable to passing on musical knowledge than seniyas were. Consequently, we hear of some sarodiyas incorporating what they had learnt from surbahar players into their performance practice. The combination of seniya and surbahar training allowed sarodiyas such as Hussain Khan, Murad Ali Khan, Fida Hussain Khan and Enayat Khan to experiment with and set about developing vilambit raag alap on their own instruments.

The Sarod

The invention of the sarod, along with the training sarodiyas received from seniyas, greatly facilitated the interpretation and transposition of dhrupad performance style and aesthetics into the playing style of some sarodiyas. As a particular quality and refinement of musical sound was required to effectively realize the performance techniques and inflections of dhrupad playing style, an increasing concern with sound production and notions of sound quality among sarodiyas crystallized into an ongoing experimentation in the design and construction of various types of sarods.

From this experimentation it becomes apparent that the early physical development of the sarod did not proceed in a single or uniform way. From the time of its invention, a number of sarodiyas continued to make modifications to the design and workings of the instrument. The outcomes that this collective activity produced in the late nineteenth century demonstrated an astonishing and rarely acknowledged variety in the designs of sarod. As there was no such thing as design patents or the mass production of musical instruments, musicians generally designed and built (or rather, had someone else build) their individual instruments. To illustrate the extent of this variation, four examples of early sarods are examined below. While noting the degree of difference between them, they also fundamentally speak of the union between the Kabuli rabab and the sursringar, an association made possible through the intermingling of the north-western and inner-India cultural orbits (Plates 5-7, 5-8, 5-9).

The cultural interaction between the two orbits did result in the invention of the sarod but the dynamics of this interaction also indicate that experimentation with musical instruments did not just proceed in this one direction. The mix-and-match process underlying the invention of the sarod meant that one of the defining features of the Kabuli rabab, namely the sympathetic strings, also appeared later on the sursringar. Further experimentation from around the same time which has recently come to light, resulted in the invention of a hybrid instrument known as the sur-rabab, a cross between the sursringar and the seniya rabab.[31] The instrument (Plate 5-10) played by the seniya Mohammad Ali Khan is another interesting outcome. For all intents and purposes it appears to be a modern sarod but is played in the vertical position of a sursringar held against the left shoulder, while the performer kneels in the customary playing position of the rabab and sursringar as prescribed by the etiquette of the courts. It is not called a sarod but is identified as a rabab.[32]

Other experimentations with sound production by sarodiyas during the late nineteenth century resulted in the previously-mentioned instrument, the surchen, invented and played by Asghar Ali Khan. Reliable descriptions of this instrument are difficult to find. However, we do know that the quality of sound that Asghar Ali Khan could elicit from this prototype instrument popularly earned it the name of the 'singing sarod'. Apparently the sound was also of appropriate quality for the performance of vilambit raag alap. Unfortunately this instrument has now faded into obscurity.

Besides this, Keramatullah Khan is credited to have sometimes played his sarod with steel thimbles on the tips of the fingers of his left hand. While these thimbles were apparently effective in helping to produce a good sound, especially in the glides of meend, they apparently were also the cause of a great deal of racket when faster passages were played. Earlier, his father Niamatullah Khan, had experimented in using dried fish scales on the fingers of the left hand, a device previously employed by seniya rababiyas.[33]

Conclusion

The migration of notable musicians to Rampur from Lucknow and other places after 1856 established this Pathan court as a major source of patronage for Hindustani musicians. The influence that the nawabs exerted as patrons over the musicians employed in their court, the concentration of sarodiyas in Rampur, and any predisposition that the Pathan nawabs may have retained towards their traditional bards, could all be cited as reasons for the improved social status enjoyed by a number of sarodiyas during this period. In Bengal, by comparison, the geographical and cultural isolation of the exiled court of Wajid Ali Shah coupled with the emergence of new zamindar patrons eager to employ Hindustani musicians, also contributed to the increased social status of sarodiyas within this colonial state.

In both Rampur and Bengal, the acquisition of social status brought sarodiyas into direct contact with seniyas. This important and potent connection has been duly emphasized in the source material on sarodiyas described in this chapter. Just as this event signified the rise in the social status of a small number of sarodiyas, it also signalled the start of their cultural metamorphosis. During the 1880s these musicians became established solo artists who played a technically and generically expanded style of music on a newly-'invented' instrument. They were employed in the houses and estates of a variety of non-Pathan patrons throughout the country. Through their association with seniyas, along with the changes in their source of patronage, their instrument and the music they played, some sarodiyas were also endowed with increased musical status. As a result, Hindustani musicians such as Niamatullah Khan and Murad Ali Khan had become far removed from their ancestors who had accompanied the military parties of Pathan mercenaries heading down from the hills of Afghanistan in the previous century, both culturally and socially. This could not be more evident than in the quality of the sound that sarodiyas now produced on their instruments, a metamorphosis that had succeeded in making their experiences of Hindustani music audible.

Notes

1 Ironically, Wajid Ali Shah's exile to Calcutta appears to have in some ways stimulated an interest in music in the city because of the retinue of expert musicians that initially accompanied him.

2 His son Nawab Kalve Ali Khan further expanded the numbers of musicians employed at the court during his reign (1864–87).

3 Bahadur Hussain and Amir Khan both continued their service in Rampur until they passed away in 1873 and 1870 respectively.

4 Another attempt by the Rampur Nawab to influence musicians is described in a story related by Garg. He states that Yusuf Ali Khan's son, Nawab Haider Ali, was so intent on receiving the 'authentic' (vastvik) training from Bahadur Hussain Khan that he gave the musician one lakh of rupees, an immense sum of money for those days. Bahadur Hussain was initially persuaded by this offer, but after some time he is said to have returned the money and imparted the training all the same (Garg 1978:500).

5 Ghulam Mohammad Khan was a qawwal who is said to have learnt from Amir Khan's father, Umrao Khan (Garg 1978:489).

6 During that time, the eastern part of Bihar, where the district of Darbhanga was situated, was considered to be part of colonial Bengal. The town of that name had been the home of the Rajas of Darbhanga since 1762. These Hindu sovereigns trace their ancestry to Mahesh Thakur, a Mughal governor of the sixteenth century (Hunter 1881, vol. 3:38–39).

7 Cf. Mukhopadhyay 1977:131

> As far as his [Ghulam Ali's] method of playing is concerned, he used to play only gats. He never played raag-alap.

8 For a full description of this gat, along with musical examples, see interviews with Dasgupta (Calcutta Doordarshan: 1982), Moitra (by B. C. Deva, New Delhi: Sangeet Natak Akademi, SNA-1267, 1972), as well as Sanyal (1959:95–96), Solis (1970:71–73) and Miner (1993). The Feroz Khani gat, as played on the sarod, is discussed further in the section on playing styles later in this chapter.

9 Mukhopadhyay is of the opinion that Asad Ali Khan and not Abid Ali Khan was the father of Ahmed Ali Khan (1977:81), which contradicts the information obtained from Mohammad Ali Khan. As Mohammad Ali Khan was the son of Ahmed Ali Khan, his version,

that Ahmed Ali Khan was the son of Abid Ali Khan, is more likely to be correct.

10 In the last half of the nineteenth century, greater Bengal comprised what is now Bangladesh, West Bengal, Bihar, Assam and parts of eastern Uttar Pradesh.

11 There is an immense body of published work concentrating on the political, cultural and social history of Calcutta during this period. The following discussion in particular draws upon works by Banerjee (1989; 1998), Bayly (1990), Chatterjee (1994; 1995), Deshpande (1987), McGuire (1983), Mukherjee (1982), Niranjana (1990), Pandey (1989) and Sundar (1995).

12 Interestingly, the patronage of vocal music was greatest in Mumbai and that of instrumental music was more pronounced in Calcutta. These preferences are still evident in the musical activity and patronage available in the two cities. Delhi tends to fall in between the two, with equal importance given to both vocal and instrumental music. There are, again probably, a number of reasons for this being so, out of which the fact that the main representatives of the seniya instrumental tradition were primarily associated with Calcutta rather than Mumbai is probably one of the most important determinants.

13 Sachindra Nath Roy (b. 1912), is the paternal uncle of my sarod teacher Ashok Roy. He was Professor of Music at Meerut University for more than thirty years. He also trained in sitar under Enayat Khan and sarod with Alauddin Khan and had occasion to witness the brothers Keramatullah and Asadullah Khan playing together. S. N. Roy's younger brother, and the father of Ashok Roy, Ananta Kumar Roy, started his sarod training with Keramatullah Khan, and later became a disciple of Alauddin Khan.

14 It is worth noting that Enayat Ali Khan or his descendants have not sought to claim credit for the invention of the sarod.

15 Alauddin Khan is a well-known figure in Hindustani music in the twentieth century. His contribution to the sarod tradition is considered in the following chapter.

16 See Pradhan (2000) for the impact of music schools on the transmission of Hindustani in colonial Mumbai; Subramanian (1999) for the same in colonial Madras; Banerjee (1989) and Capwell (1985) for colonial Calcutta.

17 The consequences of this act, and the training of Bengali sarodiyas by Pathans, is examined in further detail in the following chapter.

18 Miner (1993) has already provided substantial information on the gats played by sitariyas and sarodiyas in the nineteenth century. It is recommended that this work be consulted for more detailed explanations and descriptions of the technical terms that appear here.

19 For example, Niamatullah Khan is described as performing a short aochar and jhala to show the raag roop (Gangopadhyay in *SRA1* 1991:55).

20 It is not possible to fully understand the place of gats in all the lineages of sarodiyas as this would require thorough training in the style of each lineage. The fast gats I learnt from my teacher Ashok Roy and his uncle Sachindra Nath Roy, both of whom identify with the Maihar gharana (see Chapter 6), were primarily said to have been based on tarana that they preferred. Accordingly, a strong distinction is observed between these and those gats based on thumri and chhota khyal.

21 Literally 'the king's favourite'. Oral sources in general attribute the development of this type of gat specifically to the Rampur court.

22 Yakub Ali Khan, the late maternal uncle of Amjad Ali Khan, used to play many such gats which could be adjusted to play in either drut teentaal (fast tempo sixteen-beat cycle) or, by leaving off the last four beats, could also be fitted into drut ektaal (fast tempo twelve-beat cycle). This information was passed on during a two-year period of learning from Yakub Ali Khan.

23 For further description and examples of these gat types, see Miner (1993). For more discussion of Feroz Khani gats, see Sanyal (1959) and Solis (1970).

24 See Solis (1970:85–94) for a general introduction to the use of these musical devices by sarodiyas.

25 See Shukla (1983:147) and Manuel (1985:354–60) for further discussion of gatkari.

26 See Mukherjee (1986:passim) for a detailed description of the structure of the dhrupad raag alap.

27 There was an important difference between the bols used in seniya rabab and those used on sarod. While the vocabulary of musical syllables used on sarod are mainly da ra dire, with variations such as

drar, dirda etc., the bols used on rabab were drim, drimdo, etc (Sachindra Nath Roy, personal communication: 1998).

28 Gangopadhyay provides an example of specific pakhawaj bols used in these gats: dheta dhage te te, kredha te te dhage te te, kredha te te kredha te te, etc. (*SRA1* 1991:54).

29 For more information on the effects and meaning of this transition, see discussion in *SRA2* 1995:137–68.

30 It appears that the qawwal-bachche played a major role in the development of the surbahar. Both Ghulam Mohammad and Sajjad Mohammad belonged to this community. They had studied the surbahar repertoire with seniyas and absorbed many fundamental elements of the been, particularly in terms of sound quality and the performance practice of dhrupad alap.

31 This instrument is in the possession of the Calcutta-based musician Somjit Dasgupta who was a disciple of Radhika Mohan Moitra.

32 The possibility that this is just an instrument the musician grabbed for the sake of the photograph cannot be entirely ruled out either. Nonetheless, these sorts of examples reinforce the point about the existence of greater variation in instrument design than is currently generally acknowledged.

33 Sachindra Nath Roy, personal communication: 1998.

Sarodiyas and Sarod Gharanas

By the late nineteenth century networks of patronage located in colonial metropolises began to rival those available to musicians in regional centres. Although many regional courts such as Rampur, Jodhpur, Mewati, Jaipur, continued to maintain retinues of musicians right until Independence in 1947, the vicissitudes of coloniality along with the dwindling resources of their 'princely states' meant that, in the end, regional networks were unable to compete with the flow of capital, the range of activities and the collective promise of opportunities which the networks of the colonial metropolises increasingly had to offer.

A number of events were to accompany the gradual transition between these two networks. One of these was the recasting or restructuring of the social organization of musicians into the social clusters known as gharanas from either large-scale occupational groups or closed family lineages. This latter type of social institution effectively enabled musicians to engage the new networks and then mediated the ways and means by which this should occur. It was through the social and musical stipulations of the gharana system that, arguably, the transition between past and emerging musical practices could proceed. The effectiveness and appeal of this system as an adaptive strategy may have derived from being based on, and growing out of, pre-existing practices such as vans, baj (musical styles), vanis and khandans (Neuman 1980:146–49). Accordingly, it was not so much a brand new paradigm for the social and musical organization of musicians but a modification and recasting of existing conventions. Sarodiyas were one group among many groups of soloist musicians such as khyaliyas and sitariyas who had or were in the process of formalizing their own particular gharanas.

The social and cultural dynamics in the expanding colonial metropolis of Calcutta and the patronage which the zamindars and bhadraloks offered to Hindustani musicians generated many outcomes that were also to have an effect on sarodiyas. One of these was the revisiting of the past, a convention by which these new patrons strove to reconnect contemporary music practice with an imagined and long-lost golden age of Hindu music. Motivating this reactive trait was the desire, tacit or otherwise, to purge contemporary music practice of the moral decadence that it was perceived to have acquired from its association with Indo-Islamic courts. The other consequence concerned the institution-building spirit of modernity promoted by these new patrons which, over time, resulted in a profusion of music schools, public concerts, music circles and so on.[1] These conditions were to generate the means and opportunities for sarodiyas to make the transition from the 'domestic' contract of the mir or court musician to that of the entrepreneur. Before examining the details of the various experiences sarodiyas underwent in the course of entering these new networks, it is necessary to consider the plight of the still-influential Rampur court in the face of both British paramountcy in North India and the developments in modernity unfolding in Bengal.

The Rampur Court and Seniya Musicians

The renown of the nawabs of Rampur as patrons of Hindustani music was disrupted in the early 1870s, after the death of the seniyas Bahadur Hussain and Amir Khan. The loss of these musicians had a profound effect on the musical life of the court. This unfortunate situation was further compounded at the end of the next decade when the British resident ousted Nawab Mushtaq Ali who had ruled for only two years between 1887 and 1889. Compared to the Mughal and Awadhi courts, the paramountcy of British rule constrained any designs that the Rampur nawabs may have previously harboured about constructing a strong, independent, political and cultural identity for their rule.

Hamid Ali Khan, another member of the ruling family who was deemed, for reasons that remain unclear, to be more suitable to the colonial administration, replaced Mushtaq Ali Khan as Nawab in 1889. As he was still a minor in 1889, a Council of Regency that oversaw the administration of Rampur for the following ten years administered the affairs of the State.

It was probably the combined effect of political interference and the death of Amir Khan and Bahadur Hussain that caused the serious decline in the patronage of musicians in Rampur from 1873 to 1892. Consequently, it appears that many musicians—including a number of sarodiyas—left the court in search of other avenues. The noticeable lack of details of musical activities in the court during this period suggests a significant exodus of musicians from Rampur.

Despite this rather bleak situation, the reputation of the Rampur nawabs as cultural patrons was rekindled in 1899 when Nawab Hamid Ali appointed Amir Khan's son, Wazir Khan, as chief court musician. Wazir Khan was probably born in the early 1860s. After the death of his father in 1870, Wazir Khan spent around twelve years in his ancestral home in Benaras studying with his uncles, Nissar Ali, Sadiq Ali and Baruq Mian (Mukhopadhyay 1977:74). From Benaras, Wazir Khan went to Calcutta in 1892 where he stayed until 1899, during which time the direct administration of Rampur State was under the British Regency Council. Wazir Khan was renowned for his expert singing of dhrupad and dhamar, as well as for his playing of the sursringar, been and seniya rabab. He was the eldest of the fifth generation in the line of the famous seniya of the Mughal court, Niamat Khan, alias Saharan (Garg 1978:546). At the same time that Wazir Khan took up his appointment, the seniya rababiya Mohammad Ali Khan (1834–1927), son of Basat Khan, was also employed by the court for approximately eight years during the reign of Hamid Ali (1899–1924). Mukhopadhyay points out that Mohammad Ali, however, was primarily employed to teach Chhaman Sahib, the son of Nawab Haidar Ali and apparently did not train any other musicians during this time (1977:85).

Around the turn of the twentieth century, the Rampur nawabs enlisted many other famous musicians in addition to seniyas for their court. In this impressive list were Mohammad Hussain Khan and Nabi Baksh, both beenkars, Bundu Khan sarangiya, Hafiz Khan and Karim Khan sitariyas and Kathak dancers Maharaja Binda-Din, Kalka Prasad, Bhawani Prasad and Achchhan Prasad (Mukhopadhyay 1977:86). Over the two decades, from 1900 to 1920, the reputation of the Rampur court as patrons of music spread throughout the country.

The finale of Rampur court's leading involvement with musical patronage effectively came with the death of Wazir Khan in 1927. Although Nawab Raza Ali Khan maintained musicians and dancers after this time, his court was a faint shadow of the one that had existed at the beginning of the century.

Source Material on Sarodiyas

The Descendants of Ghulam Ali Khan: The Murad Ali Khan Lineage

At some stage the relations between Murad Ali and his brothers, Nanhe Khan and Hussain Ali, were apparently strained due to a personal disagreement. As a result, a major rift occurred in the family. As Murad Ali Khan did not have any sons, he adopted and trained the orphaned Abdullah Khan (1843–1926).[2] Like the descendants of Najaf Ali Khan, Abdullah Khan belonged to one of the sarodiya mohullas of Shahjahanpur. Most of this sarodiya's musical career was spent as a court musician along with his father, Murad Ali, in the Darbhanga court. Abdullah Khan's own son, Mohammad Amir Khan (1876–1934), grew up in that court where he learnt to play sarod from both his father, Abdullah, and his grandfather, Murad Ali. Both Abdullah Khan and Mohammad Amir Khan (Plate 6-1), or Amir Khan as the latter was more commonly known, were well known for their expertise in playing Feroz Khani and Reza Khani gats. Together, this pair of sarodiyas was responsible for introducing the playing style of Rampur sarodiyas into Bengal (Mukhopadhyay 1977:135). Amir Khan made a few commercial recordings that were reproduced on 78rpm discs in the first part of this century.[3]

At the beginning of the twentieth century, Amir Khan moved permanently to Bengal where he was initially employed by Lalit Mohan Moitra, a zamindar of a large estate in Rajshahi, now in Bangladesh. Sometime later, Amir Khan shifted to Gauripur, a nearby town, where he was employed by another family of zamindars, the Roy Choudhurys. This latter family was well known in Bengal for their patronage and, to some extent, performance of Hindustani music.[4] Finally, in the latter part of his life, he moved to Calcutta and stayed at Moitra's house. He died in 1934, at the age of fifty-eight. Little is known about Amir Khan's own offspring except that none became recognized sarodiyas. Nevertheless, Amir Khan taught sarod to a number of Bengali disciples during his stay in Calcutta.

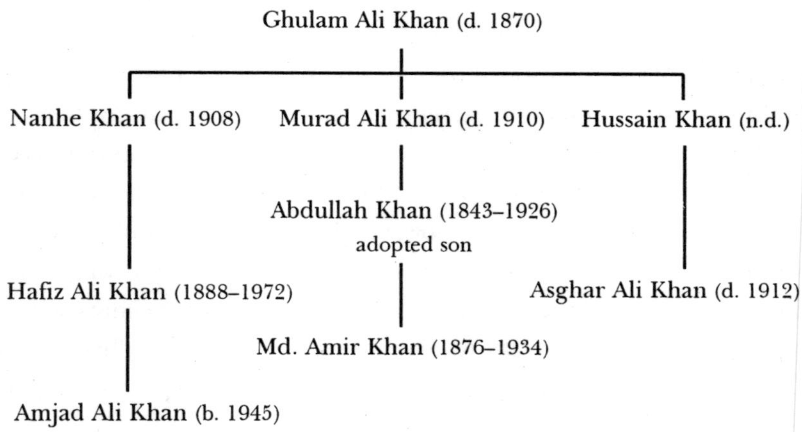

Table 6-1: Descendants of Ghulam Ali Khan

Following the death of this sarodiya, the musical style on sarod that had been developed within the Murad Ali Khan lineage was continued through various Bengali musicians, who, generally speaking, all came from well-to-do families. These were namely Birendra Kishore Roy Choudhury, Asutosh Kundu, Panchanon Ganguly, Bhola Nath Bhattacharya, Banikantha Mukhopadhyay (1912–65) and Radhika Mohan Moitra (1917–81). The last three of these musicians were the most renowned musical representatives of the Amir Khan style.[5]

The Nanhe Khan Lineage

Hafiz Ali Khan (1888–1972) began his musical education at the age of six with his father Nanhe Khan who, at that time, was employed by the Gwalior court. According to Hafiz Ali Khan (Plate 6-3), his father had introduced 'certain fast sweeping taans of the vocal style of the khyaliyas of Gwalior, Haddu and Hassu Khan.' (Khanna 1975:n.p.)[6] After his father's death in 1908, Hafiz Ali Khan also briefly studied with his paternal uncles, the previously-mentioned Murad Ali Khan and Asghar Ali Khan. After this training, Hafiz Ali Khan travelled to the Hindu pilgrimage of Vrindavan where he learnt dhrupad and dhamar from two renowned haveli dhrupadiyas, Ganeshilal and Chukkhalal Choube. These musicians were said to be the direct musical descendants of the legendary Swami Haridas and were representatives of the Dagarvani style of dhrupad (Khanna 1975:n.p.).

That a Muslim sarodiya from a Pathan background studied under brahman, Hindu temple musicians should not escape notice here. As has been noted, it was common for court musicians to acquire musical status through some level of association with the seniya line of musical transmission. In this instance, however, Hafiz Ali Khan looked beyond the musical heritage of his family and sought to study dhrupad from those musicians who represented the tradition to which seniya style in effect owed its genesis. By receiving training from the dhrupadiyas Ganeshilal and Chukkhalal Choube, Hafiz Ali Khan bypassed, to some extent, the social practices and restrictions adhered to by court musicians, both of which controlled and limited access to musical status.[7]

Hafiz Ali Khan left Vrindavan at the age of twenty-two and arrived in Rampur around 1910. He was no stranger to the Rampur court for it was here that his uncles Murad Ali Khan and Hussain Ali Khan had previously lived, trained and been employed. It was also here that he continued his earlier training in dhrupad as a disciple of the seniya Wazir Khan until 1919. In an interview towards the end of his life, Hafiz Ali related the story of how he became a student of Wazir Khan:

> The Nawab Saheb [of Rampur] was a great connoisseur of and generous to good artists, so many of the finest musicians of the time were his frequent visitors. Ustad Wazir Khan Saheb had made Rampur his

> home and the Nawab was his pupil. The first opportunity I got to perform before the Nawab, he told me to play the raag Darbari-Kanhra. In those days it was not like today when a musician himself decides what he will play. In those days when music flourished in the Courts of the rulers and aristocrats, usually the ruler would ask for a particular raag to be played. This was a great challenge, for one could not go prepared and practised to perform a particular raag. Well, it seems, by the blessing of Allah, that my performance must have displayed some unusual talent, for, after a short conversation, Ustad Wazir Khan agreed to accept me as his pupil, He was noted in the whole of India as the most deeply learned purist and a very difficult Ustad to induce to take one as his pupil. I had the honour of having the 'ganda' (sacred thread) tied on my wrist by him (Khanna 1975:n.p.).[8]

While there have been many instances in which a musician has claimed to have been a disciple of the seniya tradition, in reality these claims may sometimes have been based on a passing or casual acquaintance with this tradition. By specifying that he was formally initiated through the ganda-bandh ritual, Hafiz Ali implies therefore that he was a 'bona fide' student of Wazir Khan. The extent of this training would nevertheless have been subjected to the same rigorous restrictions seniyas placed on the transmission of their knowledge to all students from outside their social core. The grounds for Wazir Khan's decision to accept this sarodiya as his disciple are not clear. His decision may have taken into account Hafiz Ali's Pathan heritage, his family's past strong musical association with the Pathan nawabs of Rampur, his previous training in dhrupad in Vrindavan and his demonstrated performance skills on the sarod.[9] For whatever reasons, this musical association proved to be a tremendous opportunity for Hafiz Ali Khan and a sign of acknowledgment of his musicianship.

Through his training with the temple dhrupadiyas and the seniya Wazir Khan, Hafiz Ali Khan was able to develop a depth to his playing of the vilambit alap on the sarod which he rendered characteristically in dhrupad style by demonstrating due emphasis on the correct use of microtonal nuances and embellishments.[10] The emphasis he placed on the subtleties of intonation and the use of microtones meant that he was renowned for having 'maintained the purity of the notes of the raag', as such things are often euphemistically described.[11]

Due to the nature of his musical experiences and orientation, his approach to playing started to differ from his contemporaries in the Amir Khan branch of the family. His time at the Rampur and Gwalior courts led him to become well acquainted with khyal and thumri styles, yet in general he chose to highlight dhrupad above these other forms (Khanna 1975:n.p.).[12] While he is described as retaining the older and 'purer' style of sarod based on the rabab style, he is also credited with having incorporated khyal and gayaki (khyal vocal) style into his playing (Moitra SNA-1267: 1972). Even so, he is said to have generally restricted ornamentation to conform to dhrupad conventions (Garg 1978:573).

The type of sarod Hafiz Ali played was essentially of the same design as the one played by Amir Khan. However, in the course of his lifetime, Hafiz Ali Khan appears to have slightly increased the dimensions of the main resonator of his instrument and the distance in string length between the main bridge and the nut (Plate 6-3). The inspiration for the former modification at least might have been drawn from the larger, more roundly-shaped resonators of the sursringar, been and sitar. Hafiz Ali Khan also added an extra pa string to his sarod, tuned a fourth below the kharaj/low octave tonic sa.[13] This expanded the effective range of his instrument to three octaves, from pa in the ati-mandra saptak/the fifth in the extra low octave to sa in the tar saptak/the tonic in the upper octave and gave his instrument the same pitch range as the sursringar. Besides these five main playing strings, Hafiz Ali's sarod was constructed with eleven sympathetic strings, one side string tuned to sa (madhya saptak/middle octave tonic) which sounded as a drone, and two chikari strings tuned to sa (tar saptak/upper octave tonic) which were used to punctuate phrases and provided a tonic drone. Sometimes these two chikari strings would be tuned to ni (madhya saptak/middle octave) and sa (tar saptak/upper octave). Hafiz Ali Khan was mostly accompanied by tabla but occasionally he also performed along with the pakhawaj. On being asked in an interview why he favoured the pakhawaj when it was not so commonly used by his contemporaries, Hafiz Ali Khan replied:

> Well, aside from the fact that the sonorous sound of the pakhavaj pleased me, and sounded well with my playing, as it was much akin to the dhrupad style, I had also a close relationship with the famous pakhavajia family of Kadau Singhji. His family and mine played together for three generations. I was very friendly with them and did not want to sever our traditional relations (Khanna 1975:n.p.).

It will be recalled from an earlier discussion that the pakhawaj was the standard percussion instrument accompanying performances of both vocal and instrumental dhrupad. After spending around six or seven years studying with Wazir Khan in Rampur, Hafiz Ali Khan was later employed by Shrimant Madhavrao Maharaj and his successors at the Gwalior court (Garg 1978:573). Shortly afterwards, at the invitation of Maharaj Pradyot Kumar Tagore (a relative of the Pathuriaghata Tagores) and Bhupendra Kumar Ghose, he made his first performance in Calcutta in 1921. His performances in Calcutta were apparently very favourably reviewed in Bengali newspapers (Garg 1978:573). It was around this time that he also stayed for a while in the house of the famous Boral family of Calcutta (Mishra 1981:127–28). After this time he returned to Gwalior from where he regularly travelled to perform at major music conferences and other recitals throughout India.

The Amalgamation of the Lineages of Karimullah and Najaf Ali Khan

Although the descendants of Karimullah Khan trace their line of descent in India to the beginning of the eighteenth century, it has been shown that it was Niamatullah Khan (1827–1903) who was the first musician in the lineage to receive seniya training and to have played the Hindustani sarod. Niamatullah Khan's two sons, Keramatullah Khan and Asadullah 'Kaukab' Khan, also achieved reputations in their lifetimes not only for their sarod playing but also for their written commentaries on Hindustani music.

Enayat Ali Khan, the great grandson of Najaf Ali Khan, was also in Bengal at the same time as Niamatullah Khan. As previously mentioned, the son of Enayat Ali Khan, Shafayet (1848–1920), was married to Niamatullah Khan's daughter during the 1870s, an event which was to set into motion the eventual amalgamation of Karimullah's and Najaf Ali Khan's lineages. Even though Shafayet had married Niamatullah's daughter, this relationship was apparently not considered appropriate enough to convince Niamatullah Khan to impart training to his son-in-law. Therefore, it was not until Shafayet Khan's son, Sakhawat Hussain (1875–1955) married the daughter of Niamatullah Khan's son, Asadullah 'Kaukab' Khan, around the turn of this century that these lineages effectively merged (Table 6-2). Marital links between members of these two families therefore spanned two generations. It was on the basis of this prolonged association that Sakhawat Hussain was eventually formally accepted by Asadullah 'Kaukab' Khan as his disciple.[14] Therefore, after Sakhawat Hussain Khan's marriage and, more specifically, from the time of his training by Asadullah Khan, the line of transmission carried through Niamatullah Khan's lineage became common to both families, i.e. those of Najaf Ali and Karimullah Khan.

In 1926, Sakhawat Hussain Khan (Plate 6-4) was also one of the first musicians enlisted by Bhatkhande to teach amateur musicians in his music college in Lucknow, a position he retained until his death in 1955 (Mishra 1985:31). Like his grandfather Enayat Ali Khan, Sakhawat Hussain also toured and performed in Europe. During the period 1934–39 he had the dubious distinction of playing before Adolf Hitler and being awarded a medal.[15]

Commercial recordings of Sakhawat Hussain display drut gats alternating with passages of taans, with a roughly equal emphasis on melodic and rhythmic development. The speciality of Sakhawat Khan, however, was the toda consisting of bol patterns drawn from a mixture of the vast repertoire of parans that formed an important part of the musical capital of this gharana which were also combined with the bols on which the gat itself was based. Sakhawat Hussain Khan was usually accompanied by the tabla, although occasionally he would enlist the accompaniment of the pakhawaj, often played by Pandit Sakharam.

Overall, the playing style of the members of both families came to display some of the technique and playing style of the seniya rabab. This influence is evident in the clarity of the right-hand patterns and the passages of laykari that were one of the main specialities of this lineage, a taste of which can be heard on the 78rpm disc recordings of Khamaj and Pilu by Asadullah Kaukab Khan.

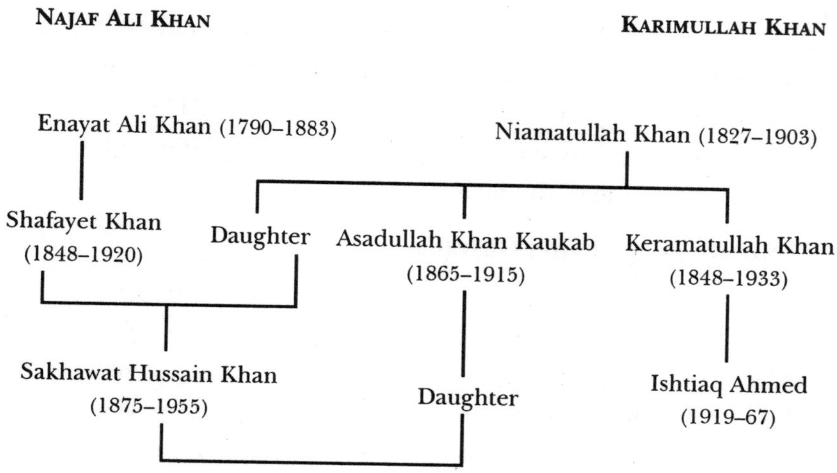

Table 6-2: Marriage links between the descendants of Najaf Ali Khan and Karimullah Khan

At the same time that the two lineages effectively merged, a number of Bengali students also began learning sarod from both Keramatullah Khan and his brother Asadullah Khan (Mukhopadhyay 1977:53–54). Among these students were Dhirendranath Bose, the Natore Maharaj, Kishorechandra Dey and Ananta Kumar Roy. Of these Bengali students, it was Dhirendranath Bose who received systematic training over a number of years from Asadullah Khan. This training began around 1900 and continued until Asadullah's death in 1912. However, the trial that Najaf Ali Khan's descendants had to endure before being accepted by Asadullah and Keramatullah Khan brings into question the degree of training that these two sarodiyas would have been willing to impart to these Bengali disciples. Nonetheless, according to Mukhopadhyay, Bose became the first recognized sarodiya from a non-Pathan family background (1977:52). Bose's own disciple, Shyam Ganguly (b. 1911), continued to maintain his style of playing.

The type of sarod played by Niamatullah Khan, with its distinctive open pegbox, continued to be used by his descendants. The pegbox of this instrument housed the four main strings tuned in ascending pitch: sa, pa (mandra saptak—tonic and fifth in the lower octave), sa and ma (madhya saptak—tonic and fourth in the middle octave) as well as the two extra drone strings tuned to the tonic. The two chikari strings (both tuned to sa) and eleven taraf strings were tied to pegs attached to the side of the fingerboard.

Sarodiyas and Sarod Gharanas

When colonial hegemony displaced premodern, feudal political structures across North India, networks of patronage in regional centres began to be either marginalized or in some other way recast. The unfolding of this political environment generated new classes and types of patrons, as well as networks and sensibilities for engaging culture. One sensibility, sometimes assigned to the bhadralok society in Calcutta at the time, was a trait of puritanism that invariably evoked a strong reaction towards a perceived social and moral dubiousness of Hindustani music in general and the 'Ustads from the North' in particular.[16] The sarodiya Buddhadev Dasgupta recalls a common belief held at the time that music was 'the surest and swiftest path to damnation.'[17] Capwell (1985:167) has mentioned another response from this period in which a 'very learned man' is reputed to have declared that '. . . he would rather see his son dead at his feet than allow him to learn music'. Notwithstanding such anecdotal declarations, Hindustani musicians were patronized by these wealthy classes, some even becoming their sincere disciples. Somehow, though, an impression of immorality firmly remained in the minds of the majority of the bhadraloks towards musicians and this issue itself is worthy of its own study.[18].

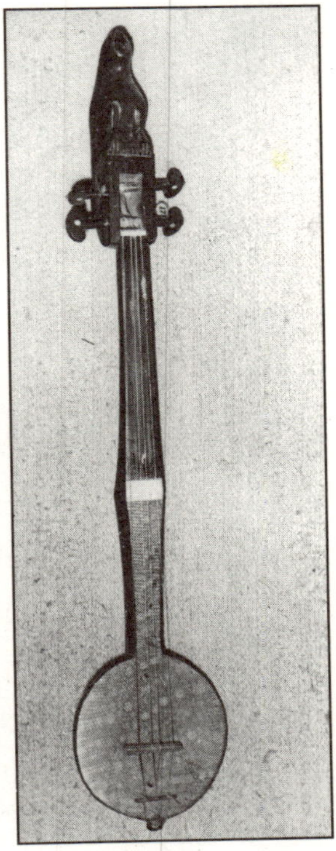

TOP LEFT *Plate 1-1* : *Rabab* (Sangeet Natak Akademi). TOP RIGHT *Plate 1-2* : *Chitra Veena*. BOTTOM LEFT *Plate 2-1* : *Lute from the Stok Monastry, Ladakh*. BOTTOM RIGHT *Plate 2-2* : *Dotara* (Sangeet Natak Akademi).

TOP *Plate 4-1 : A nautch group.* BOTTOM *Plate 4-2 : Sadiq Ali Khan playing the been.*

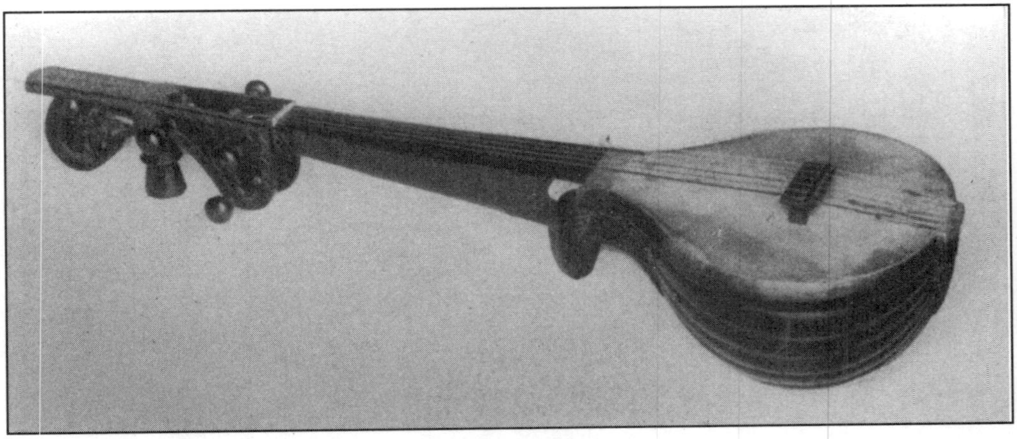

TOP *Plate 4-3* : *Seniya rabab*. BOTTOM *Plate 4-4* : *Birendra Kishore Roy Chowdhury playing the sursringar* (Sangeet Natak Akademi).

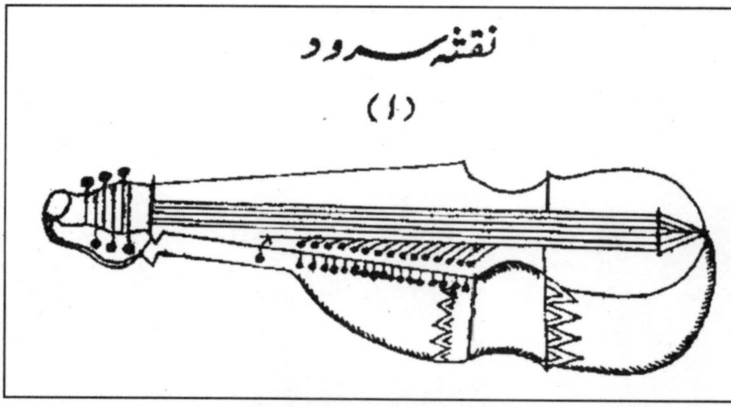

TOP *Plate 4-5a* : *Niamatullah Khan's sarod*. BOTTOM *Plate 4-5* : *Niamatullah Khan*.

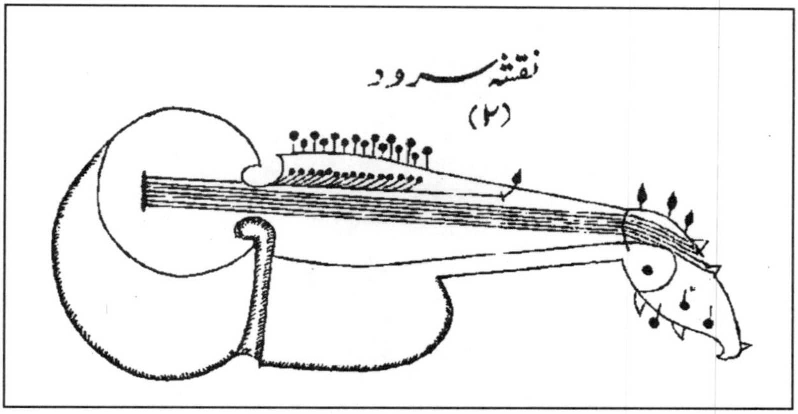

TOP *Plate 4-7a* : *Keramatullah Khan's sarod.*

BOTTOM *Plate 4-7* : *Keramatullah Khan.*

TOP *Plate 5-1* : *Fida Hussain Khan*. BOTTOM *Plate 5-2* : *Participants at the Lucknow Music Conference, 1925*.

TOP *Plate 5-4 : Keramatullah Khan and Asadullah 'Kaukab' Khan*. BOTTOM *Plate 5-5 : Keramatullah Khan with accompanists*.

TOP LEFT *Plate 5-3 : Ahmed Ali Khan*. TOP RIGHT *Plate 5-6 : Shafayet Ali Khan*. BOTTOM *Plate 5-7 : Musharaf Khan with a sarod variation*.

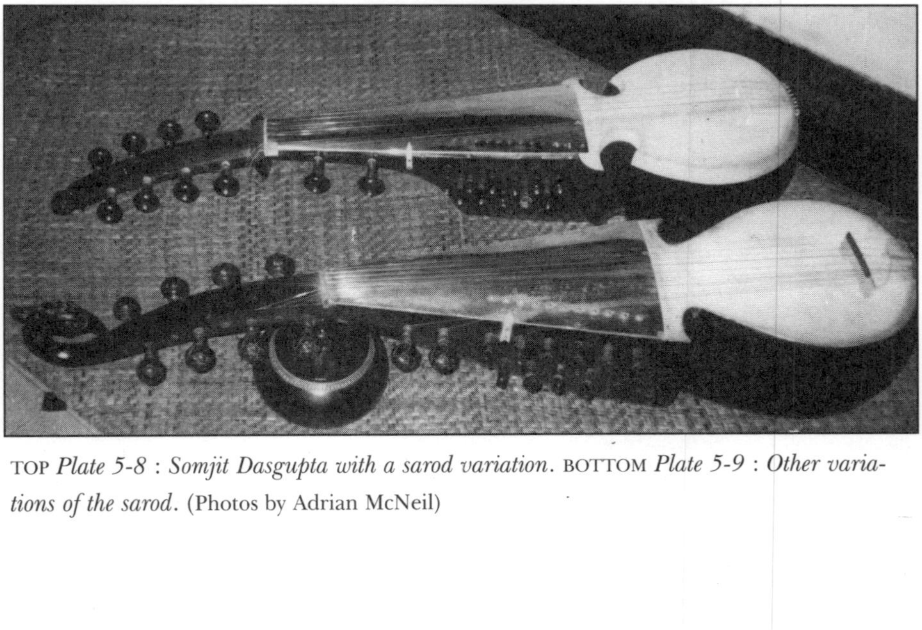

TOP *Plate 5-8 : Somjit Dasgupta with a sarod variation*. BOTTOM *Plate 5-9 : Other variations of the sarod*. (Photos by Adrian McNeil)

TOP LEFT *Plate 5-10* : *Muhammad Ali Khan and a sarod variation*. TOP RIGHT *Plate 6-1a* : *Wazir Khan*. BOTTOM *Plate 6-1* : *Muhammad Amir Khan*.

TOP *Plate 6-3* : *Hafiz Ali Khan*. BOTTOM *Plate 7-3* : *Amjad Ali Khan with accompanists.*

TOP *Plate 6-4* :*Sakhawat Hussain Khan*. BOTTOM *Plate 6-4a* : *Sakhawat Hussain Khan with Pandit Sakharam on the pakhawaj.*

TOP *Plate 6-5* : *Alauddin Khan*. BOTTOM *Plate 6-6* : *Alauddin Khan with Ravi Shankar and Ali Akbar Khan* (right).

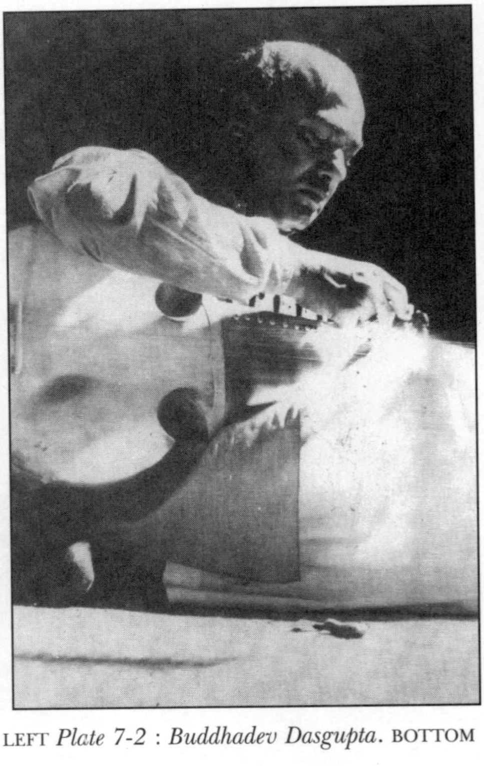

TOP *Plate 6-2* : *Radhika Mohan Moitra*. BOTTOM LEFT *Plate 7-2* : *Buddhadev Dasgupta*. BOTTOM RIGHT *Plate 7-3* : *Ali Akbar Khan*.

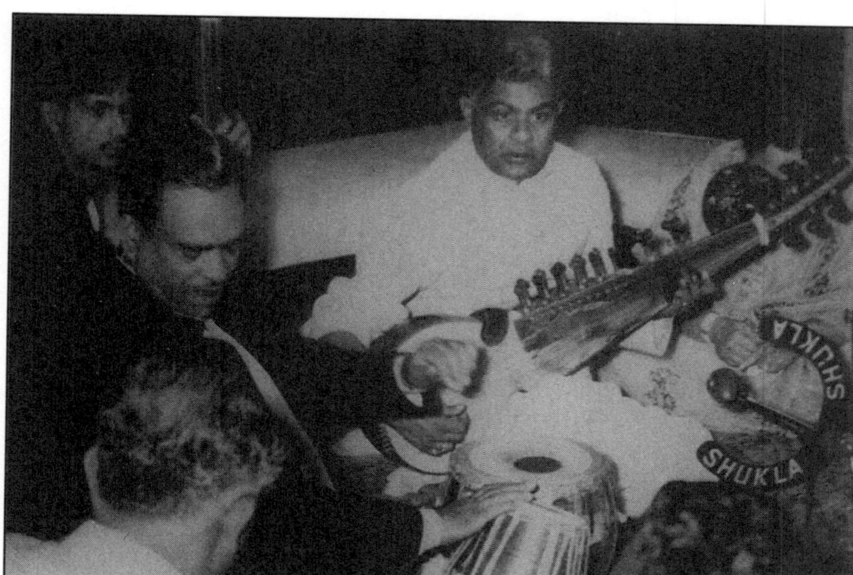

TOP *Plate 7-4 : Ishtiaq Ahmed Khan*. BOTTOM *Plate 7-6 : Umar Khan with accompanists*.

Plate 7-7 : Hemen Sen in his shop on Rashbehari Avenue, Calcutta.
(Photo by Adrian McNeil)

In this historical context it could be argued that the project of the 'Sanskritization' of culture prevalent in places like Calcutta in the nineteenth century was one strategy applied by some members of the bhadralok society to attempt to engage with Hindustani music but at the same time, filter out such undesirable elements. Perhaps there is no better illustration of this process than Sourindra Mohun Tagore's attempt to rename the sarod the 'sharadiya vina', thus simultaneously endowing the instrument with the legitimacy of an ancient Hindu past and purging the instrument of its immediate and distasteful reputation earned in the decadent courts of North India.[19] It seems that as the sarod gradually became accepted as a mainstream Hindustani instrument within that milieu, the more past associations between the sarod and its social and moral ancestry seemed to retreat, and in the process its Pathan associations were also underplayed.

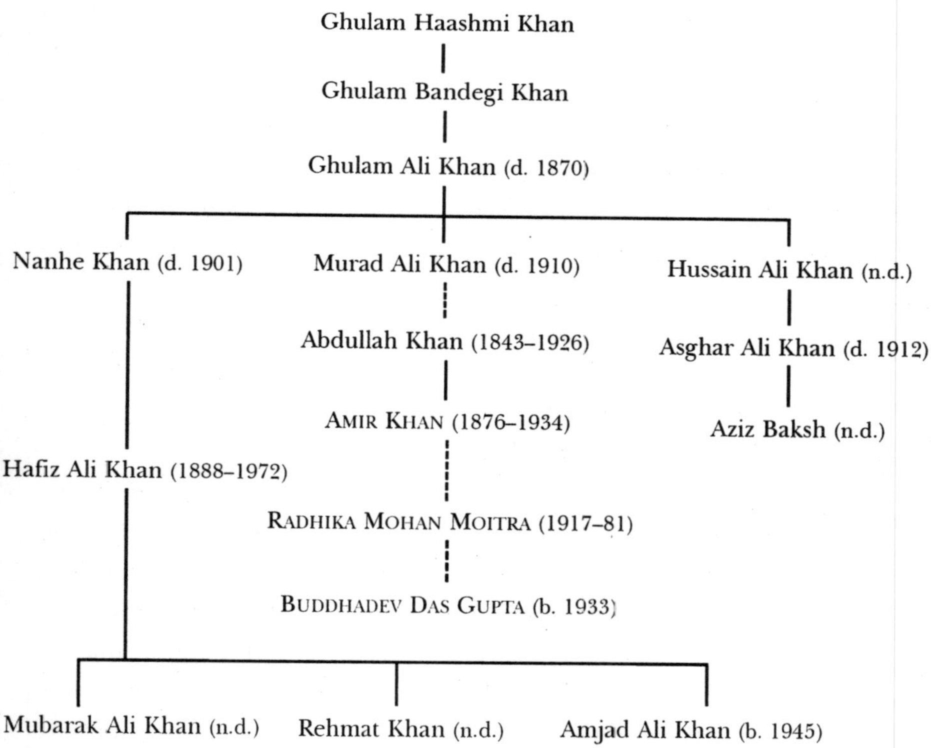

Table 6-4: The Ghulam Ali Khan/Gwalior gharana and its branches, including the Shahjahanpur gharana of Amir Khan

It was during this time of marked political transition, and perhaps also in response to these sensibilities, that the gharana system emerged as a successor to that of jajmani structures as a strategy for codifying relations between the newly-established groups of patrons and professional performers of Hindustani music. It did so through the regulation of the distribution of patronage, as well as by assigning a musician's social identity and status. With regard to this last point, Neuman (1980:169) has noted that 'aside from providing a social organization of specialized knowledge, gharanas provided a sociomusical identity for musicians . . . [who] were exposed to a wider and more diverse and anonymous public; the name of a gharana did not leave the musician similarly anonymous.'

Recent studies have examined the social and musical organization, history and workings of the gharana system,[20] therefore there is no need to dwell too much on this subject here beyond the following points. The first gharanas evolved out of family lineages of khyaliyas around the middle of the nineteenth century. In essence, a gharana can be thought of as a form of social organization structured around a core bloodline comprising a progenitor and at least two successive generations of direct descendants. The musical identity of the gharana was derived from the specialized knowledge that its participants had inherited by birth or association which became the musical capital of that gharana. A gharana's identity was also derived from the musical style, its performers and its approach to musical aesthetics. Collectively, gharanas formed a closed system which in practice served to protect and regulate this flow of musical capital.

The displacement of the jajmani structures of social organization and the formation of the gharana system generated a period of significant fluidity within the social and musical structures of Hindustani music. Apart from a general restructuring of the social organization of musician groups, it opened up new lines of access to the transmission of Hindustani musical knowledge. This opportunity was seized upon by a number of groups of musicians (including sarodiyas) who were able to position themselves in less marginal positions in Hindustani music than they had experienced when they participated in jajmani networks.

The transformation in the social organization of sarodiyas from hereditary lineages within Pathan communities to gharanas of Hindustani music was not a uniform process. By this it is meant that the formation of the various sarod gharanas did not occur at the same time, nor did their social regrouping unfold in the same manner. Attempts at documenting the early stages of sarod gharanas are further complicated by the fact that the 'birth' of a gharana cannot be traced to any one specific occasion but rather to a process of gradual acceptance over an imprecise period of time.

With the acceptance of the gharana system, a significant distinction emerged between those Hindustani musicians who could claim to be gharanedar (belonging to a gharana) and those who were not able to access this new social configuration. Within the colonial networks, the latter group were disparagingly known and referred to as mirasis. In this specific historical context the term mirasi came to signify those belonging to hereditary musician communities who not only had no legitimate 'classical' music pedigree but, worse still, were mostly likely to have accompanied tawaifs and prostitutes. The perceptions of decadence and moral turpitude with which the North Indian courts were equated in the minds of the Bengali middle class and landed classes, were now directed towards such musicians.

This was the social and moral setting in which the formation of gharanas was historically grounded. Against this backdrop, the descendants of Ghulam Ali Khan from the Gwalior branch of the family can be said to have formed their own gharana before the lifetime of Hafiz Ali Khan. Hafiz Ali Khan represented the third generation of this line of descent which, by then, was made up of Ghulam Ali Khan, Nanhe Khan and Hafiz Ali Khan. The principal steps in the transformation of this lineage into a gharana took place after Hafiz Ali had completed his training from Wazir Khan and had begun to participate in music conferences in Calcutta dating from around 1920. By this time it had begun to be called either the Ghulam Ali Khan or Gwalior sarod gharana.

The other branch of the family, descended from Murad Ali Khan, was most likely considered to have become a separate gharana during the life of sarodiya Amir Khan (1876–1934). The recognition of Amir Khan also fulfilled the criteria that a gharana must have three successive generations of acknowledged musicians in order to be regarded as one. In this case, the line of succession became Murad Ali Khan—Abdullah Khan—Amir Khan. Abdullah Khan's adoption by Murad Ali illustrates that some sarodiyas opted for the perpetuation of their family lineage as opposed to rigidly maintaining a closed hereditary occupational category solely restricted to blood descendants. Such acts were often known to create serious conflict within other members of the larger family grouping.

The initial stage in the transformation of this lineage into a gharana can be traced to the first decades of the twentieth century, when Amir Khan moved to Bengal and was quite successful in engaging the new networks and structures of patronage. He performed in the many music conferences and other public performances that occurred throughout the 1920s and became very well known and popular as a result. It was during this period that this hereditary lineage of sarodiyas became known as the Shahjahanpur gharana. It was named after Shahjahanpur because the extended family of the orphan Abdullah Khan belonged to one of the mohullas in that area. The stylistic distinctions that set the two branches of the Ghulam Ali descendants apart were manifold and were clearly determined by the type of seniya training undergone by earlier members of the two branches.

A third, more obscure, branch of the family emanated from Ghulam Ali Khan's third son Hussain Khan. He learnt music primarily from his father and spent most of his life as a sarodiya in Rampur. His son, Asghar Ali Khan (1842–1912), became the most renowned musician of this lineage. As a musician his career was contemporary with Murad Ali Khan. As Asghar Ali Khan did not have a son, the family line effectively stopped with him. Even though he had a son-in-law, Aziz Baksh, Asghar Ali did not consider their family relationship appropriate enough for training to be imparted to his son-in-law.

With their lineage effectively ending with Asghar Ali Khan, this third branch of Ghulam Ali's descendants was not considered to have formed a separate gharana. Nevertheless, it seems that Asghar Ali, strictly speaking, could rightly have made such a claim, being the third successive generation of musicians after Ghulam Ali Khan. Apart from Ghulam Ali Khan, there was little direct seniya influence on its members. Nevertheless, Asghar Ali was a recognized sarodiya who, in his later life, was employed as a court musician in Darbhanga. The members of this family did not teach musicians outside their lineage nor did they have much exposure to seniya training. For these reasons, this lineage did not develop into a separate sarod gharana.

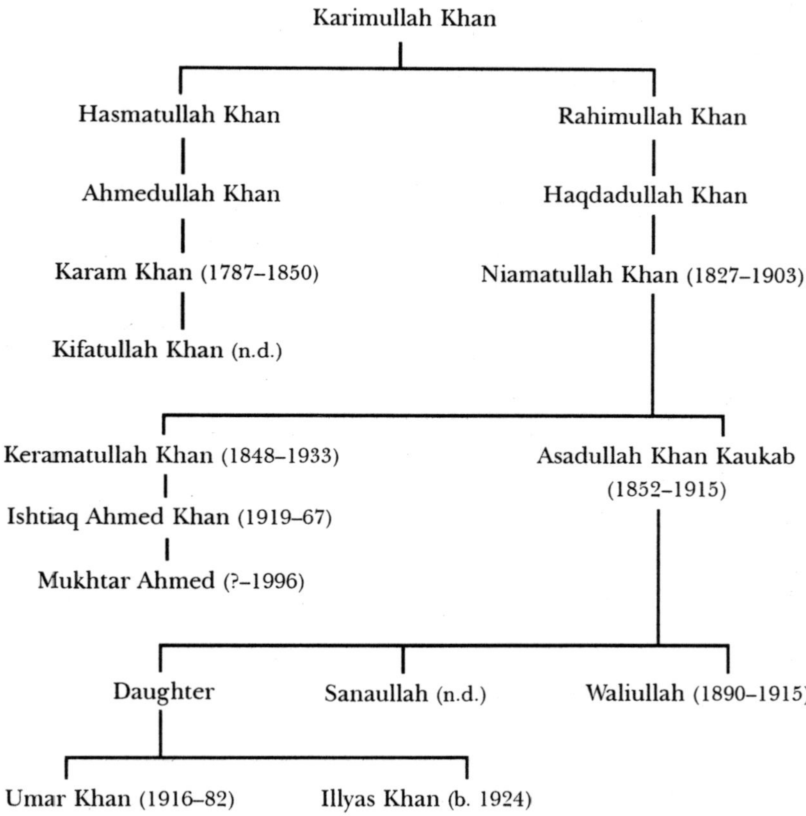

Table 6-5: The Bulandshahr/Lucknow sarod gharana

In the line of the descendants of Najaf Ali Khan, it was Niamatullah Khan who was accredited with both 'inventing' the sarod and being the first member of their family to have undergone systematic training from a seniya. It is for these reasons that he is regarded as the progenitor of their gharana which is referred to by at least three different names—the Bulandshahr gharana (named after the ancestral home of the family in India), the Niamatullah Khan gharana or, less commonly, the Lucknow gharana. Strictly speaking, it was not until the time of Niamatullah's grandson, Ishtiaq Ahmed (1919–1967), that the criterion of three generations had been fulfilled and the formation of the gharana only then completed.

Although Niamatullah's sons, Asadullah Khan Kaukab and Keramatullah Khan, could not claim to have been members of an established sarod gharana, they were, by the same token, clearly not regarded as mirasi musicians either. The social status that they enjoyed as instrumentalists could be explained in either of two ways. Firstly, as Niamatullah Khan had undergone systematic training from a seniya, this sarodiya and his sons could legitimately have claimed to be included within one of the various branches of the seniya gharana. Secondly, contemporary members of this gharana, such as Illyas Khan, have looked beyond Niamatullah Khan to Madar Khan or Karimullah Khan as the first in the line of their gharana (Illyas Khan, personal communication: 1982). The tracing of a musical pedigree to this point is probably intended to demonstrate the genealogical depth of this lineage. The rationale for doing so was to show that even during the lifetime of Niamatullah Khan, family members could claim that they fulfilled the three generations of musicians necessary for the recognition of a gharana.

Similarly, the important training which Enayat Ali Khan had received from the seniya Basat Khan, afforded him the status of progenitor in the line of Karimullah's descendants. Even so, it cannot be said that this lineage made the transformation to a gharana before the time of Enayat Ali's grandson, Sakhawat Hussain. It was only at this time that the lineage fulfilled the three generations criterion of a gharana through the line of Niamatullah—Shafayet—Sakhawat Hussain.

Again, neither Enayat Ali nor his son Shafayet were described as mirasi musicians during their lifetime. This was so because, on the one hand, they were also rightly part of the seniya gharana and on the other, could trace their musical pedigrees to Najaf Ali Khan (1705–1760). This genealogy therefore fulfilled the requirement that the recognition of a gharana can only be based on a lineage of three successive generations of musicians. For both of these reasons, members of this lineage could legitimately claim the status of gharanedar musicians in the early twentieth century. Their sarod gharana was also known as the Shahjahanpur gharana, after the town where their ancestor had lived after migrating to India. Even though it shared the same place name, it was quite distinct from the Shahjahanpur gharana of Amir Khan.

After two successive generations of Enayat Ali's male descendants having intermarried with the female offspring of Niamatullah, the members of the Shahjahanpur gharana eventually came to share the same line of transmission as that of the Bulandshahr/Lucknow gharana. This intermingling of the line of musical transmission eventually resulted in the merging of the playing styles of these two gharanas. From around the 1930s onwards, members of both lineages were usually considered to belong to the gharana of Niamatullah Khan.

Although there appeared to be a simple and objective set of criteria by which a gharana was delineated, on the basis of discussion in this chapter it is apparent that these criteria were open to some degree of manipulation. This flexibility was most evident in the interpretation of the precept that a gharana is recognized only after three successive generations of musicians. In the beginning of the process of gharana formation, the family background of individual sarodiyas was still somewhat overshadowed by their specific association with seniya musicians. This could be explained by the fact that while the seniya tradition was known and respected, few from within the Bengali patron classes would have heard of the Pathan sarodiyas Najaf Ali Khan or Karimullah Khan nor possibly even of Enayat Ali or Niamatullah Khan. Therefore, sarodiyas had a strong incentive in the last half of the nineteenth century to continue to highlight their relationship with the seniya tradition and to gain social and—depending on the amount of training they had received—musical status from such a connection. Accordingly, in addition to acknowledging their own family background, up until the last twenty years virtually all sarodiyas have, as a matter of fact, invariably claimed to represent the seniya gharana.

It seems that it was only after a sarodiya had acquired a considerable degree of recognition and social status that his relationship to his own gharana began to take precedence over his seniya affiliation. In any case this shift could not have occurred until after the progenitor and two more generations of direct musical descendants had been established. From a contemporary perspective, the progenitor was usually taken as being the first person in a family to have received systematic training under a seniya and, in most cases, to have claimed to have invented the Hindustani sarod.

Though Ghulam Ali Khan, Murad Ali Khan, Niamatullah Khan and Enayat Ali Khan were not all contemporaries, their respective lineages emerged as distinct gharanas in the 1920s. In this respect it can be said that while there had been gharanedar sarodiyas from the end of the nineteenth century, sarod gharanas were not commonly accepted until around this period. Further, the process by which sarod gharanas came into existence belies the common perception that gharanas were inflexible and hoary institutions. Indeed, the flexibility in the social dynamics within this system is exemplified by the formation of sarod gharanas. For instance, discussion in this chapter has shown how one family of sarodiyas, descended from Ghulam Ali Khan, could split into two separate gharanas, the Gwalior gharana and the Shahjahanpur gharana of sarodiya Amir Khan. Again, during the same period, two families could merge into the one gharana, i.e. the Bulandshahr/Lucknow sarod gharana.

The formation of sarod gharanas at the beginning of this century also coincided with the time that non-Pathan musicians began learning from sarodiyas. The pressure on sarodiyas to socially and musically integrate these extra members with the line of transmission of their family must have also created a need to formalize a relationship between these hereditary musicians and their new disciples. The necessity of formalizing this relationship also contributed to the necessity of sarodiyas forming their own gharanas.

Alauddin Khan and His Descendants

By the end of the nineteenth century the practice of learning Hindustani music in Bengali society either directly from the ustads of the north or through music schools had, generally speaking, become an acceptable though not widespread component of the cultural life of Calcutta. Out of the many Bengalis—mostly but not exclusively belonging to privileged families who undertook such training—was Alauddin Khan who was to become one of the most influential figures in instrumental music. He was well known in India and most details of his life have therefore been well documented.[21] The following information is intended as just a brief sketch of his biographical details.

Alauddin Khan (1882–1972)

Ali Akbar Khan (b. 1922)

Ashish Khan (b. 1939) | Dhyanesh Khan (1942–91)

Table 6-3: The Alauddin Khan/Maihar sarod gharana

Alauddin Khan (Plate 6-5 and 6-6) was thought to have been born in 1862 in the Tripura district, now a part of Bangladesh. However, more recently, this date of birth has been revised to 1882. His father and brother were reputed to have played the sitar and the tabla. Some say that Alauddin Khan did not belong to an occupational category of musicians (*JDIM* 1982:23), others say his family originally belonged to a dhaki community, professional players of the dhak, a barrel-shaped drum. His son Ali Akbar Khan maintains that they were medium-scale landholders and jute farmers. Whatever the case, Alauddin Khan's relatively humble family background placed him somewhat outside of the milieu of the Hindu, high-caste, middle-class Bengali more commonly associated with Hindustani music in Calcutta at the time.

Alauddin Khan left his small village in his early teens to pursue his interest in music, a search that eventually led him to Calcutta. After a number of years of hardship, he finally ended up as a student of Habu Dutta, a well-to-do Bengali. Habu Dutta had earlier learnt from Wazir Khan of Rampur when the latter was living in Calcutta between 1892 and 1899. Habu Dutta taught Alauddin Khan to play many different instruments, such as esraj, violin, clarinet, shahnai, mridang and tabla, and also got him an employment in the orchestra of the Minerva Theatre. This period can be conjecturally placed as some time between 1903 and 1911 when he was also employed by the Maharaja of Muktagachha and started learning from Ahmed Ali Khan. It is said that the latter accepted Alauddin Khan as his disciple on the personal request of the Maharaja. Alauddin Khan went on to stay with his ustad both in Calcutta and during tours of the north for around four to five years. Nevertheless, during these years, Ahmed Ali is said to have been reluctant to pass on much knowledge to Alauddin Khan. As Singh notes (*JDIM* 1982:4), Ahmed Ali only taught Alauddin Khan a little gatkari and always avoided teaching him alap and jod.

In 1915, Alauddin Khan had gone with Ahmed Ali Khan to Rampur where the latter sarodiya's family resided. There Alauddin Khan decided that he would try to convince the seniya Wazir Khan to accept him as a disciple. This task apparently took many weeks of concerted effort and a serious threat to commit suicide. Even after being accepted as a disciple, Alauddin Khan apparently had to wait many months before his lessons began. During this time the bandmaster of Rampur State gave Alauddin a part-time job in his orchestra on the salary of twelve rupees a month.

Alauddin Khan has related the pledge he undertook before being accepted as Wazir Khan's disciple. Such a pledge is part of the ritual ganda-bandh which signifies the bonding between the teacher and disciple. During this ritual, Alauddin Khan (1982:42) recalls, a disciple must promise 'not to give his instrument to any undeserving fellow, not to keep bad company, not to use the instrument for begging, and not teach music to courtesans or prostitutes.' As it was uncommon to hear of Bengali musicians travelling to North India to learn music at that time, Alauddin Khan has stated that he quite often found himself to be a source of derision among the many musicians of Rampur.[22]

For five years, Alauddin Khan trained under Wazir Khan and on the latter's advice left Rampur in 1918 to take up the position of chief court musician at Maihar, now in the state of Madhya Pradesh. In 1924 he returned to Maihar for a further two years of training with Wazir Khan, immediately following the untimely death of the latter's son. Alauddin Khan is credited by his descendants and followers with having used this seniya training to combine the seniya styles of rabab, sursringar and been by introducing a profusion of bol patterns, alankars and laykari into his playing style on sarod (*JDIM* 1982:46–54). Along with these adaptations of the seniya technique and musical grammar, he also devised his own innovations. For instance, he expanded the musical structure of his performance by adapting and transposing the full structure of seniya raag alap onto his sarod performances (*JDIM* 1982:18–20).[23]

Apart from the formalization of raag alap, Alauddin Khan is also credited with further developing the Masit Khani gat:

> Previously Masit Khani gats were played in what is known today as madhya lay (medium tempo). Alauddin Khan was the first to play them at the slower speed and in doing so introduced different alankars into the tal section of the performance (Perera 1994).[24]

In the course of such experimentation, Alauddin Khan developed a slower and more intricate style of elaborating on this vilambit gat. By decreasing the tempo at which the Masit Khani gat was played, he was able to exploit intricate melodic and rhythmic techniques of dhrupad style to further ornament the raag. These innovations took place in the late 1920s (Perera 1994). As many of the recordings of other sarodiyas from this time show, the most common performance style played by these musicians continued to be drut gats based on the bandish ki thumri style. By developing the ati-vilambit (very slow) teentaal gats, as well as gats in other taals, Alauddin Khan created a sarod baj that was quite distinct from those of his contemporaries.

> Nowadays when we talk of Khamaj, Bhairabi, Kafi and such other ragas we almost involuntarily think of their thumri forms or thumri ang infested applications. Yet they were originally conceived as 'Ashraya' [dependant] ragas of thats [thetas] of the same names and each of them have a large number of dhrupads. Amongst instrumentalists, Ustad Alauddin Khan was one of the very few who could play any of these ragas in a totally dhrupad-based form, devoid of any thumri expressions (Dasgupta, Calcutta Doordarshan: 1982).

Alauddin Khan named one of the types of gats he developed the Wazir Khani gat, after his teacher. Another style of vilambit gat he developed was known as 'Nawab Pasand'. Both of these compositions departed from the syntax of the bol patterns that characterized the Masit Khani gat by concentrating more on melodic intricacies and, in the latter case, rhythmic signatures rather than on the purity of the bol patterns of which the former gat is comprised.[25] Many of the fast gats that he developed were based on tarana compositions, a genre that appears to have been particularly favoured in Rampur. They were often based on complex rhythms whose accents were designed to fall at odd points of the rhythmic cycle in which they were set.

In addition to the stylistic and structural innovations he made to the playing style of the sarod, Alauddin Khan made a number of significant modifications to his instrument. Working with his cousin Ayet Ali Khan, he fashioned a new type of instrument which could more easily facilitate the style of playing he had developed. This aim was achieved by enlarging the overall dimensions of his sarod and, in particular, the size of the main resonator which became rounder in shape than was evident on other sarods at the time. More changes included lengthening the fingerboard and adding a bronze upper resonator to the back of the pegbox in the manner of the been, sursringar and surbahar. A number of extra strings were also employed on his sarod. Of these, the number of taraf strings were increased to fifteen from the existing nine or eleven along with a separate set of four jawari strings. These last strings take their name from the small flat bridge, jawari, attached to the nut of the instrument over which these drone strings pass. These jawari strings were then affixed to the extra pegs added to the extended pegbox and were tuned according to the raag. Whereas the sarods played by Amir Khan and Hafiz Ali Khan had six pegs in their pegboxes, with four main and two drone strings or five main strings and one drone string, Alauddin Khan's sarod had eight pegs which accommodated the four main strings and four jawari strings. Although five main playing strings were planned, as on Hafiz Ali Khan's sarod, only four were eventually used. Along with the two chikari strings and fifteen taraf strings, Alauddin Khan's instrument had a total of twenty-five strings. Physically, the instrument devised by Alauddin Khan significantly varied in structure, tone and appearance, not only from the sarod played by Niamatullah Khan's descendants but also from the instrument developed by individuals within Ghulam Ali Khan's lines of descent.

It is on the basis of the innovations Alauddin Khan made both in his playing style and the physical changes he made to his instrument that his descendants and disciples claim that this particular sarod owes more to the influences of the seniya rabab and sursringar than it does to the Kabuli rabab. Foremost among these proponents is Alauddin Khan's son Ali Akbar Khan who asserts that 'the sarod played by Hafiz Ali Khan is based on the Pathan instrument but his was based on the ancient chitra vina.' (Personal communications: 1983, 1990)

Therefore, it is precisely this assertion that has created the polemic surrounding the origin of the sarod. On the one hand, the sarod-playing descendants of Pathans maintain that their sarod essentially developed from the Kabuli rabab. On the other, the descendants of Alauddin Khan contend that the type of sarod they play is just a further modification of the sursringar and has little if anything to do with that rabab. In effect, Alauddin Khan successfully combined selected elements of existing categories of sarod in his own instrument to which he also added a number of new touches. These innovations created a type of sarod whose tonal quality and physical design were distinct from the two other sarod types of his contemporaries. It is on this basis that Alauddin Khan is credited with establishing another gharana of sarod. The method of formation of this gharana differed from those of the Pathan sarod gharanas.

When he first came to Calcutta to perform in the late 1920s, Alauddin Khan's affiliation with the seniya gharana through Wazir Khan meant that, like his contemporaries Hafiz Ali Khan and Keramatullah Khan, he was generally, but not always, regarded as a gharanedar musician. For this reason, and also due to the obvious musical proficiency he displayed in his performances, the extent of his musical status was undoubted. Nevertheless, some detractors would question his social status on the basis of his family background. Solis (1970:31) has recorded an oft-quoted criticism, 'Who is he? He has no family tradition [khandan]'. This sentiment lingers on even today among some musicians of other sarod gharanas.[26]

Shifting from Dhrupad to Khyal

Even though khyal had displaced dhrupad as the dominant genre of Hindustani vocal music by the beginning of the twentieth century, dhrupad continued to be the idealized form guiding instrumental music practice until at least the middle of the twentieth century. Up to this time sarodiyas generally sought to emulate the sound of dhrupadiyas and to systematically learn raags in dhrupad style, the structure of dhrupad alap, dhrupad compositions, instrumental technique and the musical grammar, syntax and approach to improvisation associated with dhrupad. This they did by learning from and copying seniyas and later musicians from the qawwal-bachche community such as the surbahar player Sajjad Mohammad.

This orientation towards dhrupad was reinforced by the perception at the time that those sarodiyas who came closest to emulating the vocal qualities of dhrupad in their own music, particularly raag alap, were the ones generally considered the most competent performers. This is apparent in the comments on the lives of sarodiyas described earlier in this chapter. Further, sarodiyas who had learnt dhrupad compositions were regarded as possessing significant knowledge because this material, among other things, gave them a powerful resource to compose instrumental gats which at that time were derived from the inventory of such a repertoire.

While the idealized form guiding sarodiyas did not change through the period during which sarod gharanas first appeared, there were other major developments in music that did coincide with this event. These were notably the organization of recitals in public performance spaces and the advent of sound recording. It is fair to say that both of these developments had a major impact upon not only sound production but, perhaps more portentously in the case of the latter, it started to raise questions over who owned and controlled the sound produced.

In performances arranged by newly-formed musical institutions and music circles in halls and other public spaces in urban centres, the 'representation' of Hindustani classical music was significantly recast from the cloistered exclusivity of the chambers of the elite to an array of public spaces. These latter spaces were, generally speaking, physically larger in size and attended by a greater numbers of listeners who had purchased their admission and who remained anonymous to the performer. The shift in performance practice from chamber to hall presented a series of new challenges to a musician among which sound production would have been the greatest concern. Although historically this is a matter that has not figured prominently in the study of music in the early twentieth century, it nonetheless is an issue that perhaps deserves some serious documentation.

The same cannot be said about the advent of sound recording which has been reasonably well documented. The widespread use of recording technology from around the turn of the twentieth century enabled musicians for the first time to hear and copy music they repeatedly heard on a disc or received through the radio. Whereas sarodiyas might previously have practised behind closed doors lest others may hear and copy their music, the intervention of technology meant the exclusive practices which had regulated transmission of musical knowledge to that point were now challenged. The phenomenon of repetition was to necessitate some form of strategy on the part of musicians to transpose and modify existing musical practice and aesthetic conventions into this modern setting.

The first recording made of a sarodiya took place in 1906, and sarodiyas also started to broadcast on All India Radio (AIR) from the 1920s. Before Independence, the list of recordings by sarodiyas was rather modest, amounting to a total of less than two dozen.[27] Those sarodiyas with Pathan ancestry who were recorded before 1947 were: Chunnu Khan (Pilu matrix no. 16251/4300e, Tilak Kamod 16255/4302e. Recorded 1906, re-released 1916. HMV P59), Asadullah 'Kaukab' Khan (Manj Khamaj, Zila, Bhairav, Bhupali, Brindabani Sarang, all recorded in 1912) and Jangla Pilu (recorded in 1916),[28] Sakhawat Hussain (Tilak Kamod, Pahadi Jhinjhoti, recorded some time in the 1920s) and Mohammad Amir Khan (Kafi and Jhinjhoti, also recorded some time in the 1920s).

The first recording by non-Pathan sarodiyas was made by the Bengali Rajendra Nath Chatterjee and was released by the Gramophone Company on a single-sided 78rpm disc in 1912 (Record No. 8-16521; matrix No. 11705v). This was followed by two recordings made by P. N. Roy in February 1915 (8-16252/4377y; 8-16523/4378. Kinnear 1992).[29] In the late 1930s Amir Khan's disciple, Banikantha Mukhopadhyay also recorded two 78rpm discs (Pilu, Khamaj, Bihag, Lalit).

The most significant consequence of sound recording technology was that for the first time the musical sound of sarod could be disembodied and disconnected both from the instrument and the musicians themselves. The ability to reproduce music on demand facilitated by the gramophone meant that the sound of the sarod could now be heard in the houses and drawing rooms of literally thousands of people who had never even seen the musician or the instrument before. The technology of recorded sound meant that the sound of sarod could be stored, retrieved and repeated on demand; musical sound was now exposed as a resource capable of mass production. This mass production and commodification meant that music had entered into a new form of economic transaction that was to have significant and ongoing ramifications. 'This mutation would profoundly transform every individual's relationship to music.' (Attali 1985:88) According to Mathur:

> Although the long-playing record was still far off, old masters continued to derive some income, but far less satisfaction, from the brief recordings they were able to give. In such a situation, it was doubtful whether high-class Indian music could survive as a form of art and entertainment (1976:98).

Sound recording technology would also introduce issues related to the ownership and control of music, concerns that have now very much become a major part of every musician's professional life.[30] These issues were in many ways related to the embracing of modernity by the Indian elite. At the same time, the arrival of sound recordings made the arrival of modernity audible. However, the impact of modernity on performance practice in Hindustani music is, of course, a complex issue and one that can give rise to many interpretations.[31] While it is not the intention to address this topic here, the following two observations do hint at some of the divergent dimensions to this condition. On one hand, Attali raises a cultural-materialist approach which, although made in the context of Western music, is also relevant here:

> In representation, the musician . . . ceased to be a domestic [read mirasi here] becoming an entrepreneur of a particular kind who received remuneration from the sale of his labour. The musician's economic status and political relation with power changed in the course of the great political upheaval of the time [i.e. modernity], as did aesthetic codes and forms in which the new audience wished to see itself reflected (1985:57).

On the other hand, a hint of the epistemological shift that accompanied the arrival of modernity appears in Moitra's comments below, made in the course of a general commentary on Hindustani music:

> Thus, while the old masters concerned themselves with the realization of pure beauty in Art, the modern artists are primarily satisfied with creating beauty through Art. To the old masters technique was just a means to an end, the end being the realization of eternal beauty in Art, which transcends all techniques. Technique to the modern artist is not only a means but also an end in itself, the end being the creation of beauty in Art, which is imminent with and not independent of technique (1998:n.p.).

The impact and scope of these consequences took on a new turn when public address systems began to be used in concerts and radio broadcasts were introduced in the 1930s. While the role of the radio is discussed at a later stage, it can be noted here that two things began to happen when sound amplification was used in public concerts. First, because the instrument needed to be heard by a large audience in a large physical space, the overall volume of sound produced by musicians had to be electronically increased. The quality of this sound was in turn then reliant on the efficiency of both the 'sound system' involved and the skill in its application. In other words, the musicians had relinquished their total control over their sound. Second, because under these conditions sound now physically travelled further from the instrument, the immediacy of the experience of the music for the performer and the listener was somehow altered and, as noted above, so too were the aesthetic codes of performance.

Responses and Strategies

Some musicians formulated strategies for dealing with the new recording technology while others appeared to largely ignore it. Irfan Khan had commented that, over the decades, the members of his family dealt with this situation by being consciously selective of the music that they played for recordings. These sarodiyas did not want their khas (special) material to be recorded because of the 'danger' of anyone copying it.

A quick perusal of the body of these recordings reveal that most of the raags which appear on these discs were those typically associated with the 'lighter' musical genre, thumri. There may have been two reasons for this. Firstly, this music was believed to be better suited to the contingencies of the medium, in the sense of having only two minutes to record and no control over who ended up listening to the music.[32] Secondly, it meant that they were not placed in positions that would compromise their musical inheritance to any major extent. Another strategy was to refrain from playing a composition in its entirety for such recordings[33] or to steadfastly maintain a reluctance to record, in the manner of sarodiyas Keramatullah Khan and Hafiz Ali Khan. When at the end of his life Hafiz Ali Khan was asked by Lalita Khanna why he never made a commercial recording, he responded,

> You know very well what my attitude to Music is, . . . I have looked on it as prayer—as my humble way of glorifying my Maker. I could

> not endure the thought that a disc of mine could be bought by some unworthy people and played casually anywhere—in pan [paan] shops, and wedding parties with people jesting and making merry the while. This is an insult to the Art of Music which had been given to us by God to worship Him with. Once I was nearly caught by the record company people. Yes, several of them came together to Gwalior and persuaded the Maharaja to make me record for them. I was in a terrible quandary. I could not refuse my gracious patron. Very tactfully I explained my feelings to him adding that when my records would be played in pan shops. etc., and jeered at by people to whom my classical music is something to laugh at, those records would bear the name of 'Hafiz Ali Khan of Gwalior' and the name of his Darbar [court] would be subjected to the same indignities as my name and music. This last aspect appealed to the Maharaja and he stopped importuning me and I was able to get rid of the record company people (Khanna 1975:n.p.).

Despite his personal reluctance to record, Hafiz Ali Khan did make many radio broadcasts over a few decades and some of these recordings are held in the archives of All India Radio. Eventually HMV released some commercial recordings drawn from these radio broadcasts.[34]

The new networks of patronage offered many professional musicians the potential for social mobility, a situation that also favoured sarodiyas. From being somewhat marginal in feudal networks, many sarodiyas quickly adapted to the new conditions, and with the backing of influential figures in colonial society, sarodiyas such as Keramatullah Khan, Asadullah Khan Kaukab and Amir Khan quickly became part of the mainstream of Hindustani instrumental music. Their past association with the feudal courts of North India was also invaluable because it afforded them a 'use value' among their new patrons. Having been granted this social status, the sound they produced also came to constitute and define the sound of mainstream Hindustani instrumental music. There has been an interest in the experimentation of sound production by sarodiyas throughout the twentieth century, probably due to these new conditions of performance practice. The combined efforts of individual sarodiyas from each gharana has significantly expanded the range of, and added many more nuances and subtle qualities to, the palette of musical sounds heard on sarod. Those musicians who could not or did not adapt to these new conditions were also marginalized or alienated from sources of patronage.

Changes to the Sarod in the Early Twentieth Century

The basic division between sarod types noted previously, i.e. those connected with the seniya rabab and those with the sursringar, continued into the twentieth century. This difference was most apparent in the designs of the sarods played by Asadullah Khan Kaukab, Sakhawat Hussain Khan and Ishtiaq Ahmed Khan on the one hand, and those played by Hafiz Ali Khan, Amir Khan and Radhika Mohan Moitra on the other.

Physical differences in sarod types were at the time also audible and they have remained so due to sound recordings from that period. The difference in design determined that each type had a different quality of sound. Preference for a particular 'type' of sound was in turn linked to the content and style learnt and developed by its progenitors. Nevertheless, constant experimentation by individual musicians with the sound of their instrument and the content and style of their music were ongoing, meaning that difference between sarod types was not static but constantly being redefined.

Probably due to the influence of the sursringar, the sarod played by Hafiz Ali Khan had an extra main string called laraj which was tuned to pancham in the ati-mandra saptak (the fifth in the extra-low octave).[35] However, as it was hard to keep in tune, this sometimes interfered with the overall sound and tuning of the instrument and was eventually discarded. He also attached a small wooden tumba (gourd resonator) behind the pegbox of his instrument. The tumba was a principal design feature of the been and the sursringar. While it effectively served little or no acoustic function on the sarod, it did act more as a marker/signifier of the past association of sarod with these instruments, and the seniya tradition in particular. Radhika Mohan Moitra also adopted the same extra tumba even though it was not present on the sarod of his teacher, Amir Khan. By way of contrast, the Bulandshahr and Lucknow gharanas did not opt for this device.

Throughout his playing life, Hafiz Ali Khan, like his antecedents, reportedly used handmade steel strings on his instrument because of his preference for their tonal quality. Even when mass-produced piano wire, which was also suitable for sarod, became available, he apparently continued to use handmade strings. The importation of mass-produced German and English piano wire eventually led to the disappearance of indigenous string makers some time between the two World Wars (Barlow 1996:3).

In the 1920s a third type of sarod was constructed by Alauddin Khan in collaboration with his cousin Ayet Ali Khan that augmented the rabab-derived sarod of Niamatullah Khan's gharana and that of Ghulam Ali Khan's gharana. As previously mentioned, Alauddin Khan experimented with the sound production of the sarod by enlarging the resonator, adding more taraf strings, adding a new jawari bridge, four new drone strings and a brass tumba. Significantly, he is also said to have raised the tonic tuning of the instrument from around A or B flat to C.

His innovations were audible in the 'brighter' sound of his sarod due to the increased production of upper harmonics and partials that the extra strings and higher tuning facilitated. These extra partials provided his instrument with a rounder tone. In addition, the overall sound of the instrument was modified by the new layer of sound which emanated from the jawari bridge and strings. The enlargement of the main resonator increased the volume of sound, sustain and tonal clarity of the instrument. The brass tumba, like the gourd tumbas on other sarods, added little if anything acoustically to the overall sound. Performers within this gharana have largely retained this feature because it acts as a counterweight to the resonator when the instrument is held in playing position.

Besides Alauddin Khan's experiments with instrument making, other sarodiyas were also known to have built their own instruments. Asghar Ali Khan is said to have experimented with the design of the sarod to come up with the surchen and Abdullah Khan, besides his

'Indian banjo', is credited with building at least two sarods which although 'not laboriously finished still have a completeness and originality in their forms and . . . play excellently.' (Barlow 1996:5)

- Najaf Ali Khan (1705–60)
  - Khaler Khan (1730–82)
    - Hussain Ali Khan (1752–1801)
      - Enayat Ali Khan (1790–1883)
        - Shafayet Ali Khan (1848–1920) + *daughter of Niamatullah Khan*
          - Sakhawat Hussain Khan (1875–1955) + *daughter of Asadullah Khan Kaukab*
            - Umar Khan (1916–82)
              - Shahid Khan (n.d.)
              - Irfan Khan (b. 1956)
            - Illyas Khan (1920–89)
      - Hasan Ali Khan (n.d.)
        - Fida Hussain Khan (1855–1927)
          - Taj Mohammad (n.d.)

Table 6-6: The Shahjahanpur gharana

Conclusion

It has been contended that there are two types of sarod traditions in Hindustani music which can be differentiated on the basis of the cultural background of its performers, the type and extent of seniya training that the respective members received as well as the design of their respective instruments. Distinctions point to those gharanas featuring sarodiyas of Pathan descent along with their disciples on the one hand, and the sarod gharana established by the Bengali Alauddin Khan on the other.

For the musicians of the former category, i.e. the Shahjahanpur, Lucknow, Gwalior and Murad Ali Khan gharanas, a number of factors combined to effect the transition of their social organization from hereditary lineages of Pathan descent to sarod gharanas. The pivotal point in this process occurred in the first two decades of this century and was due to the seniya training that a number of Pathan sarodiyas had received over the preceding forty or fifty years. These sarodiyas and their descendants were subsequently included, albeit to varying degrees, within the seniya line of transmission. In the eyes of the indigenous urban elite in Bengal, this association with the seniya tradition recast sarodiyas such as Enayat Ali, Niamatullah and Amir Khan, by investing them with a social and musical status which clearly set them apart from those musicians who accompanied either vocalists or tawaifs. Those sarodiyas with seniya training along with their descendants, therefore, became known as gharanedar musicians.

In the 1920s the need arose for sarodiyas to define and formalize the social and musical relationships of their non-family disciples in order to provide an overall cohesion to what would otherwise be a socially disparate group. Thus it is no coincidence that the formation of sarod gharanas also occurred at a time when Bengali musicians were being included in the lines of musical transmission of sarod lineages. The final formation and recognition of these sarod gharanas, however, was neither uniform in timing nor in internal social dynamics.

Notes

1 See Banerjee (1989), Capwell (1985), McNeil (1992), Pradhan (2000), and Tagore (1876) for further discussion of this consequence.

2 This practice was mentioned earlier by noting that the seniya Pyar Khan, the brother of Basat Khan and Jaffar Khan, did not have any male offspring of his own. Pyar Khan adopted his sister's son and fully initiated him in the seniya style as if he was his natural son.

3 One of these discs was recorded in 1934 and contains Kafi and Pahadi. These recordings can be heard on ME 8-1 and 8-2. A limited stylistic study of Murad Ali Khan's gharana has been covered in the MA thesis of Solis in which he has transcribed an excerpt of Kafi, in its entirety, into staff notation (1970:103–109).

4 Some of the personal observations and anecdotal material used in this chapter have been taken from the writings of Birendra Kishore Roy Choudhury and Harendra Kishore Roy Choudhury, both well-known members of this family earlier in this century.

5 These sarodiyas are commonly acknowledged as having been disciples of the sarodiya Amir Khan. But as is the case with all sarodiyas discussed in this chapter, it is not possible to clearly specify in what capacity and to what standard they had learnt from their teacher.

6 This interview by Lalita Khanna appeared in the programme notes to commemorate the third anniversary of the death of Hafiz Ali Khan, organized by the Indian Music Society, Mumbai, 3–12 September 1975.

7 This experience speaks volumes of the intermingling, tolerance and mutual respect that oral history suggests was commonplace within the domain of Hindustani music.

8 For general information on this initiation ritual of musicians, see Silver in Metcalfe ed. (1986:315–29) and Neuman (1980:55–58).

9 Harendra Kishore Roy Choudhury in *Musicians of India: Part 1* (n.d.: 48–9) expresses a rather uncommon account of Hafiz Ali Khan's family background: 'Nanhe Khan married in Nika form [temporary marriage] a Domni, the mother of Hafez [sic] Ali Khan, when Hafez was a boy of three years of age. The Domni, in her professional career, was in the employ of His Highness the Nawab of Rampur as a player of the harmonium.'

10 Mukherjee (1986:12–15) and Van der Meer (1980:30–49) have provided useful descriptions of the stylistic and structural elements of dhrupad.

11 Prafulla Mohan Dasgupta had noted of Hafiz Ali Khan's playing in an article entitled 'Reminiscences of a Music Lover': 'The other merit was the ineffable quality of his strokes (toka) which produced from the sarode deep, solemn notes, which fell on the ears like the chime of golden church bells and they became still more enthralling

when he began to play "jhala". The first stroke of the "jhala" rang out with crystalline purity and the next three were delivered after a slight and inimitable pause, the thrilling effect of which will haunt me to my dying day.' (Moitra SNA-1267: 1972)

12 Amjad Ali Khan is quoted in Mishra (1981:126) as saying that Hafiz Ali Khan learnt thumri from the famous harmonium player and doyen of thumri, Bhai Ganpatrao. This information is confirmed in Khanna's interview with Hafiz Ali (1975:n.p.).

13 This extra string was later removed by his sons from their sarods.

14 Mishra alternately states that Sakhawat Hussain was born in Shahjahanpur in 1877 and that he was initiated into the sarod early in his life by his father, Shaafat [Shafayet] Khan. After this initial training he went on to learn from Keramatullah Khan and only later received guidance from Asadullah Kaukab (1981:34).

15 According to Irfan Khan (personal communication: 1998), Sakhawat Hussain did a series of sound recordings for the German Nazis during this period, which may still survive. There was also a short film made on his playing by Wadia Studios in Mumbai around the same time.

16 Banerjee (1989:58) lists some of the defining features of bhadralok society: a basic standard of income; residence in a 'pucca' house either through ownership or renting; attention to one's sartorial style in public; use of a chaste Bengali and a noticeable knowledge of English language and manners. For a general discussion of Bengali society in the nineteenth and early twentieth centuries, see Banerjee (1989, 1998), Deshpande (1987), Capwell (1985, 1991) McGuire (1983), Mukherjee (1982) and Niranjana (1990) among others.

17 Personal communication: 1999.

18 See Banerjee (1989 and 1998) and Chatterjee (1994) for further descriptions and analysis of this puritanism in the collective disposition of the Bengali urban elite in the late nineteenth century. Also see Tagore (1876) in particular, for a nineteenth-century contemporary insight into the sensibilities of this patron group towards music.

19 See Sourindra Mohun Tagore's *Yantrakosha,* for example.

20 See Neuman (1977; 1980), Deshpande (1973), Mukhopadhyay (1977), Silver (1986) and Van der Meer (1980).

21 Out of the many books and articles in journals on this musician and

teacher, Alauddin Khan's narrated autobiography, *Meri Katha* ['My Story'], provides one of the most interesting insights into his life. Also see articles by various authors in *JDIM*, 1982, vol. 2. Additional information is provided by Bhattacharya (1979), Garg (1978:439–44), Mishra (1981:59–69), Debnath (1980:passim) and Shankar (1973:9–16).

[Alauddin Khansaheb narrated his autobiography in Bengali to Subhomoy Ghosh and the first Bengali edition of *Amaar Katha* was published by Debkumar Basu as part of the 'Ratnasagar Granthamala' series from Grantha Jagat, Calcutta, in 1958. Ananda Publishers Private Limited, Calcutta, later published an edition in 1980. The author, however, cites all his references from the Hindi version *Meri Katha* in his own translation.–ED.]

22 In this autobiography, Alauddin Khan cites a couple of examples of this attitude. In Bengal, the staple diet includes fish and one of the usual taunts directed at him by fellow Muslim musicians in Rampur because of his Bengali background was 'machhe ka pani pinewala', literally 'drinker of fish water.' (1982:44–45). Another source of derision also centred on his eating habits but called into question his religion. In this vein he was taunted by the remark, 'You have the name Alauddin and yet you do not eat beef or mutton; you must be a Hindu.' This argument was inevitably followed by the advice: 'Eat beef and mutton and only then you will be able to play sarod' (1982:44–45).

23 It is sometimes stated that Alauddin Khan is said to have been the first sarodiya to play the full structure of dhrupad alap (viz. alap, jod and jhala) in a public performance (Periera, personal communication: 1986). While he was certainly known to play a full alap in his early performances, it also true that other sarod gharanas hold that their ancestors were playing full alap before the 1920s. Therefore it seems that Alauddin Khan's contribution in this regard came more from the establishment of a systematic approach to alap than from actually being the first to introduce the full raag alap on sarod.

24 The details of the structural innovations he effected are outlined by Dhar Chowdhury (*JDIM* 1982:46–54) and Ravi Shankar (*JDIM* 1982:26–27).

25 See Ravi Shankar (*JDIM* 1982) for a technical discussion of these gats. Also see Debnath (1980:175) and Dhar Chowdhury (*JDIM* 1982:46–49).

26 At the 1948 Jodhpur All India Music Conference, Alauddin Khan for example, received a higher performance fee than many of the top musicians of the day. According to Erdman (1985:149), he was paid Rs 2,500. Other performers and their fees included: Omkarnath Thakur (vocal Rs 2,400); Faiyaz Khan (vocal Rs 2,200); Vilayat Khan (sitar Rs 1160); Pannalal Ghosh (flute Rs 1,000); Dabir Khan (been Rs 980); Mushtaq Ali Khan (sitar Rs 820); V. G. Jog (violin Rs 700); Ahmedjan Thirakwa (tabla Rs 800) and Umar Khan (sarod Rs 306).

27 Personal communication with the discographer Michael Kinnear, 1992.

28 Information concerning these dates was kindly provided by Michael Kinnear. Asadullah Khan recorded Chammach Manj [Manj Khamaj] on his previously-mentioned 'Indian banjo'.

29 I have yet to come across biographical details of these two musicians.

30 When the first 78rpm discs were commercially produced, musicians would sometimes yell out their name at the end of the recording to affirm their ownership so that no other musician's name would be put on their recording either accidentally or intentionally. I have some recordings of the sitariya Enayat Khan in which this takes place

31 Currently some attention is being afforded this topic. Lakshmi Subramanian, University of Calcutta, has explored the impact of modernity on Karnatic Music; Aneesh Pradhan, University of Bombay, has undertaken research on modernity and Hindustani music in Mumbai. This topic was also a theme of a major conference at the Centre for Studies in Social Sciences, Calcutta in January 1999. See also McNeil, 'Making Modernity Audible: Sarodiyas and Their Strategies' in Amlan Das Gupta ed. *Enterprise, Innovation and Tradition: Indian Music in the Age of Reproduction* [forthcoming from Thema, Calcutta].

32 Irfan Khan, personal communication: 1998.

33 A. Roy, personal communication: 1990.

34 The recordings of Hafiz Ali Khan in the archives of AIR in New Delhi are: Multani (SPM TS 20269) recorded 25/7/57; Eman (details not available); Chandrabhankar (SPM TS 20268) recorded 23/7/57 and Desh (SPM 20266) recorded 23/9/57. Chandrabhankar was later

commercially released. In 1989 HMV and AIR released another cassette of Mian ki Malhar, Sanjh Tarini and Bhairavi (STC 850154).

35 The fifth degree in the octave that is even one lower than the lowest heard on a contemporary sarod.

Sarodiyas and the State

AS PART OF THE ENDEAVOUR of nation building following Independence in 1947, a series of national cultural policies and objectives were formulated by the Government of India. These objectives were, of course, not unrelated to broader national political goals, such as the wide-ranging policies of national integration and social unity and the preservation and promotion of India's cultural heritage. Networks of patronage were established through State institutions and bureaucracies with the aim of furthering such objectives. At the same time, the regional and social diversity that existed among the proliferation of educational, media and arts bodies that emerged after Independence often meant that there was no real uniformity or agreement within the collective endeavour of State cultural patronage on how such objectives might be attained. Despite any difficulty in assigning a singular character to State networks, it can nevertheless be said that, once in place, State cultural policies and cultural bureaucracies presented new opportunities and challenges for professional musicians. Even so, it is not uncommon for senior musicians to recall today that the two or three decades after 1947, during which the transition between the two networks had already begun, is often characterized as a period of financial struggle.

As during previous ruptures in the networks of patronage of music, the establishment and expansion of State networks after Independence did not immediately displace those already in existence. Instead, they gradually came to assume a greater presence and role in the lives of musicians as resources of the zamindars dwindled and their networks increasingly became marginalized after

Independence. Simultaneously, State networks of patronage were expanding and privately-run music circles, along with private sponsorship of concerts and festivals by wealthy individuals and industrial houses, also played an important part in supplementing the role adopted by the State.[1]

The most immediate point of contact between musicians and the State after Independence was via the government-run radio service, All India Radio. The role of AIR as cultural patron amounted to an unprecedented shift in the ways that musicians earned their livelihood and the consequences of this phenomenon is in many ways a neglected area of research in Indian music.[2] In 1957, J. C. Mathur, a former Director of AIR, commenting on the impact of AIR on Indian music said:

> The absence of the paid concert in most parts of India added to the importance of the radio as a patron . . . Having thus emerged as a vital patron of Indian music (the annual output of Indian music on AIR is 50,000 hours and the number of artists on its rolls is nearly 10,000), it was natural that the radio should have influenced musicians and their mode of expression to some extent directly or indirectly (1976:98).

Perhaps the most immediate and compelling challenge that radio posed to musicians was the audition process through which aspiring classical musicians needed to pass in order to secure full time or casual employment. A musician's performance ability was established through a formal process of audition presided over by a selection of judges who were often senior performing artists themselves. The gradation of artists by AIR was, and to some extent continues to be, a powerful way of assigning musical status. This grading was done according to a set scale, viz. A-high, A, B-high and B.[3] The artistic grading determined not only their musical status relative to other artists, but also fixed their pay scale and determined how often they would record,[4] and '. . . the gradation given in AIR is more or less the accepted standard which determines the quality of the artiste's performance anywhere in the country' (Mathur 1976:99). The grade assigned to a musician was not a permanent assessment and it was possible for musicians to periodically apply for re-audition in order to improve their ranking.

The regular recitals and income from AIR was also a fixed primary source of income for most sarodiyas. This could be supplemented by recitals and tuition but these sources were seasonal and, therefore, could not be solely depended upon. Besides casually-employed artists, a few sarodiyas were employed as permanent staff artists by AIR in major urban centres such as Calcutta, Delhi and Lucknow. These permanent employees would often receive the same entitlements as other government officers such as accommodation, a pension on retirement, leave entitlements and so on. Apart from the major cities, casual sarodiyas would also regularly record and broadcast from AIR centres in regional cities and towns such as Ajmer and Najibabad.

Besides broadcasting, the State provided broad-based cultural patronage through another bureaucratic channel, the Indian Council for Cultural Relations (ICCR). After registering with the ICCR, musicians could apply for assistance with overseas air passage if they could demonstrate that they had the required number of concerts arranged abroad. Besides this individual sponsorship, the ICCR has, over the decades, regularly organized and sponsored *Festivals of India* overseas in which sarodiyas have often featured as principal artists. Through the ICCR, the Indian government also established a number of ongoing overseas cultural missions among the Indian diaspora in Fiji, Mauritius, Afghanistan, Trinidad and so on. Some sarodiyas were known to have been given fixed-term contracts of upto three years in these missions. The cultural bureaucracies of individual states in India still continue to regularly organize and present music festivals and competitions which provide occasional support for some sarodiyas. Teaching positions also opened up for some sarodiyas in government-run cultural institutions and universities and in private elite secondary schools. In recognition of an individual's service to the country, the State formulated and dispensed the much-coveted national titles and awards, such as Padma Shri and Padma Bhushan, which have also been conferred upon well-known sarodiyas over the last few decades.

Another avenue of State patronage was opened for musicians with the setting up of State-run television, Doordarshan, in the late 1970s. Besides appointing a number of permanent staff artists, senior artists continue to receive casual employment through the occasional live broadcast of their music on television and, more significantly, via the prestigious National Programme of Music which is still broadcast weekly. To secure an appearance on television was a sign of recognition and status for sarodiyas and was often an important step in establishing their credentials as a prominent artist.

Social Organization

The dominance of State networks of patronage also gave rise to a number of other consequences felt, not least of all, within the social organization of musicians. In this respect, a fundamental change emerged at the core of most gharanas, arising both from the marginalization, or de-emphasis, of ethnicity as a defining element of a gharana along with the continued process of accommodating non-khandan artists (those not belonging to the hereditary occupational lineages of musicians) within the gharana system.[5] Somehow, there seems to be a link between these two situations; a de-emphasis of ethnicity not only facilitated but proved to be a necessary step for the expansion of membership to gharanas, while the expansion of gharanas in the metropolises increasingly made a musician's ethnicity less relevant as a social marker. The cultural logic and functioning of the policies and procedures of State cultural bodies after Independence, in which ethnicity was overshadowed by the greater imperative of national integration and unity, had the effect of reinforcing and institutionalizing this trend. In the process, past inflections of 'Pathan-ness' in the ancestry of sarodiyas appeared to have been simply merged into, or subsumed by, the cultural eclecticism of the larger pool of Hindustani musicians. As the descendants of Pathan musicians socially and musically assimilated into the patchwork of diverse ethnicities that had come to characterize Hindustani music culture so too, it seems, their Pathan heritage was assimilated into this patchwork and eventually, almost forgotten.

For sarodiyas, the relevance of the gharana system in premodern times was in the identity and status it conferred on them within the patronage networks of the colonial metropolis. However, under State patronage this changed; sarodiyas were now graded against institutionally-established criteria and accordingly, received a ranking and hence, an institutional identity within the functioning of State networks. After Independence, a sarodiya's institutional grading can therefore be said to have been more important than his gharana affiliation for securing State patronage and determining the returns that could be expected.

It is not unreasonable to suggest that the institutionalization of patronage after Independence, by and large, tended to favour educated middle-class musicians over those perceived to belong to the 'old ways', a term which carried a host of connotations ranging from illiterate, uneducated, morally suspect to just trapped in the past. Individuals identified as such were necessarily at a disadvantage when dealing with the new bureaucratic milieu that emerged after Independence. Therefore, the climate of institutionalization seems to have marginalized those sarodiyas belonging to the 'old ways' but, at the same time, it could be seen to have benefited those who may have otherwise occupied marginal spaces in the tradition but who had the particular social skills, language and contacts necessary to deal with State cultural institutions. In other words, the unfolding of the institutionalization of patronage under the State constructed a new set of parameters by which the status of a musician was determined and this itself created the potential for individual musicians to pursue mobility within their larger groups.

An increase in the numbers of non-khandan sarod players, coupled with a de-emphasis in the ethnicity of musicians, contributed to the transformation of gharana from a model that initially served both as a social institution organized around distinct bloodlines and as an encapsulation of a musical style to a model that primarily functioned at the level of an identifier of musical style.

At the same time it could be argued that the interest taken by bhadralok Bengalis in learning and performing on the instrument also helped to propel the sarod into the mainstream of Hindustani music. Taken together, all these conditions generated a fluidity in the social organization of musicians which translated into an upward mobility for some sarodiyas and marginalization for others. Nevertheless, the ways and means by which this process unfolded was by no means uniform or tension-free.

Shifting Idealized Forms

Not long after Independence, khyal began to seriously challenge and displace the paramountcy of dhrupad as the idealized form for instrumental music. For whatever reasons this may have transpired, the transition from dhrupad to khyal represented a significant and far-reaching paradigm shift for instrumental musicians. As part of this shift, the basic foundations of performance practice such as musical content, aesthetics, voice production and technique became open to re-evaluation and re-interpretation. Instrumentalists engaged the fluidity produced by this stylistic and aesthetic shift in a number of individual ways. For example, from the 1950s, the famous sitariya Vilayat Khan had started to introduce new innovations within his musical style which later came to be commonly known as gayaki ang. This development in musical style and content was also assisted by advances in material culture and technique, both of which allowed instrumentalists greater scope in exploiting meend on their instruments. This facility enabled them to more closely approach the vocal musical style of khyaliyas and the execution of the taans characteristic of khyal.

This is not to imply that there was no evidence of a 'singing style' on instrumental music in general, and sarod in particular, prior to the 1960s. It will be recalled that Asghar Ali was renowned for his 'singing sarod' and that the primary quality of Amir Khan's sarod was its sustain and resonance which ideally lent itself to the emulation of the voice. Further, the strength of the vocal quality that is evident in recordings of Hafiz Ali Khan is perhaps one of the most distinctive aspects of his playing. Equally so, a similar degree of vocal quality is evident in the recordings of Alauddin Khan's playing. Personal musical influences along with the nuances of sound production by individual musicians determined that there were many distinct interpretations of vocal style on the instrument prior to the 1960s. However, the singing styles followed by many sarodiyas before this time more closely followed dhrupad conventions. The common usage of the term gayaki ang in reference to instrumental music coincided with experiments by instrumentalists to incorporate the vocal style of khyal into their music, a development made possible due to new instrumental techniques.

Also concurrent with this paradigm shift was a loosening up of the aesthetic conventions determining what was, or was not, an appropriate instrument for the solo performance of Hindustani instrumental music. From the early 1960s, musicians innovated with the technique and sound quality of a number of instruments, viz. Pannalal Ghosh with the flute, Bismillah Khan with the shehnai, V. G. Jog with the violin, Brij Bhushan Kabra with the Hawaiian guitar, Shiv Kumar Sharma with the santoor and Ram Narayan with the sarangi. While the general acceptance of such instruments can in no small part also be imputed to the talent and creativity of a number of remarkable individuals, it is equally true that the cultural liminality of the time probably ensured that such experiments had a greater chance of success than might have occurred at another time. The eventual acceptance of these new voices in Hindustani music can be argued to have assisted, underlined and accented the shift in idealized forms from dhrupad to khyal. This was probably so because all these instruments were primarily, but not necessarily, exclusively played according to the structural and/or stylistic conventions of khyal.

In the midst of such musical change and social fluidity, the sarod found itself repositioned within this newly-expanded domain of instrumental music. From its own marginal position relative to the been, seniya rabab and sursringar a century before, the sarod had now been recast into a position which, for want of a better term, may be called 'high-classical' compared to the other 'newcomers'. In this sense the sarod, having displaced its predecessors, now became, along with the sitar, one of the core instruments on which Hindustani music, at its most profound level, could be realized. In other words, it had not only become totally assimilated but now also represented the pinnacle of Hindustani instrumental music.

Source Material on Sarodiyas: 1947 to the 1970s

Detailed information on the lives of sarodiyas professionally active during this period is readily circulated through interviews, articles, Internet sites, publicity and marketing material. Where possible, references to more extensive biographical accounts of these musicians have been provided. The depictions given below are therefore intended only as thumbnail sketches and should be approached in this light. Given both the scope of this study and the sheer numbers of sarodiyas, it is unfortunate that a number of worthy sarodiyas from this period cannot be mentioned in the following discussion. This is an omission that one hopes will not be judged too harshly.

Gwalior Gharana

Hafiz Ali Khan's professional life straddled premodern networks, the networks of the colonial metropolis and those of the modern State. At various stages, during the course of the six decades or so of his career, he was able to move backwards and forwards between them.[6] Towards the end of his illustrious career he finally settled in Delhi where, in 1955, he received, among the many awards he was presented, the Padma Bhushan from the Government of India. The Visva-Bharati in Santiniketan awarded him the title Desikottama and Khairagarh University in Madhya Pradesh awarded him a Doctorate in Music (Khanna 1975:n.p.).

During the latter stages of his career, he made a few recordings for broadcast by All India Radio, played at the major music festivals and performed for the most prestigious music circles, such as Suresh Sangeet Samsad in Bengal. The main beneficiaries of Hafiz Ali

Khan's teaching were his three sons, Mubarak Ali, Rehmat Ali and Amjad Ali Khan and his nephew Ahmad Ali Khan (Khanna 1975:n.p.). He was also known to have taught, among many others, the Bengali musicians Viswa Chand Boral (the second son of the famous singer Lal Chand Boral) and Kumar Jaganath Mitra. In addition he is well known for having helped such luminaries as the vocalists Bhimsen Joshi and D. C. Vedi and tabla player Masit Khan (father of the famous tabla player Keramatullah Khan) in the early parts of their careers. However, according to Mukhopadhyay (1977:135), his real disciple was his son Amjad Ali Khan (Plate 7-1), who today is among the most high-profile musicians of Hindustani music. Even though Mubarak Ali Khan and Rehmat Ali Khan both figure strongly in this bloodline, for whatever reasons, they did not receive the status within Hindustani music attained by their father. Both of them have careers as professional musicians but, unlike their younger relative Amjad Ali Khan, there are not many details of their lives that are publicly available.[7] Rehmat Ali Khan still performs in concerts and on television and radio and he has toured overseas. Although he does perform well he is perhaps better known as a teacher for which he is well respected.

Born in 1945, Amjad Ali Khan, no doubt, is currently one of the most well-known names in contemporary Hindustani music.[8] From an early age he began to experiment with, and finely develop, the playing technique and stylistic potential of the instrument, innovations that apparently met with the hearty approval of his father. As Vilayat Khan had succeeded in doing on the sitar before him, Amjad Ali Khan stylistically re-oriented his performance model towards the sound production, forms and aesthetics of khyal.

Most notably, Amjad Ali Khan developed the ekhara (literally 'once each') taans of khyal onto sarod. The bolkari on sarod traditionally used for taans was based on a combination of dire or dire-dara strokes. In practice this meant that a series of notes would often be sounded through two strokes of the plectrum (dire or da-ra) on each note. In an ekhara taan, each note would be sounded by a single separate note. While this type of taan was common on the sitar, it presented great technical challenges for sarodiyas. Amjad Ali Khan has received much recognition for incorporating such taans onto his playing style. Apart from these, he also directly transposed and adapted khyal-based compositions to the sarod, in a manner similar to that undertaken earlier by Vilayat Khan. His impressive experiments with the vocal technique and ornamentation, gamak, also extended the playing style of the instrument. Taken together, these innovations have been effective in re-aligning the sarod towards the aesthetic and stylistic paradigm belonging to khyal. In this respect Amjad Ali Khan is sometimes credited with 're-inventing the sarod'.[9] At the same time it must be said that there was not a complete break with dhrupad influence in his playing which, among other things, remained most evident in his retention of the performance structure of alap, jod and jhala. While it is not possible to readily differentiate the stylistic influence of dhrupad or khyal in a performance, it would not be incorrect to characterize Amjad Ali Khan's innovations as a judicious blending of the two idealized forms.

In the face of the changes made to the performance style, sound and repertoire of the instrument, it is often mentioned that Amjad Ali Khan has effected a distinct break between his playing style and those of other family members. Those within the gharana, such as Rehmat Ali Khan and Mubarak Ali Khan, who did not embark on such a transition nor otherwise sought to devise major innovations, today find themselves somewhat marginalized.

On the other hand Amjad Ali Khan, based in Delhi, has been in constant demand to perform at all major musical festivals around the country since the 1970s. From this time he also began to tour overseas and establish an international reputation. He has many disciples, some of whom have become accomplished and recognized performers in their own right. In contrast to his father, Hafiz Ali Khan, Amjad Ali Khan has made dozens of commercial recordings over the last thirty years or so.[10]

Other sarod-playing members of the family include Yakub Ali Khan, the maternal uncle of Amjad Ali Khan's first wife. Yakub Ali Khan in the latter part of his career used to play at the government-run Ashoka Hotel in Delhi where he was appointed as a permanent staff artist. After the marriage of his daughter, he migrated to Australia where he eventually passed away in 1987. Yakub Ali Khan's father, Mohammad Aziz Khan, was a sarodiya as well whose family belonged to Shahjahanpur and whose ethnicity was also identified as Bangash Pathan.[11]

Shahjahanpur Gharana

Amir Khan was known to have taught many disciples, out of whom the Calcutta-based sarodiyas, Banikantha Mukhopadhyay and Radhika Mohan Moitra, were the most well known. By the middle of this century, Radhika Mohan Moitra had emerged as the main representative of Murad Ali's lineage. Radhika Mohan Moitra (Plate 6-2), was a son of Lalit Mohan Moitra, the principal patron of Amir Khan in Calcutta. They belonged to a zamindar family who had prospered under early colonial rule and had rural estates in pre-Partition Bengal and a mansion in Calcutta. Amir Khan did not produce any progeny who became recognized sarodiyas. Due to this, the musical inheritance of this khandan transferred from the Pathan bloodlines of the Shahjahanpur gharana to bhadralok Bengalis who now assumed the mantle of principal interpreters and developers of this inheritance. It was also at this point that ethnicity became overshadowed by musical style as the marker of this particular gharana.

In addition to his training with Amir Khan, Moitra was also known to have studied with a number of other musicians among whom Dabir Khan (1905–72), the last recognized direct descendant of Tansen, and sitariya Inayat Khan (1895–1938) were the most famous. Through this contact Moitra incorporated elements of these different styles with the knowledge he had inherited from the sarodiya Amir Khan. While Amir Khan was renowned for his medium tempo Feroz Khani gats, and fast tempo Reza Khani gats, Moitra was credited with introducing the slow tempo Masit Khani gat and toda into this gharana. Through his association with Dabir Khan, he is said to have collected a large number of dhrupad compositions. His competence in dhrupad form and style was also evident in his playing of the seniya rabab and sursringar.

Perhaps due to his training with the seniya Dabir Khan, Moitra's playing style differed from other Bengali disciples of Amir Khan, such as Banikantha Mukhopadhyay, who tended to display a style more closely to aligned to that of their teacher.[12] Moitra's style was eclectic and innovative and, in addition to his thorough grounding of the dhrupad form, he also introduced many influences of khyal into his performance style. Apart from completing a master's degree in philosophy, he also wrote a number of articles on music, aesthetics and the sarod in Bengali and English.[13] He earned a reputation for his systematic approach to teaching and, over the course of his career, is known to have produced dozens of professional sarodiyas. Radhu-babu, as he was and still is known to his students and admirers, was a popular performer in all major festivals in India. He toured overseas on a number of occasions and commanded the respect of his seniors and colleagues alike. He broadcast regularly from AIR and also made a number of commercial recordings, mostly of 78rpm discs which are still in circulation in India along with a 33rpm LP disc he recorded with the sitariya, Kalyani Roy.[14]

Today, the most celebrated exponent of Murad Ali Khan's lineage is Moitra's disciple Buddhadev Dasgupta (Plate 7-2).[15] He was born in Bhagalpur, Bihar, in 1933 into a non-musical family background of civil servants and advocates. He began serious training with Radhika Mohan Moitra from the age of eleven and, by the time he was twenty-eight, had performed solo in the National Programme of Music. However, he also studied engineering, his 'real' profession as he puts it, eventually retiring as a senior engineer in a West Bengal Government enterprise.[16] All the while he continued to professionally perform on the sarod and teach a number of students.

Buddhadev Dasgupta has described the 'speciality' of his gharana's style of playing as its command over the many Feroz Khani gats that have been handed down by members of his lineage.[17] These days, the Feroz Khani gat is not as commonly heard in the contemporary repertoire of sarodiyas as in the past. Buddhadev Dasgupta is otherwise generally respected for his knowledge of gats and insight into different playing styles on sarod. He has released a number of commercial recordings and, since the mid-1980s, has regularly toured overseas and is today considered one of the most senior and knowledgeable figures within the tradition.

Maihar Gharana

Not long after Independence, the descendants of Alauddin Khan could legitimately claim gharana status as the primary criterion required for such recognition had been fulfilled, namely that of three generations of musicians (in this case Alauddin Khan—Ali Akbar Khan—Ashish Khan). Ironically, though, by this time the primacy of the bloodline in defining a gharana had been largely overshadowed within State networks by the functioning of the gharana as a denoter of musical style. So, almost from its inception, the Maihar gharana has displayed more of this particular aspect of the gharana system than those involving Pathan ancestry. Musicians who have learnt from this source of Hindustani music are said to belong to the Alauddin Khan, Maihar, or the Maihar seniya gharana.[18]

Alauddin Khan made a valuable and diverse contribution to the development of Hindustani music and his legacy is still felt today.[19] One example of this is the performance model he pioneered which is still the principal form followed in contemporary instrumental music. Like Hafiz Ali Khan, he was awarded the Padma Bhushan in 1958. Some years later this was followed by another prestigious award, the Padma Vibhushan, in 1971. He taught many dozens of students in the course of his lifetime until his death in 1972 at the age of ninety. His son, Ali Akbar Khan and son-in-law Ravi Shankar, are the most famous of his disciples. His other well-known students included his daughter Annapurna Devi (surbahar) and his nephew Bahadur Khan (sarod), Nikhil Banerjee (sitar), Timir Baran (sarod), Sharan Rani (sarod) and Jatin Bhattacharya (sarod). Besides close family members he taught a considerable number of non-family students in institutional settings in Maihar and Almora.[20] Nevertheless, Annapurna Devi, Ali Akbar Khan and Ravi Shankar have been credited with receiving the most intensive taleem.

As mentioned earlier, perhaps with the exception of Radhika Mohan Moitra, Ali Akbar Khan (Plate 7-3) began to dominate performance on the sarod from the 1950s. He began his professional career in earnest as a court musician at the palace of the Maharaja of Jodhpur just before Independence.[21] After this support ended he was employed as a permanent staff artist with All India Radio in Lucknow for a couple of years. From there he based himself in Maihar for around a decade while regularly travelling all over India for performances. From the mid-1960s, after a disagreement with a State institution in West Bengal, he shifted to the USA although he continued to regularly tour India and play at major festivals.[22] Around this time he set up his own music schools in both Calcutta and California.

Ali Akbar Khan had introduced a new panorama of tonal quality in the sarod during the early part of his career. While this was a continuation of the important innovations in sound quality, the structure of performance and vocal style of playing initiated by his father, he had nevertheless refined this inheritance further through his own compelling interpretation and approach. On this particular point, one thing that can be mentioned is his experimentation with the angle at which the jawa strikes the string and the timing used in the execution of a stroke, both of which had the effect of dramatically increasing the overall tonal range of the instrument. The round, full and penetrating sound that he captured on his sarod in turn enabled him to exploit, especially in alap, the sympathetic strings and their harmonic overtones to produce a full and delicate sound that enabled the clear articulation of subtly revealed srutis (microtones). Building upon this fundamental innovation, he significantly expanded the amount and depth of melodic detail that could be realized on the instrument, a development that quickly earned him a reputation for introducing a new sense of poetics to instrumental music.

Ali Akbar Khan had made more than two dozen commercial recordings on 78rpm discs from the late 1940s to the 1960s. He has also recorded dozens of LPs and cassettes both in India and abroad.[23] He has taught a countless number of students over his long career both through his music schools and privately.

Lucknow and Bulandshahr Gharanas

It was noted earlier that the bloodlines and the lines of musical transmission of these two gharanas effectively merged at the beginning of the twentieth century. By the middle of this century, the senior musical representatives of these combined lineages were the son of Keramatullah Khan, Ishtiaq Ahmed Khan (1919–67) and the son of Sakhawat Hussain Khan, Umar Khan (see Plates 7-4, 7-5, 7-6).

Ishtiaq Ahmed Khan was an A-grade permanent staff artist at AIR in Delhi. Although he had made one or two commercial recordings during his career, his playing is more readily heard through the archival material of AIR who periodically broadcast some of the many recordings he made over the years. The instrument played by Ishtiaq Ahmed Khan seemed to be larger in size than the sarods played by preceding generations in his gharana. It also differed in design, construction and sound quality from those played by Hafiz Ali Khan and Alauddin Khan. Ishtiaq Ahmed Khan was well known for the clear and bell-like sound quality he developed on his instrument, reminiscent of the focused tonal clarity that Hafiz Ali Khan displayed.

Generally speaking, Ishtiaq Ahmed Khan's playing style continued to accommodate the rabab heritage of this gharana and he was one of the few sarodiyas to have successfully kept this dimension of the sarod tradition intact. The preservation of the style that Ishtiaq Ahmed and Umar Khan followed was expressed in terms of a desire to remain true to the strong dhrupad orientation and style of the seniya rabab tradition, elements of which underpinned the style and content of their performance practice. It was this very feature that had been so painstakingly developed by earlier members of these families. It was also the treasure that had invested this gharana with its musical and social status in the nineteenth and early twentieth centuries.

However, in seeking to maintain the specialities of the gharana and its musical inheritance, its members did not appear to adapt as readily to the conditions of patronage and performance practice after Independence as did the other sarod gharanas. While there have no doubt been a succession of contingencies and personal experiences that have contributed to the present position of this gharana, it is nevertheless reasonable to contend that the effective marginalization of these lineages was apparent even by the 1960s.[24] With the death of Ishtiaq Ahmed Khan, the legacy of the family continued through his son Mukhtar Ahmed Khan who, like his father, was a permanent staff artist for many years at AIR in Delhi, from where he regularly broadcast until his death in 1996. His own son, Rafi Ahmed, who lives in Delhi, also occasionally broadcasts from AIR.

Umar Khan (1916–82) belonged to the other branch of this gharana and most, if not all, of his professional life was spent in Calcutta. He was awarded an A-grade rating by AIR and made regular broadcasts throughout his career. Apart from this, he was largely a freelance artist who regularly participated in major music festivals throughout the country and taught a number of students. He is not known to have made any commercial recordings during his lifetime.

Irfan Khan (b. 1956) and his elder brother Shahid Khan, currently represent the Bulandhshahr lineage of this gharana. Both perform professionally in Calcutta. In the 1980s, Irfan Khan was sent by the ICCR to their cultural centre in Kabul where he performed and taught sarod and Hindustani music for three years. A knowledgeable and revered teacher, he is not only a professional sarodiya based in Calcutta, but is also in charge of the music department in an elite private secondary school in Assam.

While members of this gharana from the time of Keramatullah Khan were known to have taught a lot of students, there are no recognized non-khandan musicians carrying on this tradition today (Mukhopadhyay 1977:114). Perhaps this situation could be explained in terms of the restrictions on the transference of music capital between the Lucknow and Bulandshahr gharanas that were transcended only after two generations of marriage between their bloodlines. Granted this was the case, it seems more likely that outsiders to the family were not in a position to inherit the full specialities of tradition, which have remained with the respective families till today. Equally so, the marginalization of this gharana can be imputed to close adherence to a sound quality and musical style that simply started to go out of fashion in the 1960s, relegated in the end to what became known as the 'old style'.

Perhaps another contributing factor is that although these gharanas were established by sarodiyas and have always centred on the sarod, a number of core family members over the last century or so opted to become sitar players. This includes in recent times Umar Khan's younger brother, Illyas Khan, who remained in Lucknow where he was a respected and popular performer and teacher of sitar until his death in 1989. Besides this musician, other members of the family, such as Illyas Khan's son, Idris Khan, is also a recognized performer on sitar. Irfan Khan's maternal uncle Nurullah Khan, who still lives near Matiyaburj, plays sitar and composes light classical music.

Other Sarodiyas

During the first half of this century, the instrument and its musicians had spread to many more locations across the country and could be heard in Almora, Dehra Dun, Jodhpur, Meerut, Maihar and Ajmer, primarily due to the increase in the number of non-khandan musicians who had taken up the sarod. It is not possible to know exactly how many sarodiyas were now professionally pursuing careers in North India in the few decades after Independence. Even so, the bulk of sarod activity, in terms of the numbers of performers and performance opportunities, was concentrated in the metropolises, out of which Calcutta was by far the most notable for the numbers of sarodiyas it produced. Outside this city, sarodiyas were also resident in or around Delhi while, on the other side of the country, Mumbai continued to be renowned more for its cultivation of vocal rather than instrumental music culture. Even though performances of sarodiyas would be periodically organized in Mumbai, these were comparatively few in number when compared to those that regularly took place in Calcutta.

Besides spreading across the country, the sarod was to be heard in new performance contexts. The growth of institutionalized State patronage meant that some sarodiyas were also inducted into orchestras such as the Vrindavadhya of All India Radio, and various other types of institutions. Besides its inclusion in this type of ensemble, the sarod was commonly used in the orchestration of the music for Bengali films. In this setting it could be part of an ensemble or played solo. However, this practice was not just confined to Bengali films but was also sometimes used in music ensembles that recorded soundtracks for Bollywood Hindi films in Mumbai. Outside the film industry it was used in the small ensembles that would accompany a performance of Kathak dance and even in five-star restaurants, entertaining guests while they dined.

While the instrument had almost exclusively been associated with and played by men, it was also around this time that two notable exceptions, namely Sharan Rani Bakliwal and Zarin Sharma (nee Daruwala) became professional sarodiyas. Sharan Rani was born in Delhi, studied dance from the age of six, after which she learnt vocal music (Garg 1978:561). Later, she went to Maihar for some time to study with Alauddin Khan and accordingly, became a well-known figure in the Maihar gharana.[25] She subsequently received an A-grade rating from AIR, performed on radio and television, played at major concerts in India and abroad and made some commercial 7 inch 45rpm recordings. Sharan Rani is also known for her donation of a large collection of rare musical instruments, including some sarods, to the National Museum in New Delhi.

Zarin Sharma belongs to the Parsi community of Mumbai. She learnt music from a number of teachers, mostly vocalists, of whom S. N. Ratanjankar and Lakshmanprasad Jaipurwale are most well known. She has performed Hindustani music widely in India since the 1960s, and is a well-known artist in Mumbai. Her performance style is well grounded in the khyal-based training which she has technically developed to a high degree as is especially evident in her gamak taans. Besides this, the sound of her sarod would be familiar to people in India due to her performances on Hindi film soundtracks.

Other women sarodiyas, well-known performers or teachers include Sipra Banerjee, a student of Ananta Kumar Roy now living in Assam, and Uma Guha, the daughter of Shyam Ganguly, living in Calcutta.

Recent Sounds

Roughly concurrent with the shift in idealized forms from dhrupad to khyal, successful innovations in the quality of sound production were initiated by a number of instrumentalists. Among sitariyas and sarodiyas, the contributions of Vilayat Khan, Rais Khan, Ali Akbar Khan, Amjad Ali Khan and Nikhil Banerjee are particularly remembered in this regard. Even though it may be possible to establish a direct connection between these two developments, it is perhaps sufficient for the present purpose to make a few observations about the conventions and practices of sound production around the time that khyal started to be positioned as the principal idealized form for instrumentalists.

As mentioned earlier, performing in auditoriums and concert halls presented the artist with new challenges and expectations that varied substantially from the mehfil or chamber setting. The preference for concert halls and other large public spaces for performance increased after Independence possibly because there was a greater number of such venues constructed which lent themselves to the institutionalized sensibilities of cultural patronage otherwise prevalent at the time. Improvements in the technology of sound amplification within such large venues in the 1960s, and the skills musicians displayed in exploiting this technology, created the potential for exploring and developing innovations in instrumental technique and tonality. The refinement of playing technique was particularly relevant to the task of transposing the stylistically-complicated meend of khyal, along with its highly-ornamented melodic style and ekhara taans, on to instruments. It therefore seems that one could not really have taken place without the other.

Those sarodiyas who most successfully negotiated these performance conditions prevailed over those who, as it is often put, retained the 'old style' of playing. Therefore, from around the 1960s, there has been an opposition set up between the gayaki style of instrumental music and this so-called 'old' style; the particular sarods played by the former group gained precedence over those instruments audibly associated with the musicians who persevered with these outdated performance practices.

Meanwhile the arrival of new technology in the form of long-playing records, reel-to-reel tapes and cassettes opened up new possibilities for extending not only the project of the mass production and commodification of recorded sound, but also the length of recordings. The increase in the number of sound recordings produced and sold created further consequences concerning the regulation of the transmission of musical knowledge. Never had it been easier to hear recorded artists and imitate their playing, or to privately copy their music from one recording medium to another. From the 1960s, such sound recordings have become a valuable resource for aspiring musicians and, in a sense, many of the recordings issued have collectively over the years become a type of unofficial 'textual' source informing contemporary music practice.

The Instruments

Whereas it was not uncommon to discover diversity in, and experimentation with, the construction and design of the sarod in the nineteenth century, by the 1970s the instrument had become standardized into two distinct types. These two types are those now associated with the Maihar gharana and the Gwalior gharana. The instrument played by Radhika Mohan Moitra and now by Buddhadev Dasgupta is effectively the same as that played within the Gwalior gharana and therefore has also been included within the latter group.

Generally speaking, the sarod played by members of the Maihar gharana is slightly bigger in size than its counterpart. However, the string length from the bridge to the nut, which varied widely in the past, is more or less identical on both contemporary versions of the instrument. The main resonating chambers of both types of sarod also exhibit a similar round shape in contrast to the more elongated design of earlier sarods. The most palpable difference between the two concerns the numbers of strings each employs.

In the case of the Maihar instrument, there are twenty-five strings divided into four baj (main) strings, two chikari strings, four jawari (drone) strings and fifteen taraf strings. The Gwalior version does not employ the jawari strings and varies between nineteen and twenty-one strings which can be identified as four baj strings, two drone strings, two chikari strings, and between eleven and thirteen taraf strings. Due to the difference in the function and the number of drone strings, the pegboxes of both instruments are distinct, with the Maihar version having eight pegs and the Gwalior version six. This last factor creates an easily recognizable difference in their overall appearance and is perhaps the quickest way to visually distinguish between them. In the past an extra tumba was also affixed behind the main pegbox on the instruments played by Hafiz Ali Khan, Radhika Mohan Moitra and Alauddin Khan. These days, preference for this extra appendage remains with performers from the Maihar gharana. There is also a distinct preference expressed over the type of wood used in the two versions. The Maihar gharana tends to prefer a type of wood known in India as tun, while those of Gwalior generally, but not exclusively, play on instruments made from teak. According to Buddhadev Dasgupta: 'toon gives a softer sound, teak gives you a harder sound so the bols are more crisp and sharp edged.'[26] The greatest number of professional quality sarods are today built and supplied by Hemen Sen, whose workshops and retail premises are on Rashbehari Avenue in South Calcutta (Plate 7-7). Hemen learnt at least some of his craft from Mohindar-babu of Comilla, a student of Ayet Ali Khan, who had a shop at Manicktala in North Calcutta: Aside from Hemen Sen, Rikki Ram of Delhi is also an important contemporary supplier of sarods.

In the past, however, it was not unusual for sarodiyas to design and oversee the construction of their own instruments. Asghar Ali Khan and Abdullah Khan are probably the most well-known examples of this. Ayet Ali Khan, the younger brother of Alauddin Khan, was a surbahar player and gifted luthier. The brothers started an instrument making business in the Brahminbaria district of what was then East Bengal. Ayet Ali made a series of sarods that culminated in the instruments he made for his nephew Ali Akbar Khan and his son Bahadur Khan. These were made from a log of tun wood that had been lying in their pukur (fish pond) for years.[27]

Gopal Mistry and his younger brother Durga were the chief sarod makers in Calcutta since the 1920s. They were from North India but had spent most of their lives in Bengal. They made instruments for Hafiz Ali Khan, Timir Baran and the students of Keramatullah Khan and Amir Khan. Radhika Mohan Moitra made many instruments with the help of Gopal Mistry, including his own. Durga Mistry's son, Mohan, still works in Calcutta. Dulal Chandra Kanji, the youngest of successful sarod makers, originally learnt his craft from Hemen Sen and for a number of years now, has worked with Buddhadev Dasgupta who has supervised the construction of many of his instruments.

Conclusion

Over the course of the twentieth century, the sarod, along with the sitar, have become the two most important solo instruments in Hindustani music. In the last few decades, the sound of the sarod has become one of the principal carriers of the Hindustani instrumental music tradition. Considering its position of relative obscurity a century ago, the arrival of the sarod at this pivotal point in Hindustani music marks the progress of what has been quite a major social, cultural and musical metamorphosis.

Apart from inheriting the sound and the 'voice' of Hindustani instrumental music from the been, seniya rabab and sursringar, the sarod now also accommodates many of the physical features of its dhrupad antecedents. For example, the straight design of the main pegbox of the sarods played by members of the Maihar and Gwalior gharanas is derived directly from the been and the sursringar. The 'lips' which are affixed between the upper neck and the pegbox and the lower neck and the main resonator on the underside of the neck of the sarod are taken from seniya rabab and sursringar. These lips had a practical application on the sursringar which was generally held while kneeling. In this position, the upper lip conveniently rested on the left shoulder of the performer and helped to keep the sursringar in the correct playing position. Of course this design feature is of no practical benefit to the sarod and was not part of the Afghani rabab either but has, for whatever reasons, become a defining feature of modern sarods. The steel plate and metal strings, the major innovations that gave birth to the sursringar in the 1820s, are also integral components of the sarod. Further, the preference for the roundish design of the main resonator of the sarod which has now replaced the more elongated resonator of the Afghani rabab and earlier sarods, is arguably derived from the seniya rabab. To this list can be added the chikari strings, the design of the pegs of the main strings and the jawari bridge of the Maihar instrument, all part of the legacy of the earlier dhrupad instruments.

At the same time, many definitive design features of the Afghani rabab are present on modern sarods. The taraf, in particular, are perhaps the most significant manifestation of this historical past. Also, the characteristic 'cutaway' sections on either side of the main resonator as it joins with the neck on the rabab, have been retained on the sarod.

The design of the modern sarod therefore demonstrates physical evidence of both the legacies of a Pathan past and the inheritance of Hindustani instrumental music. The various design features of the modern sarod are indicative of the intercourse which has taken place between these two streams since the middle of the nineteenth century. The modern sarod is now the prized offspring of this liaison.

Notes

1 There are many music circles still active in India. For example, the Bhowanipur Music Circle established in the late nineteenth century

continues to organize regular programmes in its own premises in Calcutta.

2 Studies by Goswami (1996), Mathur (1976), Mukherjee (1955) and Neuman (1980) provide most of the material available on the musical patronage provided by AIR.

3 When this system first began, there apparently was a C grade as well, denoting an amateur status.

4 For example, in the early 1990s, musicians listed as top grade (above A-grade) could record 6 times a year, A-grade artists 5 times a year, B-high grade artists 4 times year and B-grade artists, 3 times a year. The fee fixed for each grade was Rs 3,250 (top grade); between Rs 1,200 and 3,000 (A-grade); between Rs 700 and 1,100 (B-high) and Rs 500 (B-grade).

5 Ethnicity is used here to denote both a specific community, such as Pathan, Bengali, Rajput, etc., and different hereditary occupational groups of music specialists such as qawwal, kalawant, mirasi and so on.

6 See Garg (1978), Malhotra (1973), Sanyal (1959) and http://www.sarod.com among others for further details on Hafiz Ali Khan.

7 Brief biographies of these musicians can be found in Garg (1978).

8 Further biographical information on Amjad Ali Khan as well as further bibliographic, discographic and filmographic references can be obtained through the official web site of Amjad Ali Khan: www.sarod.com. Also see Mukhopadhyay (1977) and Garg (1978).

9 See, for example, the headline of *The Times of India Sunday Review*, 29 September 1996.

10 Further details of his later career are discussed in the following chapter.

11 Personal communication: 1984.

12 The strong similarity in the playing style, tonal quality and presentation, between Amir Khan and Mukherjee can be heard in their respective 78rpm disc recordings of Kafi.

13 See bibliography for references to some of these articles. Moitra also published a book in Bengali, *Jantrasangeet Prabeshika,* in 1951.

14 A selection of Moitra's recordings is housed in the archives of the American Research Centre for Ethnomusicology (ARCE), New

Delhi. There is also a performance and a taped interview with B. C. Deva (SNA-1267: 1972).

15 Buddhadev Dasgupta discusses his life and musical influences with Ira Landgarten at http://www.raga.com/210int.1html

16 It is not uncommon for musicians from middle- and upper-class backgrounds to have degrees or post-graduate qualifications in areas other than music. This phenomenon is perhaps indicative of both class expectations and the generally low regard in which university music courses in India are held.

17 Interview for Calcutta Doordarshan, 1982. For further discussion of Feroz Khani gats, see Sanyal (1959) and Miner (1993).

18 Maihar is a town in northern Madhya Pradesh where Alauddin Khan had settled after coming from Rampur. Before 1947, he had been employed as chief court musician by the local raja for more than two decades. Radhika Mohan Moitra had observed that Alauddin Khan and his students prefer to call themselves disciples of the seniya gharana (SNA-1267: 1972).

19 See Alauddin Khan (1982), Bhattacharya (1979), Debnath (1980) and Garg (1978) among others for further biographical details on Alauddin Khan and his music.

20 A controversial documentary film on this institution, *Maihar Rag,* was made by Sunil Shanbag and Arunabh Bhattacharjee (Setu Films, Mumbai) in the early 1990s. The documentary itself won a National Award in India in 1994 for the best non-fiction film of the year.

21 He had begun performing solo by at least 1938 when he was included as one of the artists at the Allahabad Music Conference in the same year.

22 See Ken Hunt's interview with Ali Akbar Khan in *Roots,* June 1995, no. 144, for the background to this disagreement.

23 See Kinnear (1985) for a comprehensive discography of both Ali Akbar Khan and Amjad Ali Khan during this period.

24 For example, this view was put forward as early as 1972 by Radhika Mohan Moitra (SNA-1267: 1972).

25 In a popular television programme 'Sa Re Ga Ma', screened on Indian cable TV in February 1998, Sharan Rani was the adjudicator of this music talent quest. When asked by the compere Sonu Nigam about her musical training, she claimed that she had taught herself

sarod and, in recalling her musical career, chose not to mention the name of Alauddin Khan.

26 Interview with Ira Landgarten, at www.raga.com/210int.1html

27 I am grateful to Jon Barlow for supplying most of this information on instrument makers through both personal communications over a period of a few years and, more formally, through an unpublished paper 'In Search of an Instrumental Voice: The Sarod' presented at the conference *Music in the Age of Reproduction: Tradition, Innovation and Enterprise* at the Centre for Studies in Social Sciences, Calcutta, in June 1999.

Marketing Sarodiyas

In recent times, professional Hindustani musicians have seen corporate finance steadily and assuredly becoming the most substantive source of funding for contemporary musical events. While empirical studies have yet to confirm the exact degree and extent to which corporate networks have so far displaced State patronage in India, a casual observation of the contemporary scene will nevertheless reveal that a coterie of high-profile Hindustani musicians have been quick to both appreciate the significance of such a shift and to try and formulate strategies for dealing with it.

This is not to imply that State networks have now become inactive as sources of patronage—it is just that the greater capital resources of corporations has meant that the concerns of the market, rather than those of the State, impel the modes through which contemporary patronage of music proceeds. Conversely, professional musicians within India who have managed to engage and exploit expanding corporate networks have found themselves, to varying extents, in better positions both in professional status and financial security than those who, for whatever reasons, have been unable or unwilling to do so.

Alongside corporate sponsorship, other networks located outside India have also provided a lucrative source of income and professional standing for musicians from at least the 1960s. While corporate networks in India are primarily derived from locally-based companies and are tempered by local concerns, global networks tend to be embedded in, and operate across, more levels of activity which therefore makes them not so easy to account for. Until now, global networks, in which musicians travel from one international city to another and from one patron-organizer to another have been sustained through, among other things, the resources of a substantially large Indian diaspora, overseas cultural and educational institutions, foreign promoters, record companies, interested individuals and students of music. On another level, the globalization of the distribution networks of multinational music companies, along with the potential of the Internet, have opened up a host of other future possibilities for the wider propagation of Hindustani music. However, it remains to be seen what future possibilities these new domains will offer musicians and to what extent local corporatization and economic globalization are interlinked and mutually self-serving.

While the necessity to participate in corporatized and globalized networks has increasingly become a matter of day-to-day reality for Hindustani musicians, the consequences of doing so, on culture in general and music in particular, have still not been fully anticipated or understood. The following comments and observations on corporatization and globalization are not intended as a detailed critique of the economic forays of transglobal corporations into India or the internationalization of Indian companies, but rather are approached in the light of their immediate and long-term impact on the lives and concerns of contemporary sarodiyas. How the corporatization and globalization of networks of patronage has effected their other instrumentalist and vocalist colleagues in Hindustani music, is itself worthy of a separate and much more indepth study.

Corporatized Networks

Out of the many points of intersection between the marketing needs of private corporations and the day-to-day requirements of musicians, it is the sponsorship of music festivals and concerts that is perhaps the most visible and also significant. The genesis and growth of corporate parlance and euphemisms in the language of promoters, musicians and media are no doubt symptomatic of the growing influence of corporate networks on the lives of musicians. From the corporate perspective, concerts and festivals are increasingly referred to as 'events'.

Event sponsorship has rapidly evolved in post-liberalization India [post 1991] from a 'nice thing to do' to a 'need to do' activity for companies. Clearly this has been the result of increased competition in the marketplace . . . There are many diverse ways of sponsoring an event —title sponsorship, co-sponsorship, official supplier, et al. Depending on the scope of sponsorship and category, the sponsor usually gets a host of benefits and rights. These generally include signage, tickets, hospitality, product category exclusivity, the right to leverage its association with the event through advertising, promotions and publicity and acknowledgment in event-related promotional activity. Association with a world-class international event can give a company the kind of credibility and competitive advantage that no other medium can.[1]

The channelling of corporate resources into cultural patronage in India appears to have generated two major outcomes. One of these is evident in the changes in how important annual music festivals, many with a long history, are now costed and underwritten. Until 1960, the revenue for major music festivals was primarily derived through ticket sales. However, since then, the cost of staging such festivals of Hindustani music has substantially escalated. This increase can largely be attributed to the present scale of performance fees paid to 'celebrity' musicians who are routinely known to charge upwards of one lakh of rupees (approx. US$ 2,300) for each local performance.[2] If a festival stretches over two or three days and presents four or five such celebrities besides a selection of other lesser-known or debuting artists, the outlay of putting on such an event can reach fifteen lakhs of rupees or more (approx. US$ 38,000). In most instances, the costs of staging such an event makes it difficult to recoup more than a third of the outlay from ticket sales. It is then imperative that promoters of concerts and festivals secure a substantial corporate sponsorship in order just to break even.[3]

Another area in which the influence of corporate networks is felt directly by musicians lies in the holding of a 'celebrity' musical event to serve a specific corporate purpose. It is nowadays not uncommon for a classical musical performance to provide a backdrop but also a drawcard to a product or service launch—the announcement of a stock report or a 'new management initiative'—or otherwise to help improve a corporation's market position by courting clients and powerful individuals or organizations. A new and influential cadre of brokers known as 'event managers' largely manages the interface between this corporate world of endeavour and that of aspiring musicians. The intervention of professional brokers between musician and patron marks a significant development in the patronage of Hindustani music, an engagement that in the past had been more or less characterized by a direct exchange between the two groups.

Recast as an element in a corporate setting, musical events can sometimes provide a greater utility as part of a strategy for marketing and publicity rather than as a cultural happening. On one such occasion in Calcutta in January 1998, a large media conglomerate organized and lavishly promoted a performance in the arts precinct in Calcutta by a high-profile celebrity sarodiya. He was accompanied by an equally famous tabla player.[4] Even though the concert was widely advertised in both Bengali and English major daily newspapers, only a small percentage of the tickets were made available to the general public.[5] The majority of the seats were reserved for the business clients and other guests of the organizers. This led to a violent incident in which an angry crowd, who had queued for some time to collect tickets, smashed the glass front of the Nandan theatre complex at Rabindra Sadan when it was announced that the few tickets which had been made available to the general public were exhausted.

In another instance, a concert was organized for a Calcutta-based sarodiya at the prestigious Kala Mandir auditorium in the same city by a media conglomerate in February 1998. At the event, the musical performance was preceded by a presentation of the annual report of the company and future sales forecasts by an executive who, when it was time to introduce the main artist of the programme, had to be reminded of the latter's name. Similar scenes of violence were witnessed outside the north Calcutta newspaper office of the media conglomerate who sponsored the event, when it was announced to the crowds queuing outside that tickets had been exhausted after only 200 or so had been distributed to the public.[6] Such incidents are not that common but irrespective of this they point to the nature of these events which are more often than not mutually beneficial to corporate patrons and celebrity musicians alike. But their effect on music itself and the relationship of music to its avid aficionados is difficult to assess. At any rate it cannot be doing either music or its aficionados any good.

Besides the direct funding of specific events, corporations have been an important source of finance in the running of private institutions such as the ITC-sponsored Sangeet Research Academy (SRA) in Calcutta and Mumbai. In Calcutta, the SRA has played an important role in training vocalists, organizing concerts and conducting a limited research programme. Recently, the SRA in Calcutta has also started to include instrumental music in their instruction. The western chapter of the SRA at Mumbai organizes and funds research activities including conferences and seminars, awards prizes and produces a number of publications.

Individual musicians also receive support through corporate networks by undertaking product endorsement, partaking in private programmes organized by a corporate firm or through developing useful contacts with corporate identities and event managers. Over the last few years, some powerful alliances have been forged between celebrity musicians, on both professional and personal levels, and the owners of large media, technical or industrial companies in ways that are reminiscent of the association that once existed between zamindars and khandan musicians during the late colonial period.

Globalized Networks[7]

Hindustani musicians have travelled and performed outside of India from at least the late nineteenth century. However, it was from the late 1950s that networks of patronage from outside the country started to figure seriously as a lucrative source and generator of prestige in the local domain. Overseas touring by Indian musicians was initially made possible because of patronage dispensed by the Indian government through the ICCR for *Festivals of India* abroad, overseas touring grants and the setting up of cultural missions in several countries. In addition, overseas support for Indian artists initially came from socio-cultural organizations, commercial sponsors and individuals of the Indian diaspora and from the arts and educational institutions of host countries. Today, musicians are invited to tour overseas by a range of organizations including international music festivals, ashrams and gurudwaras, non-resident Indian community organizations and individual entrepreneurs and local institutions such as universities and companies.

It is now increasingly commonplace for contemporary Hindustani musicians to travel abroad regularly for performances. Overseas tours and ongoing participation in globalized networks provides the local musician with a use value which then translates into increased professional status in the Indian market. Accordingly, these two networks—the cosmopolitan and the local—overlap in the lives and practice of many musicians. For those musicians who are not yet recognized as celebrities in India, the opportunities provided by global networks are also increasingly providing an income with which they can maintain a reasonable lifestyle. These income opportunities are not only confined to live and recorded performances but also involve commodity sales and the range of prospects opened up by the Internet.

The growth of both local corporate and global networks has been helped substantially by recent and rapid developments in communications and transport. While these have been the most immediate catalysts, their confluence also reflects the wider political and economic patterning of globalization. Thus musicians, at some level or another, are compelled to respond to the economic codes of transaction and organization mediated through the corporate paradigm. In other words, there are pressures on musicians to learn how to adapt to this state of affairs and respond in ways appropriate to its modus operandi. As to how, and to what extent, individuals are successful in doing so, especially in the marketing of themselves or the commodities they are involved with, is being observed with great interest and scrutiny by aspiring musicians.

State Networks of Patronage

While corporate and globalized networks now dominate contemporary cultural consumption in India, State networks, although marginalized, are far from redundant. Significantly, the musicians who have not adapted to the modalities of corporatized and globalized networks are still supported at national and international levels financially and in terms of exposure by the government. In fact, a majority of professional Hindustani musicians still rely upon State networks for support. Further, it is also not uncommon for musicians with high profiles within corporate networks to participate regularly in State-funded cultural promotions and events in India and abroad.

State-run radio and television continue to play an important role in providing a parallel forum for Hindustani musicians, not so much financially any more but in terms of prestige and exposure. For staff artists still employed by State-funded institutions, the provision of a tenured job, accommodation and a pension on retirement provides substantial and much-needed support for many individuals around the country. For others, regular recording and broadcast fees are an important component of their income. Despite sustained media focus on celebrity musicians, there are also a number of artists of extremely high musical status largely unknown outside their immediate locale who continue to rely on the support provided by State-funded broadcasting and educational institutions.

State-run television still broadcasts Hindustani classical music through its National and Regional Services (i.e. Bengali, Marathi, Gujarati, etc. Doordarshan channels) and these now compete with broadcasts by private cable TV channels such as Zee TV, Star TV and Music Asia. As one would expect, Hindustani music programmes on cable TV have noticeably better production inputs than similar programmes aired on the State-run Doordarshan. As Doordarshan enjoyed a monopoly in broadcasting until the 1990s, it is now facing tough competition from cable TV companies flush with advertising incomes and is itself in the throes of change.

At the same time it is not uncommon for free market politicians, public opinion and those with sundry vested interests to target State institutions and networks with accusations of inefficiency and cronyism.

> To be a good patron, it is not enough to have money . . . In most of our states the ministers of culture and directors of culture departments lack knowledge of, and feel for, quality in art. The claims of caste and sub-region count for too much. When there is imagination we have organizations like the Bharat Bhavan in Bhopal, but Madhya Pradesh has not been able to prevent that institution from getting tied up in squabbles. At the Centre, the Department of Culture is forced to spend too much time in anticipating and dealing with parliamentary questions.[8]

Despite any merits that such accusations may contain, the audition and grading system that has been the characteristic of State patronage for so long has ensured support for a greater and a more diverse number of musicians and musical diversity than is currently witnessed in the corporate domain. A musician's State grading holds little significance within corporate networks, either in terms of financial reward or even access to the media. In the private arena, musicians must not only be talented but equally well connected at political and personal levels and able to engage in aggressive marketing. In short, they must have entrepreneurial skills.

Perhaps the most enduring features of State patronage in contemporary Hindustani music are the awards conferred by the State to recognize and honour artists for contributions within their respective fields of endeavour. These awards, not always separated from those given to politicians, businessmen and high achievers, have an intrinsic worth and hence are valued by musicians and the public alike. Apart from the public recognition that they generate for an artist, the award also carries a financial reward. Sizeable as this cash was initially, it has lost a little of its lure for the highly-paid celebrity musicians and, of late, awards given to a musicians sometimes attract strong charges of political favouritism or bad judgement.[9]

Contemporary Trends in the Social Organization of Musicians

It is not surprising for the new corporate and global networks to tend to favour logic and procedures that reflect their own modus operandi and sensibilities. Hence, some professional musicians find themselves having to devise and create their own series of responses to these networks and to define and promote an identity. What has happened is that alliances and understandings between patrons and musicians are in a constant state of negotiation and open-endedness. This is also having an impact upon the social fabric of Hindustani music. Sarodiyas, like other Hindustani musicians, have felt the need to invent strategies that would sell their music in the private market. In the article 'The Decline of Gharanas', noted Mumbai-based vocalist and musicologist Vidyadhar Vyas notes:

> The 'market economy' conditions and considerations with motivated 'trade practices' are entering in the music field very rapidly. For [the] young or old [musician], it is not enough now to learn and produce good music, but it is more important to know how to 'sell' it (Vyas 1995:18).

The couplings of the market economy with the endeavours of music, entertainment and sport have created a new need—that of the media celebrity. Observing how collective corporate activity and globalization have valorized selected commodity 'brand names' in the marketplace, it is not surprising that within the 'business' of Hindustani music, a coterie of musical celebrities have also been valorized by the media and turned into brand name products. The end result is that the rest of the musicians, young or old, established or aspiring, turn into unbranded commodities or even 'non-commodities'. The media celebrity figure is now the dominant and public sign of success and an icon for aspiring musicians.

What, or even who, exactly confers or withholds 'celebrityhood' on a musician cannot be described with any precision. The two dozen or so current celebrities possess no single criterion with which their celebrityhood can be associated. Further contemplation on this particular subject brings into the focus of inquiry broader and more compelling issues, such as the role of the celebrity in advertising; the influence of advertising in the electronic and print media; the influence of editorial preferences on shaping cultural discourse; the consequences of 'market practices' on cultural traditions and production;

accountability, corruption and ethics and so on. Such questions will no doubt frequent our future concerns but, for the time being, a musician's celebrity status fundamentally exists within, and is generated by, media and other commercially-driven agendas such as advertising, with the actual amount of media exposure given to a musician at any given time determining the degree of their 'celebrityhood'. A musician's skill, artistry and musical status no doubt can go a long way in the conferral of celebrity status but it is certainly not the sole criterion by which a celebrity is created these days.

On the other hand, as is the case with entertainment and sport, there are major and minor celebrities, either of whom can seem to appear overnight or disappear from public view in a similar fashion. One can only guess that access to media makes for a celebrity. Musical celebrities are of use to the media in that they sell other products. Perhaps this use value decides their market value and hence, their celebrity status.[10]

Beyond an ongoing high media profile, it is commonly expected for celebrity musicians to: regularly perform at major music festivals, often as the drawcard; regularly perform at corporate events; have a substantial number of commercially-released recordings and often function as chief guest or judge at competitions, on television chat shows and the like. Once created, a musical celebrity can become a hub through which work is dispensed or distributed to students and other affiliates. In instrumental music, a disciple's affiliation with a celebrity musician now has increasingly less to do with following a shared musical style, or even playing the same instrument as the celebrity, as it does with establishing useful contacts and learning how to engage networks of patronage. In such an arrangement, the celebrity becomes the 'brand name' and the affiliates assume a position not unlike that of a franchisee of that name. Promoters do not always know much about music, or even who is a good musician, but they can avoid taking a risk by employing affiliates of celebrity musicians. This association by name provides an identity for otherwise unknown talent. Established celebrities of Hindustani music now form an important part of the galaxy of sports and entertainment media celebrities in Indian urban popular culture and imagination.

The new modes of affiliations between celebrity musicians and their disciples are often casually referred to as 'groups'. This term is commonly used to describe an alliance between established musicians and other disciples with a musical celebrity who, in the logic of corporate sponsorship, assumes the identity and function of a corporate brand name. It is difficult to say whether these 'groups' are a further modification of the gharana system or a new development operating as a parallel system in competition with gharanas. While the minutiae of this debate will no doubt continue for some time, the relevance of gharanas is meanwhile being seriously challenged by new economic realities. Tension between previously-held understandings of how gharanas operate and the modes of exchange through which corporate or cosmopolitan networks dispense patronage is becoming increasingly apparent. Either way, this phenomenon, like similar ruptures in economic codes in the past, holds significant implications for the identity of musicians, the modes of transmission of musical knowledge and the rights to the ownership of that knowledge. It is also something that is attracting attention among musicians, musicologists and music lovers. The eminent musicologist Ashok Ranade observes, 'It is likely that a new alignment of musical elements will take place and a new way of grouping musical ideologies will be attempted, which happens to be the main function of the concept of the gharana as it developed in the modern period.' (1997:120)

The lure of new and very lucrative resources and the development of 'groupism' as strategy needed for engaging them, have not been passed up by sarodiyas. Each individual experience varies according to many factors, such as personal preference and the resources at hand at any given time, the level and quality of musical training that one receives, one's social and cultural background and most of all talent.

Among sarodiyas, two broad strategies for engaging contemporary sources of patronage can be discerned. Aspiring sarodiyas have attempted to affiliate with, or otherwise invoke the name of, one of the current 'celebrity' sarodiyas; more experienced sarodiyas, it seems, have sought to establish direct personal links with an events manager, corporate sponsor or, preferably, with executives of the large print and electronic media companies.

Sarod gharanas, as social units, have faced the obligations of this new set of affiliations in which considerations of musical training, style and past social sensibilities and modes of exchange have given way to the demanding market economy. It would not be unrealistic to anticipate that the consequences of 'groupism' can be potentially as far reaching as those set in motion by the gharana system a century or so earlier, when it had been developed as an analogous strategy for negotiating the transition of musicians into modernity.

Gharanas, Groups and Celebrity Sarodiyas

Currently two senior sarodiyas can be counted among the celebrities in Hindustani music, Amjad Ali Khan and Ali Akbar Khan. They share a similar professional status in the sense that both are khalifas (leading authoritative figures) of their respective gharanas. But they also depict two different aspects of how celebrityhood works. Ali Akbar, who resides in the USA, is the senior of the two in terms of age and experience and can be rated as more successful in his engagement of global networks. Amjad Ali Khan lives in Delhi, has strong connections with local networks and is perhaps the most well-known sarodiya in India. While one must research their lives and experiences in a sustained manner to account for how they attained celebrity status, their high public profiles have meant that information on their lives is easily accessible. Their marketing and publicity materials over the years have more than amply documented their biographical details. The following discussion uses this material to raise one or two issues concerning celebrityhood and its consequences for the sarod tradition.

Gwalior Gharana

Among the contemporary sarodiyas, Amjad Ali Khan has unquestionably the highest profile as a media celebrity in India. His comprehensive engagement with local corporate networks, in conjunction with ongoing support through State networks, contributes strongly to his high profile in India. The faultless professionalism, personal charisma and unquestionable musical talent have no doubt contributed to his success as a public figure and to his induction into the ranks of celebrities in the Indian media. Like most celebrities, information on his professional life and background is readily available. This can be accessed through the documentation accompanying sound recordings, of which he has produced dozens during his professional career; on a web site;[11] in many print and electronic media interviews; in journals; in documentary films, of which at least three have been made and even a glossy celebratory book. His family's musical history has been preserved in a museum at Amjad Ali Khan's ancestral home in Gwalior. Memories of the history of his lineage are further reinforced through the annual Hafiz Ali Khan Awards which honour musical excellence. While his domination of the local scene continues, he has also developed a significant presence in global networks and is regularly invited to perform in major cities and cultural festivals overseas.

The lineage of Murad Ali Khan—Nanhe Khan—Hafiz Ali Khan—Amjad Ali Khan is now the principal branch of the Gwalior gharana. It is fair to say that it overshadows other bloodlines of the gharana belonging to Hafiz Ali Khan's other sons, the previously-mentioned Rehmat Ali Khan and Mubarak Ali Khan. Recently, however, Rehmat Ali Khan's son, Amin Ali Khan has started to perform professionally and has received press coverage.

The musical and technical innovations Amjad Ali Khan introduced into the sarod repertoire have become a model for emulation for many of the current generation of sarodiyas. Apart from the large contingent of musicians he can count as his disciples, the particular stamp of his playing can often be heard from sarodiyas who do not belong to this gharana. From among his students, his two sons, Amaan Ali and Ayaan Ali Bangash have by far the highest public profile. Both of them are at the beginning of their professional careers and both receive frequent media exposure and promotion. They regularly accompany their father in concerts and also perform solo in their own right at major music festivals. Besides preparing his sons, Amjad Ali Khan has taught many disciples over the years, including non-sarodiyas. He has also established a scholarship for talented students. Among the best known of his other disciples are Biswajeet Roy Choudhury, Mukund Sharma and Narendranath Dhar.

In the case of Amjad Ali Khan, the intersection of media celebrities, the market economy and the functioning of the gharana system have generated an interesting conundrum. On the one hand, there is the seniormost and respected figure of a musical tradition in which ritualized social relations and codes of behaviour, such as adab[12] are still very strong and expected to be observed by students, other musicians, music aficionados, rasikas and so on. On the other hand, there is the public figure, one of an array of media figures from music, film, stage, fashion ramps, sports and other arenas, whose utility in the corporate networks is not necessarily a musical one. A high media profile means that it is not uncommon for a photograph of him to appear in the Indian media shaking hands with the Dalai Lama or meeting the Pope, attending or judging a beauty pageant or Mr Universe Contest or otherwise being involved in high-profile sponsorship and product endorsement. On one level, the Gwalior gharana still operates according to past understandings of what a gharana should be, in terms of encapsulating a core bloodline, musical pedigree and musical style. However, an earnest engagement with the corporate world has meant that a new set of obligations and transactions have intruded into, and are beginning to transform, the foundations of this social institution.

The behavioural and social responsibilities and obligations expected within a premodern or traditional, professional musical setting somehow do not always successfully make the transition to the domain of the market economy which is invariably engrossed in its own concerns and discourse. As a result it can said that two levels of discourse intersect in the celebrity. On one hand, there is the artist steeped in the cultural authority of a musical tradition and, on the other, there is the celebrity public media figure. This dual identity creates a situation complicated by there being no clear demarcation between the two spheres in the eyes of the general public. This in turn can permit a past action, a contemporary event, a piece of history or whatever, to be simultaneously and ambiguously exposed to two discourses of interpretation and meaning. Consequently, this has led to the occasional unabashed act of self promotion by a contemporary musician being vehemently criticized by senior musicians for clashing with past sensibilities of behaviour and protocol but, perhaps at the same time, lauded as a clever marketing strategy. The problem of how to deal with the transposition of values and sensibilities from one domain and their reconstitution in another is one of the most complex issues facing Hindustani music culture today.

There is another issue that has raised controversy regarding the historical representation of sarodiyas. This has to do with the revival of the title 'Bangash' appended to the names of Amjad Ali Khan's two sons. Given that Bangash appears to be a recent construct relative to other Pathan koums, and also that sarodiyas from other gharanas can claim a continuous and direct Bangash family history,[13] the question arises as to why it was felt important to highlight the term Bangash within this particular lineage at this time. For whatever reasons this may have been done, its most immediate effect has been to revive ethnicity as a parameter within the social organization of musicians, something the gharana system had tacitly overridden over the last few decades. The claim also has the more direct effect of emphasizing the Pathan history of the sarod, and through implied association, also the centrality of this lineage in any such history. The revival of the term Bangash in this way injects the distant past into the present and implies notions of cultural legitimacy and authority through blood for the descendants of this lineage. In so doing, it carries with it, intended or otherwise, an unshakeable implication of cultural ownership.

The meaning and implications of Bangash in the context of the market economy in contemporary India, take on a different connotation that is not historical. Marketing practices are generally not renowned for accommodating nuances and subtleties of historical narratives due to the prerogative of 'straightening out' complicated facts under the pressure of preparing a short publicity statement, media release or liner notes for a CD. In this the relationship of Bangash to the sarod tradition gets collapsed into a simplistic assertion that acquires other meanings.

It is almost inevitable that some distortion in the imagining of a celebrity's historical past should occur when terms and concepts are transposed from the universe of discourse of premodern historiography to that of marketing. Whether intended or otherwise, a contemporary or historical event tends to acquire meaning and representation in line with marketing practices. Not knowing whether to interpret a piece of historical or cultural information as a self-referential construct of a commercial marketing exercise or as part of the contestatory dynamics of a larger historical narrative remains a hidden conundrum for the outside observer.

Maiḥar Gharana

The Maihar gharana, as it exists today, can probably claim affiliation of the largest number of professional musicians in Hindustani instrumental music.[14] Besides sarodiyas and sitariyas, through this gharana a significant number of professional musicians of other instruments have also received their musical training to varying degrees. Many current celebrity instrumental musicians have, or once had, some affiliation with it. To name but a few: Hariprasad Chaurasia and Ronu Majumdar (bansuri), Shiv Kumar Sharma (santoor) and Vishwa Mohan Bhatt (guitar). While in the past the musical identity of the Maihar gharana was strongly derived from, and grounded in, its association with the sarod, in contemporary Hindustani music the Maihar gharana is certainly not exclusively a sarod gharana in the same way, for example, as the Shahjahanpur gharana might be so regarded.

In practice, the Maihar gharana currently functions as a rather loose and diverse affiliation of musicians with three identifiable main branches and many sub-branches spread across India and abroad. One main branch effectively centres on Ali Akbar Khan, while another branch revolves around Ravi Shankar. A further branch can be attributed to the daughter of Alauddin Khan, Annapurna Devi. In addition to these three primary branches, a number of sub-branches can be identified. There were two sub-branches particularly relevant to Calcutta; one connected to the late Bahadur Khan and the other to the late Dhyanesh Khan. Another more recent sub-branch has formed in India and the USA around Ali Akbar Khan's eldest son, Ashish Khan. The branches of the Maihar gharana connected to Ali Akbar Khan and Ravi Shankar have by far the largest number of affiliates.

Out of all these branches, Ali Akbar Khan is the current khalifa of the Maihar gharana and, as Alauddin Khan's son, is ideally held to have the final word on matters related to the family's musical inheritance. The numbers and types of musicians that have some form of affiliation with the Maihar gharana over the last few decades seem to have stretched and transformed the definition, functioning and utility of the term gharana.

Among the many non-family disciples who currently represent the different branches of the Maihar gharana are: Anindya Banerjee and Tejendra Narayan Mazumdar (both of whom reside in Calcutta), Rajeev Taranath (Bangalore) and Ashok Roy (who lives in Sydney, Australia).[15] Other important sarodiyas belonging to the Maihar gharana but who received their musical training from different branches are Sunil Mukherjee (Delhi) and Parthasarathi Choudhuri (Calcutta), both of whom studied with Ravi Shankar. Pradeep Kumar Barot, Basant Kabra and Suresh Vyas (all in Mumbai) learnt from Annapurna Devi. Besides the coterie of established professional musicians there are many dozens of sarodiyas in India who currently learn from, or at the very least identify with, the Maihar gharana.

As is also the case with the Gwalior gharana, there is no dearth of information currently available on the principal figures of this gharana. There are articles, books, interviews, academic studies, at least two documentary films, a web site and the publicity information that accompanies sound recordings.[16] The amount and accessibility of this material makes it unnecessary to reproduce this information here, for the discussion concentrates primarily on sarodiyas and the core lineage of the gharana associated with the sarod, a focus which invariably centres on Ali Akbar Khan.

Although based in the United States for more than three decades, he has continued to make regular visits to India for performances and also to teach many disciples. Ali Akbar Khan's engagement with local corporate networks and media houses in India is less close than the patronage he receives from corporate networks in the United States and elsewhere. This has meant that despite being a musical celebrity in the Indian media, he is not a significant part of the corporate musical nexus there. Yet the regard for him as a senior artist continues to ensure that his performances in India are in high demand and that his professional status remains in the uppermost ranks of artists in India.

After Ali Akbar Khan are his elder sons, sarodiyas Aashish Khan (b. 1939) and the late Dhyanesh Khan (1942–91). Dhyanesh Khan spent his professional career in Calcutta where he was a well-liked and respected teacher. Ashish Khan resides mostly in the United States but returns to teach for a time every year at the Ali Akbar College in Calcutta. During these visits he also performs regularly around the country and is beginning to get inducted into the local corporate networks. Besides his sons, Ali Akbar Khan has taught many dozens of sarodiyas who are, or at one time were, professional musicians in India.[17] Residing in California, Ali Akbar Khan has attracted the maximum number of foreign students from outside India to study the sarod.[18]

During the course of his career, Ali Akbar Khan has also made dozens of commercial recordings. The length of his career can almost be marked by the stages in the development of sound recording technology. While his first recordings were produced on 3 minute 78rpm discs in India in the late 1940s, his latest recordings have been issued on 75 minute compact discs. In the early 1980s, along with his American associates, Ali Akbar Khan established his own music publishing company AMMP which among other things has released a number of his live concert recordings. Alongside signalling a significant development in the economy of Hindustani music, this action effectively amounts to a strategy for responding to broader changes taking place in the business of music. In the larger scheme of the mass production of sound, it signals that the musician can also assume the role of producer, distributor and retailer of his own products.[19]

Two major consequences of this development should be noted here. One is the renegotiation of the economic modes and transactions that exist between musicians and contemporary sources of patronage. Another is the pressure it exerts on the need to rethink previously-held concepts about the utility and functioning of the gharana system. One more outcome relates to the treatment of historical representation in a market economy, the means by which history can be unwittingly or otherwise exploited in the business of selling commodities. The inner narrative of the Maihar gharana has always emphasized a direct musical identification with the seniya tradition. This connection was based on the pivotal ustad-shagird relationship between seniya Wazir Khan and Alauddin Khan. However, apart from this undoubted musical identification with seniyas, there has been no familial or blood ties that have connected these two figures who otherwise belonged to quite distinct communities originally from opposite sides of the country. However, in the liner notes of a recent commercial recording, Alauddin Khan is described as a direct descendant of Tansen, the progenitor of the seniya tradition.[20] It is unimaginable that Ali Akbar Khan should ever assert such a familial connection that would have tremendous implications on the history of Hindustani music and, further, would be something easily dismissed as untrue. The allusion or direct implication of such a familial connection is therefore an overstatement by some over-zealous and ill-informed copywriter, hoping to add a little more edge to the marketability of the product. If it were Ali Akbar Khan who made such a statement, he would be answerable to the community of musicians to correct the remark; this copywriter is not.

This tiny incident brings into focus a number of things. This is yet another example of the problems of employing sensitive historical material in the service of the market economy. It shows that the ascendancy of the market economy has translated into social and economic pressure on musicians. What this and other such overstatements falsifying musical history end up doing is making the stretching of history a de rigueur act in the process of creating a celebrity and establishing a 'group'.

Shahjahanpur Gharana

By comparison with the Maihar gharana, the Shahjahanpur gharana is considerably smaller and has far less coverage in the mass media than the Gwalior gharana. It now effectively operates as a main branch with some sub-branches in Calcutta where it is centred. After

Radhika Mohan Moitra, Buddhadev Dasgupta became the principal representative of this lineage. Currently he has the highest professional status among all its members. He is the best-known performer of the gharana and has the highest number of students. The main branch of the gharana now emanates from him. In this respect he has effectively assumed the role of the khalifa of the gharana, although modesty may prevent him from describing himself as such.

Buddhadev Dasgupta continues to live in Calcutta and is adored by many as a respected performer, teacher and arbiter of musical matters in general. In fact, he is counted today as the seniormost authority on sarod in Calcutta, the city that for the last century had been the centre of sarod activity in India. In musical matters he is articulate and thoughtful; he is recognized as a compelling performer, and his music is inculcated with a depth of knowledge of rare and beautiful gats which have characteristically formed part of the inheritance of this gharana.

Like his teacher, Buddhadev Dasgupta displays a very effective technical command of the instrument, enabling him to produce an appealing tonal quality, well-balanced sound and crisp ekhara taans.[21] His playing contains a combination of khyal and dhrupad styles, structures and artistic sensibilities. He has performed at most, if not all, major festivals in India and, since his retirement as an engineer, he has given many performances overseas and made several commercial recordings. In 1998, he was the principal organizer of the first Radhika Mohan Moitra Memorial Music Festival lasting four days at Uttam Manch in Calcutta. Over the years he has trained many students both privately and through his involvement with the Sangeet Research Academy in Calcutta. His son, Anirban Das Gupta, received extensive training on the sarod from his father and is an accomplished player. He lives in the USA and, like his father, is committed to another professional career. Those currently professionally performing in India are Pratyush Banerjee and Debasish Bhattacharya, both residents of Calcutta.

Another senior figure and long-time student of Radhika Mohan Moitra is Kalyan Mukherjee. As with his gurubhai Dasgupta who juggled two careers as an engineer and a musician for several years, Kalyan Mukherjee is both an accomplished sarodiya and a mathematician of international standing. He is particularly remembered for his delicate tone and intelligent command over the performance idiom. A resident in Calcutta, Mukherjee has now retired from performance. Although he has never released a commercial recording there are plenty of private recordings of his programmes in circulation.

Other senior figures of the gharana include Anil Roy Choudhury, who although a contemporary in age with Radhika Mohan Moitra, was also his long-time student. He taught scores of students and was quite well known in Calcutta in the 1950s and 1960s. There are other students of Moitra, such as Samarendranath Sikdar who is still an active performer and teacher in Calcutta. Narendranath Dhar, who is based in Lucknow, had learnt extensively from Radhika Mohan Moitra and also performed with him; however these days he is more generally known as a disciple of Amjad Ali Khan. Somjit Das Gupta spent his childhood growing up in Moitra's house in Calcutta and received intensive training from him, not only on sarod but also sursringar, seniya rabab and in dhrupad. He is an excellent teacher and performer who has collected and cared for many priceless old instruments. Despite this background and his well-grounded knowledge of the history of the sarod, he struggles to maintain a living in that city. Besides these, and many other sarodiyas of this gharana not mentioned here, there are sitariyas, among them Sanjoy Mukhopadhyay, who received their training under Radhika Mohan Moitra and are accomplished representatives of the Shahjahanpur gharana. Since the late 1960s, a number of foreign students have also found their way into the fold of this gharana.

However, to date, Buddhadev Dasgupta has been the most successful from this gharana in engaging and working within both local corporate and global networks. His international reputation has been enhanced by a series of concert tours overseas and, more recently, by the sound recordings published by the New York-based Raga Records. Even so, he has lived with a relatively low public profile and this is one reason he is generally not counted among the caste of celebrity musicians. His public recognition appears to be derived from his authority both as a performer and as the principal representative of the gharana, his own musical talent along with extensive professional association with colleagues and institutions.

The Shahjahanpur gharana has so far maintained itself as part of the sarod tradition. This can be partly imputed to it not having received the same attention in the media and corporate networks over the last decade as the Maihar and Gwalior gharanas. There are no doubt other reasons why this may be the case—lack of engagement with corporate networks, lack of a fully-fledged celebrity, the upper-caste identity and the Hindu social background of its main representatives and so on. Nevertheless, as the senior maestro of the sarod tradition resident in Calcutta, Buddhadev Dasgupta is attracting a group around him which does overshadow other musicians of this gharana. On both the social and stylistic level, the Shahjahanpur gharana still continues to operate as a gharana in the way that term was previously understood and has strongly retained its primary identity as a sarod gharana.

Lucknow and Bulandshahr Gharanas

In the nineteenth century, when the sarod occupied a position on the margins of Hindustani music, these two gharanas represented the central core of that tradition. Ironically, now that the sarod itself is firmly ensconced at the centre of Hindustani music, these two gharanas find themselves on the periphery. They had thrived under premodern networks and survived under early modern networks but lost their primacy once State networks became ascendant. More recently, members of this now amalgamated joint gharana have not had any notable engagement with local corporate and global networks. At the same time they are finding it increasingly difficult to depend on pre-existing sources which are steadily declining.[22]

There are essentially only two dwindling branches that remain today of this amalgamated gharana, now commonly known as the Lucknow gharana. One of these is localized in Calcutta and the other in Lucknow. No one from either branch has celebrity status so far. Further, after the death of Illyas Khan in the late 1980s, there are no well-known performers who can represent this heritage or further its position in the contemporary music arena. Irfan Khan in Calcutta, currently the main representative of this heritage, is not able to get more than a few engagements a year and relies on teaching in increasingly disinterested private schools to earn a livelihood. Idris Khan in Lucknow is striving to establish himself as a concert artist. Other family members who follow music professionally are fading away and there are now few left to carry on this heritage or to give voice to its history and musical experiences.

The struggles that current representatives face in maintaining the viability of the gharana makes the transition to corporate patronage or global patronage remote. Yet, whatever remains of the Lucknow gharana still strongly carries the memories of a more privileged and successful past. Its members remain justifiably proud of their ancestors' contribution to the development of sarod, and hope it will be acknowledged as equal alongside other more powerful voices currently heard.

Meanwhile, there remains a wealth of musical knowledge in these gharanas that is as valuable as it is unknown and unappreciated by contemporary musical practice. Apart from a clear and precise knowledge of the forms and architecture of the major raags, the musical inheritance of this gharana comprises a huge collection of gats, parans and todas that particularly highlight the seniya rabab heritage of this lineage. To these possessions can be added the knowledge of an extensive list of rare raags and, most of all, a unique body of recorded written work of historical importance. It has to be said that it is both true and unfortunate that, being caught up in the maelstrom of rapid change and re-invention that characterizes contemporary patronage, this gharana is now seriously in danger of vanishing totally and a unique body of musical performance practice and attendant repertoire might be lost forever.

Other Sarodiyas

Brij Narayan is the son of the famous sarangi player Ram Narayan. Ram Narayan has played a leading role in pioneering the sarangi as a solo instrument in Hindustani music. Brij Narayan, who lives in Mumbai, mentions that although he initially received some very basic training on the sarod from Ali Akbar Khan, his musical training was imparted to him by his father.[23] This explains why he has introduced many new elements, derived from the sarangi and its technique, into his sarod playing. Of these, two details in particular are worth mentioning. The first is the right-hand technique developed for crossing from one string to another in fast passages that avoids breaking the flow and continuity of alternating up-and-down plucking patterns. The second concerns the design, agility and clarity shown in the execution of ekhara taans, which draw heavily on khyal and sarangi patterns.

Although Brij Narayan regularly performs overseas, his performances in India over the last few years have not been commensurate with his experience and musical background. He survives as a professional musician in India with the help of the niche he has cultivated over the years in global networks. In his case, local patronage has been much harder to come by.[24] He has made a number of commercial recordings which are readily available in India. Further, he broadcasts regularly on the radio and cable TV and periodically performs at important concerts and festivals in India.

The globalization of networks of patronage for some sarodiyas has thrown up another interesting outcome—the study, practice and performance of sarod by non-Indian students from all over the world. A handful of foreign sarodiyas have made commercial recordings in the last few years and also perform routinely in India.

Experiencing Sound

Alongside new forms of patronage and strategies for dealing with them, there are new fundamental shifts in the way we hear and experience musical sound. Broadly speaking, it is possible to discern at least two significant dimensions to this shift. One of these has to do with the replacement of recorded analog sound with digital technology, and the new modes of the distribution of sound that this technological shift has generated. The other change has to do with improvements in the technology used in live performances and the greater potential this has created for the exploitation of live sound.

The digitization of recorded sound first occurred on a widespread level with the arrival of the compact disc. More recently, digital storage and retrieval technology, especially with MP3 players, has meant that recorded sound has now been developed into a well-suited medium for distribution through the Internet. Already there is a significant impact on the way in which recorded and live music is distributed. This change has come so rapidly upon us, that efforts to plot directions for the future of recorded sound, let alone the details of how it may be done, remain assuredly speculative. While the long-term impact and consequences of these developments still remain largely in the future, we can, from our current position, at least ponder on the astonishing degree by which this technology has dramatically extended the project of the mass production of sound begun around a century ago.

The Internet promises new modes of transaction and exchange between musicians and potential patrons of Hindustani music. It lays down new challenges to the broadcasting, copyrighting and commodification and distribution of sound recordings. Like most things in flux, these can be characterized as a melange of gains and losses for musicians. On the one hand, large multinational music companies can exploit the Internet for better distribution of mass-produced commodities. On the other hand, it becomes economically possible for individual musicians to distribute their own music directly thereby negating the necessity of dealing with record companies. While the potential of a new economy of exchange opens up so many possibilities for musicians, at the same time it unleashes some issues of concern. The technology that allows for the relatively easy distribution of recorded sound also makes it difficult to monitor let alone control what happens to it once it is distributed.

Performance Practice

Khyal is well entrenched now as the idealized form guiding the aesthetics and sensibility of Hindustani instrumental music. Compositions and stylistic elements of khyal are now being increasingly included in instrumental music and this is audible in the music of many upcoming sarodiyas. A lack of opportunity for younger sarodiyas to learn dhrupad has meant that the knowledge of the forms, structures, compositions and aesthetics of this genre are now almost lost, barring a handful of contemporary beenkars. For the last few decades, the primary legacy of dhrupad had been retained in the alap–jod–jhala format of instrumental music performance. However, questions even about the relevance of alap have started to be raised. This is evident for example in the observation of a well-known contemporary sarodiya from Mumbai:

> Today, the reason why artists are more prone to showing off their virtuosity is because the audience prefers this. People become bored listening to a long alap; they want their music to be like fast food.[25]

Although this may be the case, it is not uncommon to hear the comment that an emphasis on virtuosity often occurs at the expense of musical content. Apart from obliging sections of the audience in a concert, the emphasis on virtuosity and technique has another dimension which has to do with the style of music that is possible, and desirable, for performers to produce on their instruments. Now, a conflict has arisen in the twenty-first century—how much time should be given to technique and how much to the presentation of real music in a performance . . . technical perfection will bring out better musical effects. Once you can produce these musical effects, it has a lot of value in the markets—not only here but abroad.[26]

Apart from these developments, other strategies are starting to appear in contemporary Hindustani music which appear to emphasize and value novelty per se. Such diversions have included jugalbandis (duets) of unusual combinations such as sarod and voice, collaborations between Hindustani musicians with local or international popular musicians, as well as with overseas classical, jazz, traditional and 'world' musicians.

In the wake of these manifold changes there has not been, as yet, a dramatic change in the physical design of the instrument. This may have been a typical response to similar significant developments in Hindustani music in the past; the current mode for tackling the same problem translates into a concern over controlling the technology of sound production. This comes in the wake of a slowly-dawning awareness of the importance of sound technology among Hindustani musicians for their professional image and the success of their programmes. It is not uncommon to hear the charge that many artists go to great efforts to cultivate a particular sound quality and tonal production, yet they feel that this accomplishment can often be destroyed in an instant through bad equipment or an incompetent technician and, not least of all, due to their own lack of understanding of the technology. This situation has been met with a desire by musicians to exercise greater control over this domain with some like Ashish Khan experimenting with a fixed microphone or Amjad Ali Khan using known and dependable sound technicians wherever possible for his concerts in India.[27]

Perhaps this development can be imputed to a greater sensitivity among musicians towards sound production on their instruments. The expectation of high quality sound in India has increased with the availability of good quality home and professional sound equipment. Instrumental technique has adapted to, and more effectively exploited, the technology which reproduces the sound of the instrument rather than attempting to change the design of the instrument. As is also evident in the aesthetic codes of popular music, artists increasingly need to sound like the CD in a live performance. Conversely, the live performance takes on the character of a forum or promotion for these commodities.

The diversity in design and playing styles of the sarod tradition over the last few decades has meanwhile significantly decreased. Accordingly, in contrast to the many different types and designs of sarod played at the beginning of the twentieth century, there are currently only two designs of the instrument in circulation today, one of which is associated with Amjad Ali Khan and the other with Ali Akbar Khan.

Conclusion

Over the last 300 years it has become evident that a period of social and aesthetic fluidity appears to occur at the point of transition between a pre-existent and an emerging network of patronage. In this respect, changes currently unfolding follow a similar magnitude and patterning to those observed in the past. Current developments in the economic and social organization of Hindustani music are seriously challenging the continued viability of the gharana system. The Gwalior and Maihar gharanas have now forged a secure engagement with corporatized and global networks of patronage, and it is in this sense that some of their members can also be said to have made the transition to the group structure. To some extent the same can be said about the Shahjahanpur gharana. However, as contemporary members of the Bulandshahr and Lucknow gharanas have not forged these connections, they still identify with prior notions of the function of the gharana and accordingly, have now become effectively marginalized in the contemporary setting. These changes are not restricted to the experience of sarodiyas but appear to be a widespread trend in Hindustani instrumental and vocal music.

Notes

1 Ravi Krishnan, *The Economic Times*, Mumbai, Brand Equity Supplement, 2–8 June 1999.

2 At the end of the 1990s, some top celebrity musicians were known to be charging up to Rs 8 lakh per performance (approx. US $18,500)—more than a middle-level government employee in India could hope to earn through seven years of service.

3 Personal and ongoing communications with festival and concert organizers in Mumbai, Delhi and Calcutta (1996–2000).

4 This concert featured Amjad Ali Khan and Zakir Hussain.

5 A personal contact within the media group estimated that only 10 to 15% of total tickets available were distributed to the general public (January 1998, soon after the event).

6 Personal observation. Kala Mandir has a seating capacity of approximately 2000 people.

7 Much of the material in this section is based on the group discussion sessions which arose during a conference *The Impact of Globalization on Culture: The Case of Music* organized at the Centre for Studies in Social Sciences, Calcutta, in February 1998. The conference was con-

vened by Partha Chatterjee, Sugata Marjit and myself.

8 Taken from *The State of the Arts* by H. Y. Sharad Prasad, former Information Adviser to the Prime Minister of India. Printed as a feature article in *The Asian Age*, 25 February 1998.

9 The very public quarrels in recent years between Jasraj and Ravi Shankar, highlighted in the media, over the awarding of the title Bharat Ratna, and that between Vilayat Khan and Ravi Shankar over the awarding of the Padma Vibhushan are well-known examples of this (*Indian Express, The Express Magazine,* Mumbai, 13 February 2000).

10 For example, the former Indian cricket captain, and one-time coach of the team, Kapil Dev, was the chief guest at a media launch of a new CD featuring a famous sarodiya and his sons. See *The Telegraph,* Calcutta, 24 January 1998.

11 http://www.sarod.com

12 See Metcalfe ed. (1986) for a detailed discussion of adab.

13 As mentioned before, the Bulandshahr and Lucknow gharanas are also directly descended from Bangash forefathers. During many interviews and meetings with Illyas Khan, Irfan Khan, Nurullah Khan and other family members of these gharanas, it was repeatedly mentioned with regret that even after so many generations living in India, they were now unable to recall any details of their Bangash past, let alone make any comments on what such a past means historically.

14 This does not include the tabla gharanas.

15 Ashok Roy has been my teacher and mentor for more than two decades. A long-time disciple of Ali Akbar Khan, he started his musical training with his father Ananta Kumar Roy, himself a disciple of both Keramatullah Khan and Alauddin Khan. Ashok Roy served as a staff artist at AIR in Delhi for a number of years before shifting to Dehra Dun and then migrating to Australia, Ashok Roy's paternal uncle, Sachindra Nath Roy, was a disciple of Inayat Khan and Alauddin Khan, and his younger brother Chandan Roy was, and cousin Robi Roy currently is, an A-grade artist with AIR.

16 Further biographical details of Ali Akbar Khan can be accessed through his official web site: http://www.ammp.com/aak.html

17 It is not possible to mention them all here; apologies for these omissions.

18 Recent publicity material for the Ali Akbar College in San Rafael, California, claims that an incredible 7,000 students have passed through the college since it opened in the late 1960s. There is no indication, however, as to how many of these studied sarod. An affiliated branch of the Ali Akbar College was opened by his student Ken Zuckerman in Basel, Switzerland, in the 1980s.

19 Diversification into such commercial activity conforms to the concept of the 'entrepreneur musician' put forward by Attali (1985).

20 *Hindustani Music from the 17th and 18th Centuries,* Ali Akbar Khan/Asha Bhosle collaboration.

21 Ekhara taans are fast passages that, on sarod, are executed with one right hand stroke to every note. There are many different types of taan patterns in the sarod repertoire. Most of these rely on either two (double) strokes to a single note or a combination of double and single strokes. The ekhara taan is basically adapted from taans developed in the khyal vocal style, and is one of the most technically challenging to perform on the sarod.

22 Irfan Khan, personal communication: 1999.

23 Personal communication: Melbourne 1987.

24 Personal communication: Mumbai 1999.

25 Brij Narayan, *SRA2,* 1995:113.

26 Bimal Mukherjee, *SRA2,* 1995:106–07.

27 Some musicians with a solid understanding of currently available digital technology such as Zakir Hussain, are known to use digital special effects as part of their solo performances (viz. Kala Ghoda Arts Fest 2000, Mumbai, 13 February 2000, with Sultan Khan).

Conclusion:
'Do We Deserve the Sarod?

THE HISTORY OF THE SAROD evokes an imagery of a dynamic and transformational journey beginning at the fringes of Hindustani music culture and culminating at its very core. Over a succession of generations, this journey ventured through cultural, social and musical domains that have intersected at various times and in various ways in the lives of hundreds of sarodiyas. These domains themselves were interlinked and interdependent upon each other so that changes that occurred in one were often felt elsewhere in some form or another. For example, as previously noted, a significant shift in the networks and structures of patronage prompted responses in the social organization of sarodiyas in the ways knowledge was transmitted and even in the ways that material culture and musical expression were approached.

Individuals also guided and influenced the direction of the journey, such as Niamatullah Khan who forged crucial personal associations with seniyas from the mid-nineteenth century onwards. This, and a handful of similar relationships, set about orientating the sarod tradition to the larger musical legacy of the inner-India orbit. At its most immediate level, the encounter resulted in the transference of the steel strings and metal plate of the sursringar onto the Kabuli rabab which, of course, was fundamental to the invention of the modern sarod. The connections sarodiyas formed with seniyas from the mid-nineteenth to the mid-twentieth centuries was so much an integral part of the social history of the instrument, that it is difficult to imagine how the modern tradition could have evolved without the input of seniyas.

For that matter the question also arises as to whether it is possible to conceive of the invention of the Hindustani sarod in the absence of the confluence of the Persianized north-west and inner-India cultural orbits that took place in the early eighteenth century. Even though the Pathan rabab had probably been in India since the time of the Lodi Sultans, it was the confluence of the eighteenth century in particular that somehow assembled the fundamental materials, and created the right conditions, that could provide the entry point for Pathan sarod players into Hindustani music culture.

Aside from these two major influences, the sarod also developed against a sequence of evolving networks and structures of patronage in Hindustani music, from premodern jajmani to colonial, to modern and finally, to the present. Within this sequence, the potential for social and cultural mobility appeared to be the most potent for sarodiyas, as well as for other musicians, during periods of liminality, i.e. when an existing network and structure of patronage was at the point of being marginalized by an emerging one. The most significant change in the social organization of sarodiyas, from the biradaris of premodern times to the gharanas of modern times for example, coincided with the marginalization of feudal patronage structures and networks by modern networks, signified and partly caused by the growing inclusion of non-Pathans into the social framework of the sarod tradition. The long-term effects of these and similar other shifts in patronage could also be discerned in changes in the ways specialist musical knowledge was regulated and circulated and in the places and times that Hindustani music was performed and how it was patronized.

The primary argument underlying this study, therefore, has been that the greater history of the sarod is embedded within multiple historical trajectories. This means that a fuller understanding of its past can be found in the aggregate of its social history, the history of its material culture, the history of its patronage, the history of its musical voice and of its repertoire. Yet plotting these distinct, but closely interrelated, histories is not so straightforward an exercise. For example, there can be little argument that Pathans were crucial to the invention of the instrument in the mid-nineteenth century, yet modifications made to the sarod in Bengal by Ayet Ali Khan and Alauddin Khan in the early twentieth century introduced an alternate strand to this trajectory. The former views the history of the sarod as the result of the mixing of the morphology and design features of the rabab, such as the sympathetic strings, from the north-west cultural orbit and those of the steel plate and steel strings belonging to sursringar of the inner-India orbit, highlighting the role of Pathan social history in this process. The latter views the invention as a further development of the sursringar and in so doing highlights the contribution of the instrumental tradition of the inner-India orbit. No doubt there may be many areas of contention between these two perspectives, but what is of importance here is that from this point onwards the social history of the tradition starts to career off on different trajectories. While both essentially describe the same process of cultural syncretism, they do so from two entirely different points of view.

When the parallel trajectory of the sarod's modern musical voice, style, technique and performance practice is considered, then the influence of the inner-India orbit comes to the fore. In this respect, the sarod represents a continuation of the musical voice inherited from the been, sursringar and seniya rabab. In fact, the desire to acquire a musical voice on the sarod that could potentially approximate these instruments can be identified as one of the principal motivating factors impelling the journey in the first place. Scrutiny of this particular desire, at any given point of time, will possibly reveal the reasons why things connected to the sarod happened when they did and in the ways that they did. Yet, at the same time, the historical trajectory of the musical voice cannot be disconnected from developments in the material culture of the instrument which itself was contingent upon conditions generated in the social history and broader cultural dynamics. What emerges is that firstly, each action or event has multiple reference points and secondly, that on each and every level of its cultural, social and musical history, the sarod is open to interpretation and, therefore, some form of contestation.

This is why it becomes especially problematic to formulate a single response to the vexed question—who first invented the sarod? While certainly not without significance, the actual invention of the sarod was in reality just a momentary event contained within the wider and deeper flow of all these other factors. If comment is to be made on the event itself, then it is difficult to go past the names of Niamatullah Khan and Ghulam Ali Khan as they have always figured prominently in any speculation on this issue, and there are compelling reasons to equally accept both of them as inventors of the modern sarod. This is especially so when it is considered that each ended up with markedly different types of the instrument. But at the same time the existence of other claims cannot be totally ignored. The sarod designed and built by Alauddin Khan was so different from other sarod types that he could be, and often is, also cited as an inventor of the sarod—but this of course depends on how one wants to define 'invention'. For this reason it is doubtful whether universal agreement over who first invented the sarod is something that is ever likely to be achieved. Certainly the invention could not have occurred without the fundamental input of a number of elements, at least as important to the process of invention as the singular contribution of any one individual.

Nevertheless, some will continue to assert that the invention of the sarod is essentially the product of modifications made to the Pathan rabab, while others will regard it as the outcome of modifications made to the sursringar. No matter which perspective one prefers, the point is that both end up highlighting the underlying fact that the invention and subsequent development of the sarod were the outcome of a culturally rich, syncretically complex and creative process.

Representations

In the 3000-word article 'Do We Deserve the Sarod?' in the Arts section in *The Telegraph,* a leading English daily of Calcutta, the well-known music critic Nilaksha Gupta described how the history of the sarod as asserted by Ali Akbar Khan now ran the risk of seriously damaging the whole tradition.[1] Gupta inquires, 'Why do people concoct lame theories and clothe the sarod in ancient Indian glory? The answer is fairly simple: to establish their Hindutva and deny credit to the people who built and developed them because they happened to be Muslims.'

No reason, however, is offered as to why Ali Akbar Khan, as a Bengali Muslim residing abroad, would want to establish Hindutva credentials. Instead, Gupta rather patronizingly implies that this respected maestro is being erroneously and unwittingly misled by those who would propagate such a Hindutva spin on the sarod's past. The point that is lost in all this is that Ali Akbar Khan has voiced this same claim for some decades now, long before Hindutva became such a force in the political climate of India. Nevertheless, Gupta does rightly make the point that in the current political climate this claim does sail dangerously close to what can easily be construed as a Hindutva agenda:

> We are living in times when ace sarod players feel the necessity to mouth false stories about their instrument in order to woo the public. Such is the deplorable change that has come about in the mentality of a large number of people in this country. If the nation cannot accept such a magnificent instrument because it originated from an instrument born in an Islamic nation and because the people who developed it and play it are largely Indian Muslims, then it does not deserve the sarod.

The bulk of the article sets out to reinforce this view by detailing the role of Muslims in the development of the tradition which, as this study has shown, is indeed a crucial one. In doing so he proceeds to 'tell the story of how the sarod came into being.' Unfortunately though, this story is seriously unconvincing because it is narrowly and unapologetically restricted to the version of the past associated with Amjad Ali Khan, the details and merits of which have been previously discussed. In the end, this article assumes an importance not because of the self-appointed mission it seeks to undertake but because of the range of issues that intersect within it.

In addressing these it is perhaps best to start by posing the question, why has this 'damage' not happened before? What is so different now, that such a threat could be so seriously contemplated? While this study has tried to show that contestation has always been part of the sarod tradition in one form or another, until recently the circulation of competing narratives of the past were mainly contained within the tradition and were grounded by its collectively-shared social and cultural referents. This was primarily the case because there was not that much interest in these issues outside the tradition and little to be gained by forcefully presenting them in a more public domain. It is generally acknowledged that different groups had different perspectives from which they derived a partial view of the greater and more complex whole. Contestation can be said to represent the historical complexity of the tradition's diversity in its understanding of itself. What has changed is the way this contestation is now circulated, the conduits through which this occurs and the new meanings and associations it acquires in the process.

Contestation within corporatized networks and structures is linked to, and motivated by, the endeavour of building brand equity. The trouble is that nowadays the coupling of cultural ownership to brand equity in the business of marketing, means that an event, like the invention of the sarod, can acquire a different and economically more potent meaning than it did even two decades ago. It is here that we confront the contemporary conundrum: control over the representation of the past holds serious financial consequences for contemporary sarodiyas. The utility of the past is increasingly harnessed to help with increasing one's share of the Hindustani music market. The details and lessons of the past have little if any associative meaning or utility beyond this. Further, there is no cultural space in which history can be seriously engaged with, and there is little inspiration or incentive for doing so. Rather, contestation is itself important because it is useful both in product differentiation and in providing a selling point. In this context, contestation acquires a similar disposition to what one may find in the corporate battle between Coke and Pepsi.

In the domain of Hindutva, however, contestation acquires a completely different set of meanings and consequences where it essentially gravitates around a communalist polemic of Hindu and Muslim. When it descends on culture, communalist fervour can battle on multiple fronts, be it in the ransacking of paintings by the well-known Indian artist Maqbool Fida Husain or in the destruction of the dargah (shrine) of the famous twentieth-century vocalist Faiyaz Khan. As Gupta quite rightly points out, highlighting the seminal role that

Muslims played in the formation and development of the sarod tradition through the mass media is like a waving the proverbial red rag to a bull and can easily turn into an invitation to the kar sevaks of Hindutva to start smashing sarods. This, of course, would not be the intention or sincere desire of either Ali Akbar Khan and Amjad Ali Khan, as both these great artists eschew communalist rhetoric.[2]

A further issue concerns the tendency of both the market and Hindutva to construct their discourse through the reduction of complex issues into historical singularities. This strategy ultimately succeeds in self-affirming the modus operandi of their own agendas; it also restricts them to hearing only their own concerns and voices. In the case of the market, concern with the past is focused upon who exactly invented the sarod, and this is important in the context of the market because of its utility in the building of brand equity. In the rhetoric of Hindutva, concern for the past is invariably focused on the question of 'whether the sarod is a Hindu instrument or a Muslim instrument.' Each of these singularities is concerned with a past that is both easily digestible and relevant to its concerns. They succeed because they are detached from the balance generated by the collective reference points and heterogeneity of voices within the tradition. The problem is that such singularities concentrate on issues that are essentially tangential to the tradition or are even constructed out of gross distortions of it.

This propensity for detachment from context is somewhat reminiscent of an earlier situation—the advent of recording technology—which enabled musical sound to be detached from musicians, mass produced and then sold in the market like any other commodity. This process began during the period when modern networks and structures of patronage were in the process of marginalizing feudal ones at the beginning of the twentieth century. The mass production of musical sound was argued to have made modernity audible and it was said to have been part of the consequences of the collision between modernity and tradition. Since this time, issues connected with sound recording, such as ownership and distribution, have become more complicated, especially since the development of digital technology.

What seems to be happening now that corporate networks are seriously challenging modern ones is that some of the inner narratives are being similarly detached from the cultural, social and musical frame of reference of the sarod tradition. This process of detachment also seems to be part of, and coincidental with, the rise of Hindutva. While it may be possible to argue that some sort of a link exists between the rise of the new networks and structures of patronage and the rise of Hindutva, and between the detachment of musical sound and of inner narratives, this is not the place to undertake it. What can be said, though, is that this new round of detachment is perhaps symptomatic of the collision between tradition and the current climate that we are engaged with which has been labelled as hyper-modernity.

The sound of the sarod is testament to the cultural, social and musical possibilities and potencies of sustained cultural syncretism. This attribute has been the core feature of its inception and subsequent development and until recently, overwhelmingly, been its underlying strength. In today's climate, however, it has become the characteristic that is most exposed to attack by religious fundamentalism and most vulnerable to distortion by the market. This climate, and the harsh conditions to which it can give rise, have the potential to silence the sound of the sarod, and we certainly do not deserve this.

Notes

1 *The Telegraph,* Calcutta, 19 February 1993.

2 Amjad Ali Khan stated his concern over communalism in a press interview in October 2002, which can be accessed at http://www.rediff.com/news/2002/oct/01spec.html

Glossary

alankar	the generic term for melodic ornaments.
alap	slow or medium tempo elaboration of musical ideas, unfolding the melodic character of a raag by developing key notes and phrases. Usually placed at the beginning of the performance of a raag, it is not set to a definite rhythmic measure. In instrumental music, it includes the sections designated as jod and jhala, though sometimes its use is restricted to the part preceding the jod. Different forms of alap rendition are recognized such as vistar alap, rupak alap, aochar alap and qaid alap.
anga	sub-division or part; also used to distinguish between different stylistic possibilities (i.e, dhrupadanga/khyalanga).
antara	the second part of the musical composition. See tuka.
aroha	ascending scale of a raag.
astai	from 'sthayi', used to designate the first part of the musical composition. In common usage, astai antara or even astai by itself, came to stand for the musical composition (usually the khyal composition) as a whole. See tuka.
audava	raag using five notes in either ascent or descent.
avaroha	descending scale of a raag.
baj	also baz; style of playing, especially in the context of instrumental music. Related to Hindi 'baza', meaning musical instrument.
badhat	controlled progression maintained in the elaboration of a raag.
bol	literally 'that which can be uttered'. Used to denote the verbal content of a composition and also to distinguish the various striking techniques in instrumental music.

chalan — the distictive progression of notes in a particular raag.

chamra — also khaal; skin (commonly goatskin) covering for sound box used in sarod.

chhanda — literally 'rhythm'; used in Hindustani music to distinguish the particular kinds of rhythm employed in rhythm cycles. Comparable to jati.

chikari — high-pitched drone strings on instrument tuned to the upper tonic; played for rhythmic articulation.

dhaivat — sixth note of seven note scale; abbreviated as 'dha'.

dhadhi — also dhari; originally an occupational caste of musicians from western India. In the nineteenth century, it became a term (like dom) used to describe musicians with a military association or background.

dhrupad — from dhruva meaning 'definite' or 'fixed', and pada or 'word'. Type of musical composition thought to have evolved from the earlier style of 'pravandha' singing. The major form of vocal music from the fifteenth to the nineteenth centuries. In more recent times, it has become less popular, perhaps because of the rise of the khyal, as the principal form of vocal music. Dhrupad texts are usually in a dialect of Hindi, praising gods, goddesses, kings and noblemen as well as natural and seasonal events.

dom — originally, hereditary occupational communities of musicians from the west of the subcontinent. In the nineteenth century, the term referred to musicians with some sort of military association or background.

drut — fast tempo.

ekhara — single-note melodic passages played in faster tempo using alternate strokes, with one note to each stroke.

gandhar — third note of seven note scale; abbreviated as 'ga'.

gat — fixed instrumental composition, set to definite rhythmic measure, with drum accompaniment.

gat toda — traditional form of instrumental music based on the idea of theme and variation, utilizing different bol patterns.

gamak — technique by which each note is sounded with adjacent upper and lower notes. One of the principal musical embellishments with many traditional varieties, used in both vocal and instrumental music.

gayaki — style of singing; used to distinguish the styles appropriate to particular forms of music as also to describe the styles of individual schools and performers. The term 'gayaki anga' is used in instrumental music to indicate an attempt to approximate the effect of vocal music.

gharana — literally 'family' or 'family tradition'; school or centre of musical culture possessing certain characteristic stylistic traits which are preserved in the process of transmission from teacher to pupil. The term acquired prominence from the nineteenth century.

jajman — also anudatta, literally 'patron'. The jajmani system or networks of patronage, when found in the context of music, refers to the various forms of exchange between groups of hereditary occupational music specialists, generically known as mirasis, and their traditional jajmans.

jati — literally 'class or type'; used to distinguish the basic kinds of rhythmic patterns in music. The forms usually recognized are teesra, chatasra, misra, khanda and sankeerna.

jawa (java) — triangular plectrum used for playing sarod, sursringar and rabab. Sarod jawas are made of coconut shell, sursringar ones of stiff wire and rabab jawas out of bamboo.

jawari — special bridge used for supporting the strings on tanpura, sitar, rabab, sarod, been and sursringar (referred to as sawari). Also used to designate a particular quality of resonance of the voice or the sound of the instrument.

jod — generally the second part of dhrupad alap, it is characterized by rhythmic movements but is not set a fixed time-cycle. In instrumental music, the part lying between the vilambit alap and the jhala.

jhala — third section of instrumental alap. Evolved in the beenkar style, it is characterized by rhythmic patterns which combine repeated strokes on the chikari strings with melodic improvisation. The speed of the jhala is increased creating expectation and excitement, leading up to a climax. Sometimes applied to the final section of fast gats which utilize the same technique within the bounds of the composition.

kaan — peg for securing and adjusting strings in the instrument.

kalawant — hereditary caste of musicians; also an honorific title for accomplished musicians formulated in the Mughal emperor Akbar's court.

krintan — in instrumental music, the technique of sounding a note by striking or 'cutting' a string with a finger of the left (i.e., non-stroking) hand.

khandan — literally 'family'.

khyal (khayal) — literally 'imagination', 'fancy'. Currently the predominant vocal style in North Indian classical music, commonly characterized by greater scope for improvisation, ornamentation and individual artistry when compared to dhrupad.

ladi — chain of stroke combinations (generally based on strokes 'di ri') forming continuous linked patterns.

ladijhala — combination of ladi and jhala.

ladlapet — derived from word meaning 'winding'; combination of ladi with meend.

ladant — derived from word meaning 'to fight'; interplay between main instrument and percussion, usually involving complex rhythmic patterns.

ladguthao — derived from word meaning 'to knot'; combination of ladi with clusters of notes.

laya — one of the central concepts of Indian music, commonly understood as 'tempo' or 'speed'. Classical musical theory, however, distinguishes ten different concepts in the disposition of musical time.

madhya (laya) — medium tempo.

madhyam — fourth note of seven note scale; abbreviated as 'ma'.

meend — slide from note to note, connecting their sounds through use of microtones or shrutis. In instrumental music, accomplished by left-hand movement on basis of single right-hand stroke.

mirasi — from miras, literally 'inheritance.' Originally identified with communities of traditional occupational music specialists, but in the nineteenth century it became a term associated with musicians who accompanied courtesans.

mizrab — plectrum made of stiff wire worn on fingertip; used to play sitar, surbahar and been.

murki	also known as khatka; type of musical ornamentation, usually that of 'embellishing' or highlighting a note by the use of a supporting phrase.
nishad	also nikhad; seventh note of seven note scale; abbreviated as 'ni'.
qawwal-bacchhe	musical descendants of the legendary court musician of the Delhi Lodi dynasty, Amir Khusrau.
patri	piece of wood used to cover the neck (stem) of instrument.
pancham	fifth note of seven note scale; abbreviated as 'pa'. Does not admit of vikriti or alteration.
pakhawaj	also called 'mridanga' in Hindustani music. Double-headed barrel-shaped drum used for solo performance and accompaniment to dhrupad and been.
raag	one of the central concepts of Indian music. Melodic form consisting of particular scale notes, affording distinct possibilities for combination and characterized by identifiable melodic phrases. Its individual melodic shape distinguishes it from other raags and creates an emotional impact on listeners.
rishav	also rikhab; second note of seven note scale abbreviated as 're' or 'ri'.
sampoorna	raags with complete sequences of notes, i.e., using all seven notes in ascent or descent.
samvadi	the secondmost important note in a raag.
sargam	the deployment of the abbreviated names of the notes (sa re ga ma etc.) in vocal music (principally khyal).
seniya	direct descendant of Tansen, the legendary court musician of the Mughal emperor, Akbar.
shadaj	first note of seven note scale; abbreviated as 'sa'. Does not admit of vikriti or alteration.
shadav	raags using six notes in ascent or descent.
shruti	concept of 'microtone' in the Hindustani musical scale. Between sa and ni, 22 shrutis are recognized and arranged in irregular groups of two, three or four. Sa and pa are thought to have no shrutis, and to be fixed in musical value.
shuddha	pure.

swara — musical note. One of the key concepts in Hindustani music, and used in many contexts.

taal — rhythmic cycle characterized by recurring pattern of beats arranged in definite sets of sub-divisions.

taan — fast melodic passage sung or played in khyal and in instrumental music.

tabli — piece of wood covering the gourd in stringed instruments like the sitar and the surbahar.

taleem — also talim; training.

tappa — a particular kind of musical composition or bandish. The words are rendered in a particular stylized manner, with rapid embellishments such as zamzama being used. Adjacent notes are sounded in quick succession, giving the impression of a vibration.

taraf (tarab) — sympathetic strings on string instruments such as sitar, sarod, esraj, sarangi. Not actually touched while playing.

tarana — a composition usually using apparently 'meaningless' sounds—syllables, drum and solfa mnemonics—set to a particular raag and taal. One theory holds that the sounds utilized in the tarana compositition are corruptions or fragments of Persian words. Some taranas also use distinct Persian words.

thumri — genre of classical music; usually regarded as being 'lighter' than dhrupad or khyal. Also adopted into performative style of instrumental music.

toda — instrumental counterpart of vocal taan, but incorporating a greater degree of rhythmic elaboration.

tuka — the parts or sections of the musical composition. Four parts were traditionally recognized in the dhrupad: sthayi, antara, sanchari, abhog. Khyal compositions in most cases had only the first two parts.

ustad — teacher, preceptor; used as honorific for a musician.

vadi — the principal note of a raag.

vansh — lineage, clan, family, dynasty.

vilambit — slow tempo.

zamzama — a series of embellishments (such as murki, sparsh, krintan) or combination of them played in fast succession resulting in a taan with a zigzag pattern.

Bibliography

AIM Aspects of Indian Music: A series of articles and papers read at the music symposia arranged by All India Radio. New Delhi: Ministry of Information and Broadcasting, Publications Division, Government of India [first ed. 1957].

IESHR Indian Economic and Social History Review.

IMS International Musicological Society.

JDIM Journal of the Department of Instrumental Music. Rabindra Bharati University 1982, VOL. 2 (Special Issue on Acharya Alauddin Khan Saheb).

NGDMI New Groves Dictionary of Musical Instruments (3 vols). Stanley Sadie ed. London: Macmillan, 1984.

NGDMM New Groves Dictionary of Music and Musicians (20 vols). Stanley Sadie ed. London: Macmillan, 1980.

SRA 1 Sangeet Research Academy. Published proceedings of the seminar on *Sarod*, Mumbai, 15 December 1991.

SRA 2 Sangeet Research Academy. Published proceedings of the seminar on *Tradition and Change*, Mumbai, 9 September 1995.

SRA 3 Sangeet Research Academy. Published proceedings of the workshop on *Indian Music and the West*, Mumbai, 29–30 November and 1 December 1996.

SRA 4 Sangeet Research Academy. Published proceedings of the workshop on *Bandish*, Mumbai, 25–26 October 1997.

IN HINDI

[All translations from Hindi to English are by the author, except for the occasional excerpts from *The Imperial Gazetteer*, which provided the romanized Hindi texts along with the English.]

ALAUDDIN Khan. *Meri Katha*. New Delhi: Rajkamal Prakhashan (for Alauddin Khan Music Academy), 1982.

ANAND, Keshav. 'Khyal va Sadarang' in *Sangeet*, January–February 1976, pp. 75–78.

ANANDPALSINGH, Sumitra. 'Dhruvapadgayakon aur Dhruvapadkaron ke Ashrydata' in *Sangeet* [Special number on Dhrupad-Dhamar], January–February 1964.

BANDYOPADHYAY, Shripad. *Sangeet-Bhashya*. New Delhi: B. R. Publishing Corporation, 1985.

BRAHASPATI, Acharya. *Dhrupad aur uska vikas*. Patna: Rashtrabhasha Parishad, 1951.

—. *Mussalman aur Bharatiya Sangeet*. New Delhi: Rajkamal Prakashan, 1974.

—. 'Musalman, Ghazal, Qawwali aur Khyal' in *Sangeet*, January–February 1976.

DAS, Chandrakantlal. 'Hindustani Vadhya Sarod' in *Sangeet*, June 1961.

—. 'Tarana: Ek Adhyyan' in *Sangeet*, January 1967.

DEVANGAN, Tulsiram. 'Tarana: Visheshnatmak Drishti' in *Sangeet* [Special number on Tarana], January 1968.

GARG, L. N. *Hamare Sangeet Ratna*. Hatras: Sangit Karyalay, 1978 [first ed. 1957].

HUSSAIN, Mirza Jaffar. 'Qadeem Lakhnau ki Twaifen' in *Ajkal*, New Delhi, May 1977.

KSHIRSAGAR, D. B. *Jodhpur Riyasat ke Darbar Sangeetgyon ka Itihas*. Jodhpur: Maharaja Mansingh Pustak Prakash, 1992.

MISHRA, Lalmani. *Bharatiya Sangeet Vadhya*. New Delhi: Bharatiya Gyanpith, 1973.

NAHATA, Agarchand. 'Rajasthan ke Gane-Bajanewale Koumen aur "Dhadhi"' in *Sangeet*, October 1961.

RAJOPADHAYE, Vasantrao. 'Tarana aur Trivat Bharatiya Prabandh Hai' in *Sangeet* [Special Issue on Tarana], January 1968.

SHUKLA, Shatrughan. *Thumri ki Utpatti, Vikas aur Shailiyaan*. New Delhi: Delhi University, 1983.

SINGH, Naina Ripjit. *Mushtak Hussain Khan*. New Delhi: Sangeet Natak Akademi, 1964.

TAKI, Roshan. *Lakhnau ke Bhand Parampara*. New Delhi: Vishwa Prakashan, 1993.

UMAR Khan. 'Sarodiyon ke Gharane' in *Swarn Jayanti Smarik*. Lucknow: Bhatkhande Hindustani Sangeet Mahavidyalaya, 1976.

IN URDU

KERAMATULLAH Khan. *Israr-i-karamat urf naghmat-i-n'amat*. Lucknow: Nizami Press, 1908.

KHAN, Muhammad Karam Imam. *Ma'dan al-musiqi*. Lucknow: Hindustani Press, 1925 [first ed. 1856].

MAHDI, Maulana Agha. *Tarikh-e-Lakhnau* [no pub. details].

IN BENGALI

[All translations from Bengali to English are by Sri Ashok Roy, McNeil's teacher.]

MOITRA, Radhika Mohan. *Jantrasangeet Prabeshika*. Calcutta: 1951.

MUKHOPADHYAY, Dilip Kumar. *Bharatiya Sangeetey Gharanar Itihas*. Calcutta: A. Mukherjee and Co., 1977.

IN ENGLISH

ABID HUSSAIN, S. *The National Culture of India*. New Delhi: National Book Trust, 1978.

AHMAD, Najma Parveen. *Hindustani Music: A Study of its Development in the Seventeenth and Eighteenth Centuries*. New Delhi: Manohar, 1984.

AHMED, Akbar S. *Pukhtun Economy and Society: Traditional*

Structure and Economic Development within a Tribal Society. London: Routledge, 1980.

ALLEN, Charles and Sharada Dwidei. *Lives of the Indian Princes*. London: Century, 1984.

APPADURAI, Arjun. 'Disjunctures and Difference in the Global Economy' in *Public Culture*, 1990, VOL. 2, no. 2, pp. 1–24.

ATHAR ALI, M. 'The Passing of Empire: The Mughal Case' in *Modern Asian Studies*, 1975, VOL. 9, no. 3.

ATTALI, Jacques. *Noise: The Political Economy of Music*. Minneapolis: University of Minnesota Press, 1985.

BAILY, John. *The Music of Afghanistan: Cambridge Studies in Ethnomusicology*. Cambridge: Cambridge University Press, 1988.

BANERJEE, Projesh. *Dance in Thumri*. New Delhi: Abhinav Publishers, 1986.

BANERJEE, Sumanta. *The Parlour and the Streets: Elite and Popular Culture in Nineteenth Century Calcutta*. Calcutta: Seagull Books, 1989.

—. *Dangerous Outcast: The Prostitute in Nineteenth Century Bengal*. Calcutta: Seagull Books, 1998.

BARLOW, Jon. Unpublished paper prepared for the conference *Indian Music and the West* organized by Sangeet Research Academy, Mumbai, November 1996.

BARNETT, Richard B. *North India Between Empires: Awadh, the Mughals and the British 1720–1801*. Berkeley: University of California Press, 1980.

BARTON, William. *The Princes of India*. New Delhi: Cosmos Publications, 1983.

BASHAM, A. L ed. *A Cultural History of India*. New Delhi: Oxford University Press, 1975.

BAYLY, C. A. 'Town Building in North India' in *Modern Asian Studies*, 1975, VOL. 9, no. 4.

—, *Rulers, Townsmen and Bazaars: North India Society in the Age of*

British Expansion 1770–1870. Cambridge: Cambridge University Press, 1983.

— ed. *The Raj: India and the British 1600–1947*. London: National Portrait Gallery Production, 1990.

BEVERIDGE, Annette Susannah tr. *The Babur-nama in English* [Memoirs of Babur translated from the original Turki Text of Zahiruddin Muhammad Babur Padshah Ghazi]. London: Luztac and Co., 1969 [first ed. 1922].

BHAKARI, S. K. *Indian Warfare: An Appraisal of Strategy and Tactics of War in Early Medieval Period*. New Delhi: Munshiram Manoharlal, 1980.

BHANU, Dharma. 'Promotion of Music by the Turko-Afghan Rulers of India' in *Islamic Culture*, 1955, VOL. 29, no. 1, pp. 9–31.

BHATKHANDE, V. N. *A Short Historical Survey of the Music of Upper India* [A Reproduction of a speech delivered by Pandit V. N. Bhatkhande at the first All-India Music Conference, Baroda 1916]. Mumbai: B. S. Sukthankar, 1934.

—. *A Comparative Study of Some of the Leading Music Systems of the 15th, 16th, 17th and 18th centuries*. 1941.

BHATTARCHARYA, Jatin. *Ustad Alauddin Khan and His Music*. Ahmedabad: B. S. Shah Prakashan, 1979.

BLACKING, John. 'The Problem of Ethnic Perception in the Semiotics of Music' in Wendy Steiner ed. *Sign in Music and Literature*. Austin: University of Texas, 1981.

BOR, Joep. 'The Voice of the Sarangi: An Illustrated History of Bowing in India' in *National Centre for the Performing Arts Quarterly Journal*, 1986, VOL. 15, nos. 3 and 4; 1987, VOL. 16, no. 1.

BRENNAN, L. 'Social Change in Rohilkhand 1801–1833' in *IESHR*, 1970, VOL. 8.

BRODKIN, E. I. *Rohilkhand from Conquest to Revolt 1774–1858*. Ph.D. Thesis, Cambridge University, 1968.

—. 'British Rule and the Abuses of Power: Rohilkhand and

Early Company Rule' in *IESHR*, June 1973, VOL. 9, no. 2.

BURGHARDT, Richard. *The Conditions of Listening*: *Essays on Religion, History and the Politics of South Asia.* New Delhi: Oxford University Press, 1997.

CAPWELL, Charles. 'Musical Life in Nineteenth-Century Calcutta as Component in the History of a Secondary Urban Centre' in J. T. O'Connell ed. *Bengal*: *Vaishnavism, Orientalism, Society and the Arts* (Occasional Paper no. 25). Michigan: Asian Studies Centre, 1985.

—. 'The Interpretations of History and the Foundations of Authority in the Vishnupur Gharana of Bengal' in Stephen Blum, Philip Bohlman and Daniel Neuman eds. *Ethnomusicology and Modern Music History.* Urbana and Chicago: University of Illinois Press, 1991.

CAROE, Olaf. *The Pathans 550 B.C. to A.D. 1957*. London: Macmillan, 1965.

CATON, Margaret Louise. *The Classical 'Tasnif'*: *A Genre of Persian Vocal Music*. Michigan: University Microfilms, 1982.

CHAKRABARTI, Dilip K. *Colonial Indology*: *Socio-politics of the Ancient Indian Past.* New Delhi: Munshiram Manoharlal, 1997.

CHAKRABARTI, Indrani. 'Sarod—Its Origin and Evolution', *SRA 1* 1991.

CHANDRA, Satish. *Parties and Politics at the Mughal Court 1707–1740*. New Delhi: People's Publishing House, 1972.

CHATTERJEE, Partha. 'Claims on the Past: The Genealogy of Modern Historiography in Bengal' in David Arnold and David Hardiman eds. *Subaltern Studies VIII*. New Delhi: Oxford University Press, 1994.

—. *The Nation and its Fragments*: *Colonial and Postcolonial Histories*. New Delhi: Oxford University Press, 1995.

—. *A Possible India*: *Essays in Political Criticism.* New Delhi: Oxford University Press, 1998.

COHN, Bernard S. *India*: *The Social Anthropology of a Civilisation*. New Jersey: Prentice Hall, 1971.

—. 'Representing Authority in Victorian India' in E. J. Hobsbawm and Terence Ranger eds. *The Invention of Tradition*. Cambridge: Cambridge University Press, 1983.

—. *An Anthropologist Amongst the Historians*. New Delhi: Oxford University Press, 1987.

COLE, J. R. I. *Roots of North India Shi'ism in Iran and Iraq: Religion and State in Awadh 1722–1859*. California: University of California Press, 1988.

CROOKE, W. *Races of North India*. New Delhi: Cosmo Publications, 1973.

—. *The Tribes and Castes of the North Western India* (4 vols). New Delhi: Cosmo Publications, 1974 [first ed. 1897].

DAY, C. R. *The Music and Musical Instruments of Southern India and the Deccan*. New Delhi: B. R. Publishers, 1974 [first ed. 1891].

DAYAL, Maheshwar. *Rediscovering Delhi: The Story of Shahjahanabad*. New Delhi: S. Chand & Co., 1975.

DE BARY, Wm. Theodore ed. *Sources of Indian Tradition* (2 vols). New York: Columbia University Press, 1958.

DEBNATH, Anjana. *Contribution of Acharya Alauddin Khan in Indian Classical Music*. Unpublished M.Phil. thesis, Faculty of Music, Delhi University, 1980.

DEHLAVI, Shahid Ahmed. 'Tradition and Change in Indo-Pakistani Classical Music' in *Journal of the Siam Society*, 1959, VOL. 47, no. 2, pp. 167–77.

DESHPANDE, G. P. 'The Dialectics of Defeat: Some Reflections on Literature, Theatre and Music in Colonial India' in *Economic and Political Weekly*, December 1987, VOL. 22, no. 50, pp. 2170–76.

DESHPANDE, Vamanrao H. *Indian Music Traditions: An Aesthetic Study of the Gharanas in Hindustani Music*. Mumbai: Popular Prakashan, 1973.

DEVA, B. C. *An Introduction to Indian Music*. New Delhi: Ministry of Information and Broadcasting, Government of India, 1973.

DHAR, Sheila. *'Here's Someone I'd Like You to Meet': Tales of Innocents, Musicians and Bureaucrats*. New Delhi: Oxford University Press, 1995.

DHAR, Sunita. *Seniya Gharana: Its Contribution to Indian Classical Music*. New Delhi: Reliance Publishing House, 1989.

DHAR CHOWDHURY, Sisirkona. 'Ustad Alauddin Khan: The Great Maestro' in *JDIM*, 1982, VOL. 2.

— ed. *JDIM*, 1982, VOL. 2.

DHOND, M. V. *The Evolution of Khyal*. New Delhi: Sangeet Natak Akademi, 1974.

DIKSHITAR, V. R. Ramchandra. *War in Ancient India*. Madras: Macmillan & Co., 1948.

DIRKS, Nicholas B. 'Political Authority and Structural Change in Early South Indian History' in *IESHR*, 1976, VOL. 15.

—. *The Hollow Crown: Ethnohistory of an Indian Kingdom*. Cambridge: Cambridge University Press, 1987.

DOBBIN, Christine E. *Basic Documents in the Development of Modern India and Pakistan 1835–1947*. London: Van Nostrand Reinhold, 1970.

DREIKMEIER, Charles. *Kingship and Community in Early India*. California: Stanford University Press, 1962.

ELIAS, Norbet. *The Court Society* [Edmund Jephcott tr.]. Oxford: Basil Blackwell, 1983.

ENGINEER, Ashgar Ali. *Lifting the Veil: Communal Violence and Communal Harmony in Contemporary India*. Hyderabad: Sangam Books, 1995.

ERDMAN, Joan L. *Patrons and Performers in Rajasthan: The Subtle Tradition*. New Delhi: Chanakya Publications, 1985.

— ed. *Arts Patronage in India: Methods, Motives and Markets*. New Delhi: Manohar, 1992.

FARMER, H. G. *The Rise and Development of Military Music*. London: Reeves & Co., 1912.

FARRELL, Gerry. *Indian Music and the West*. Oxford: Clarendon Press, 1997.

FAZL, Abul. *The Ain-i-Akbari* c. 1590 [H. Blochmann tr.]. New Delhi: Aadiesh Book Depot, 1948.

—. *The Ain-i-Akbari* c. 1590 [Col. A. S. Jarrett tr., revised by Jadunath Sarkar]. Calcutta: Royal Asiatic Society of Bengal, 1965.

—. *Akbar Nama* c. 1590 (3 vols, H. Beveridge tr., Bibliotheca Indica Work no. 138). New Delhi: Rare Books, 1973.

FISHER, Michael H. 'The Imperial Coronation of 1819: Awadh, the British and the Mughals' in *Modern Asian Studies*, 1985, VOL. 19, no. 3, pp. 239–75.

—. *A Clash of Cultures: Awadh, the British and the Mughals*. Maryland: Riverdale, 1987.

FLORA, Reis W. *Double-Reed Aerophones in India to a.d. 1400*. Unpublished Ph.D thesis, UCLA Michigan: University Microfilms, 1983.

GHOSH, Pradip Kumar. 'How Habu Dutta Influenced Acharya Alauddin' in *JDIM*, 1982, VOL. 2.

GOMMANS, Jos J. L. *The Rise of the Indo-Afghan Empire c. 1710–1780*. New Delhi: Oxford University Press, 1999.

GONDA, J. *Ancient Indian Kingship from the Religious Point of View*. Leiden: E. J. Brill, 1966.

GOSVAMI, O. *Story of Indian Music: Its Growth and Synthesis*. Mumbai: Asia Publishing House, 1957.

GOSWAMI, B. N. *Broadcasting: New Patron of Hindustani Music*. Delhi: Sharada Publishing House, 1996.

GUHA, Ranajit. *Dominance without Hegemony: History and Power in Colonial India*. New Delhi: Oxford University Press, 1998.

GUPT, Bharat. 'Some clarification of Lokadharmi and Natyadharmi' in *Sangeet Natak Akademi Journal*, 1990.

GUPTA, H. R. 'Rohillas' in R. C. Mazumdar ed. *The History and Culture of the Indian People*. Mumbai: Bharatiya Vidya Bhavan, 1977, VOL. 3.

GUPTA, Narayani. *Delhi Between Two Empires 1803–1931: Society, Government and Urban Growth*. New Delhi: Oxford University Press, 1981.

HABIB, Irfan. *An Atlas of the Mughal Empire*. New Delhi: Oxford University Press, 1982.

—. 'Studying a Colonial Society—Without Perceiving Colonisation' in *Modern Asian Studies*, 1985, VOL. 19, no. 31, pp. 355–81.

HALIM, A. 'Music and Musicians of the Court of Shahjahan' in *Islamic Culture*, October 1945, VOL. 19, no. 4, pp. 354–60.

HALLISAY, Robert C. *The Rajput Rebellion against Aurangzeb: A Study of the Mughal Empire in Seventeenth Century India*. Columbia: University of Missouri Press, 1977.

HASAN, Amir. *Palace Culture of Lucknow*. Delhi: B. R. Publishing Corporation, 1983.

HEAD, Raymond. 'Corelli in Calcutta: Colonial music-making in India during the 17th and 18th centuries' in *Early Music*, November 1985.

HIRIYANA, M. *Essentials of Indian Philosophy*. London: Unwin, 1978.

HOBSBAWN, E. J. and Terence Ranger eds. *The Invention of Tradition*. Cambridge: Cambridge University Press, 1980.

HOCART, A. M. *Kingship*. London: Oxford University Press, 1927.

—. *Kings and Counsellors*. Chicago: University of Chicago Press, 1970.

HUNTER, W. W. *The Imperial Gazetteer of India* (9 vols). London: Trubner, 1881.

HUSAIN, Iqbal. 'Socio-Economic Background of the Rise of Rohilla Afghans in the First Half of the 18th Century in the Gangetic Doab' in *Studies in Islam*, 1979.

IBBETSON, Denizil, H. A. Rose comp. *A Glossary of the Tribes and Castes of the Punjab and the North-West Frontier Province*. Punjab: Languages Department, 1970 [first ed. 1883].

IMAM, Hakim Mohammad Karam. 'Melody through the Centuries' [Govind Vidyarthi tr.] in *Sangeet Natak Akademi Bulletin,* 11–12 April 1959, pp. 13–26.

IRVINE, William. *The Army of the Indian Moghuls: Its Organisation and Administration.* New Delhi: Eurasia, 1962.

IRWIN, H. C. *The Garden of India or Chapters on Oudh History and Affairs* (2 vols). Lucknow: Pustak Kendra, 1973 [first ed. 1880].

JEFFREY, Robin. *People, Princes and Paramount Power*. New Delhi: Oxford University Press, 1978.

KAMAT, A. R. *Essays on Social Change in India*. Mumbai: Somaiya Publications, 1983.

Kautilya. *Arthashastra* c. 200 AD [R. Shamasastry tr.]. Mysore: Mysore Printing and Publishing House, 1960.

KHANNA, Lalita. Programme notes to commemorate the third anniversary of the death of Hafiz Ali Khan, *The Indian Music Society*, Mumbai, 3–12 September 1975.

KHOSLA, Ram Prasad. *Mughal Kingship and Nobility*. Delhi: Idarah-i Adabiyat-i Delli, 1976.

KIEL, Charles and Steven Feld. *Music Grooves*. Chicago: University of Chicago Press, 1994.

KINNEAR, Michael. *A Discography of Hindustani and Karnatic Music*. Connecticut: Greenwood Press, 1985.

KIPPEN, James. *The Tabla of Lucknow: A Cultural Analysis of a Musical Tradition*. Cambridge: Cambridge University Press, 1988.

KOLFF, Dirk A. *Naukar, Rajput and Sepoy: The Ethnohistory of the Military Labour Market in Hindustan, 1450–1850*. Cambridge: Cambridge University Press, 1990.

KUKERTZ, Joseph. 'The Origin and Development of the Rabab' in *Sangeet Natak*, 1976, VOL. 15, pp. 16–30.

KUPPUSWAMY, G and M. Hariharan. *Royal Patronage to Indian Music*. New Delhi: Sundeep Prakashan, 1984.

LATH, Mukund. *A Study of Dattilam: A Treatise on the Sacred Music of Ancient India*. New Delhi: Impex, 1978.

LEACH, Edmund and S. N. Mukherjee. *Elites in South Asia*. London: Cambridge University Press, 1970.

LLEWELLYN-JONES, Rosie. 'The City of Lucknow before 1856' in Balhatchett and Harrison eds. *The City in South Asia: Premodern and Modern*. London: Curzon Press, 1980.

LOBO, J. W. 'Patronage to Music: The Role of ICCR' in *Programme Proceedings of the Achievements in the Field of Percussive Arts over 50 years*. Bangalore: Bangalore Gayana Samaj, 1998.

MCGUIRE, John. *The Making of a Colonial Mind: A Quantitative Study of the Bhadralok in Calcutta 1857–1885* (Monographs on South Asia no. 10). Canberra: Australian National University, 1983.

MCNEIL, Adrian. *The Dynamics of Musical and Social Status in Hindustani Music: Sarodiyas, Seniyas and the Margi-Desi Paradigm*. Unpublished Ph.D thesis, Monash University, Melbourne, 1992.

—. 'Why Hindustani Musicians are Good Cooks: Analogies between Food and Music in North India' in *Asian Music* 1995, VOL. 25.

MAJUMDAR, Bimal Kanti. *The Military System in Ancient India*. Calcutta: Firma K. L. Mukhopadhyay, 1960.

MALHOTRA, L. K. ' "My Father, My Guru": An Interview with Ustad Amjad Ali Khan' in *Sangeet Natak*, 1973, no. 29, pp. 17–26.

MANUEL, Peter La Marche. *Thumri in Historical and Stylistic Perspective*. Ph.D. thesis, Michigan: University Microfilms International, 1985.

MARSHALL, P. J. 'Economic and Political Expansion: the Case of Oudh' in *Modern Asian Studies*, 1975, VOL. 9, no. 4, pp. 465–82.

MASSOUDIEH, Mohammad Taghi. *Music in Baluchistan* (2 vols).

Beitrage zur Ethnomusikologie, Hamburg: Verlag de Musikalien Landhug, 1988.

MATHUR, J. C. *The Impact of A.I.R. on Indian Music*. New Delhi: Ministry of Information and Broadcasting, Publications Division, Government of India, 1976 [first ed. 1957].

MENON, Raghava. *The Hindustan Times Presents the World of Amjad Ali Khan*. New Delhi: UBSPD, 1996.

METCALFE, Barbara. *Authority and Moral Conduct: The Place of Adab in South Asian Islam*. Berkeley: University of California Press, 1986.

MINER, Allyn. 'The Sitar: an Overview of Change' in *The World of Music*, 1990, VOL. 32, no. 2, pp. 27–57.

—. *Sitar and Sarod in the 18th and 19th Centuries*. Wilhelmshaven: Florian Noetzel Verlag, 1993. [First Indian edition published by Motilal Banarsidass, New Delhi, 1997.]

MISHRA, Shiva Shekhar. *Fine Arts and Technical Sciences in Ancient India, with special reference to Somesvara's Manasollasa* (Krishnadas Sanskrit Series). Benaras: Krishnadas Academy, 1982, VOL 3.

MISHRA, Susheela. *Great Masters of Hindustani Music*. New Delhi: Hem Publishers, 1981.

—. *Music Makers of the Bhatkhande College of Hindustani Music*. Calcutta: Sangeet Research Academy, 1985.

MITRA, Rajyeswar. 'Indian Music in the Muslim Rule in India' in A. K. Majumder ed. *The Bases of Indian Culture*. Calcutta: Ramakrishna Vedanta Math, 1961.

MOITRA, Radhika Mohan. 'Musing on the Muse' in *Sangeet Research Academy Journal*, Calcutta, September 1981, VOL. 2, no. 1.

—. 'Hindustani Instrumental Music: then and now' in *Sangeet Research Academy Journal*, Calcutta, August 1988, VOL. 9, no. 1.

—. 'The Story of Ustad Mohammed Ameer Khan Sahib, The Great Sarode-Newaj of Shahjahanpur' in *The First Radhika*

Mohan Moitra Memorial Music Conference Souvenir Booklet. Calcutta: Ballygunge Maitreyee Music Circle, 1998.

MUKHERJEE, Bimalendu. 'A Survey of Presentation of Dhrupad Style of Music Through Instruments' in *Dhrupad Annual*, 1986, VOL. 1, pp. 1–12.

— and Sunil Kothari eds. *Rasa: The Indian Performing Arts in the Last Twenty-Five Years*. Calcutta: Anamika Kala Sangam, 1995, VOL. 1.

MUKHERJEE, D. P. *The Great Masters I Have Heard*. New Delhi: Publications Division, Ministry of Information and Broadcasting, Government of India, 1955.

MUKHERJEE, Girija K. *The Indian Image of Nineteenth Century Europe*. Mumbai: Asia Publishing House, 1967.

MUKHERJEE, Nilmoni. *A Bengal Zamindar: Jaykrishna Mukerjee of Uttarpara and his Times 1808–1888*. Calcutta: Firma K. L. Mukhopadhyay, 1975.

MUKHERJEE, Sushil. *The Story of the Calcutta Theatres: 1753–1980*. Calcutta: P. M. Bagchi and Co., 1982.

NEUMAN, Daniel M. 'Country Musicians and their City Cousins: The Social Organisation of Music Transmission in India' in *IMS, Report of the Twelfth Congress*. Berkeley, 1977.

—. *The Life of Music in North India: The Organisation of an Artistic Tradition*. Detroit: Wayne State University Press, 1980.

—, Shubha Chaudhuri and Komal Kothari eds. *An Ethnographic Atlas of Music Traditions in West Rajasthan*. [Forthcoming from Seagull Books, Calcutta]

NIRANJANA, Tejaswini. 'Translation, Colonialism and the Rise of English' in *Economic and Political Weekly*, April 1990, VOL. 25, no. 15.

NIZAMI, Khaliq Ahmed. *Some Aspects of Religion and Politics in India during the Thirteenth Century*. Aligarh: Department of History, Aligarh Muslim University, 1961.

OJHA, P. N. *North Indian Social Life During Mughal Period*. New Delhi: Oriental Publishers, 1975.

OLDENBERG, Veena Talwar. *The Making of Colonial Lucknow*. New

Jersey: Princeton University Press, 1984.

PACHOLCZYK, Josef. 'The Story of Sufiana Kalam in Kashmir' in *Asian Music*, 1982, VOL. 12, no. 1, pp. 159–63.

PAGE, Helen E. 'Black Images, African American Identities: Corporate Cultural Projection in the Songs of My People' in *Identities: Global Studies in Culture and Power*, May 1997, VOL. 3, no. 4, pp. 557–603.

PANDEY, Gyanendra. 'The Colonial Construction of Communalism: British Writings on Banaras in the Nineteenth Century' in Ranajit Guha ed. *Subaltern Studies VI*. New Delhi: Oxford University Press, 1989.

PEARSON, M. N. ed. *Legitimacy and Symbols: The South Asian Writings of F. W. Buckler*, Michigan: University of Michigan, 1985.

PEMBLE, John. *The Raj, the Indian Mutiny and the Kingdom of Oudh 1801–1859*. London: Harvester Press, 1977.

PERERA, E. S. *The Origin and Development of Dhrupad and its Bearings on Instrumental Music*. Calcutta: K. P. Bagchi and Co., 1994.

PHILIPS, C. H. and M. P. Wainwright eds. *Indian Society and the Beginnings of Modernisation c. 1830–1850*. London: School of Oriental and African Studies, 1976.

PRADHAN, Aneesh. *Changing Facets of Indian Music in a Colonial Situation: A Case of Mumbai 1818–1947*. Unpublished Ph.D. thesis, Department of History, Mumbai University, 2000.

PRAJNANANANDA, Swami. *Music of the South Asian Peoples*. Calcutta: Ramakrishna Vedanta Math, 1979.

—. *A Historical Study of Indian Music*. New Delhi: Munshiram Manoharlal, 1981.

QUDDUS, Syed Abdul. *The Pathans*. Lahore: Feroz and Sons, 1987.

QURESHI, Regula Burckhardt. 'Islamic Music in an Indian Environment: The Shia Majlis' in *Ethnomusicology*, 1981, VOL. 25, no. 1, pp. 41–71.

—. 'Qawwali: Making the Music Happen in the Sufi Assembly' in Wade ed. *Performing Arts in India: Essays on Music, Dance and Drama*. Washington: University Press of America, 1982.

—. *Sufi Music of India and Pakistan*. Cambridge: Cambridge University Press, 1986.

—. 'Sufi Music and the Historicity of Oral Tradition' in Blum, Bohlman and Neuman eds. *Ethnomusicology and Modern Music History*. Urbana and Chicago: University of Illinois Press, 1991, pp. 103–20.

RANADE, Ashok Damodar. *On Music and Musicians of Hindoostan* [first ed.] New Delhi: Promilla and Co., 1984.

—. *Stage Music of Maharashtra* [first ed.]. New Delhi: Sangeet Natak Akademi, 1986.

—. *Keywords and Concepts in Hindustani Classical Music*. New Delhi: Promilla and Co., 1990.

—. *Indology and Ethnomusicology: Contours of the Indo-British Relationship*. New Delhi: Promilla and Co., 1992.

—. *Hindustani Music* [first ed.]. New Delhi: National Book Trust, 1997.

RANGACHARYA, Adya. *Natyasastra: English Translation with Critical Notes*. Bangalore: IBH Prakashana, 1986.

RAVI Shankar. 'Sweet Reminiscences' in *JDIM*, 1982, VOL. 2.

RAY, Rajat K. 'Political Change in British India' in *IESHR*, 1977, VOL. 14, no. 4, pp. 493–517.

RICHARDS, J. F ed. *Kingship and Authority in South Asia* (Madison Publication Series no. 3). Wisconsin: University of Wisconsin, 1981.

RIDGWAY, R. I. I. *Pathans*. Calcutta: Government Press, 1918.

RIZVI, S. A. A. *Religious and Intellectual History of the Muslims in Akbar's Reign: With Special Reference to Abul Fazl*. New Delhi: Munshiram Manoharlal, 1975.

RIZVI, S. N. H. 'Music in Muslim India' in *Islamic Culture*, 1941, VOL. 15, pp. 331–40.

ROUSSELET, Louis. *India and its Native Princes: Travels in Central India and in the Presidencies of Bombay and Bengal* [revised and edited by Lt. Col. Buckle]. London: Bick ers and Son, 1882.

ROWELL, Lewis. *Music and Musical Thought in Early India*. Chicago: University of Chicago Press, 1992.

ROY, Bimal. 'Alauddin Khan Saheb and Aesthetics' in *JDIM*, 1982, VOL. 2.

ROY, Sukumar. *Music of Eastern India: Vocal Music in Bengali, Oriya, Assamese and Manipuri with Special Emphasis on Bengali*. Calcutta: Firma K. L. Mukhopadhyay, 1973.

ROY CHOUDHURY, B. K. 'The Seniya Gharana of Rampur' in *Sangeet Natak Akademi Journal*, 1973, VOL. 29, pp. 5–8.

—. *Mian Tansen and Indian Music* (n.d.1)

—. *Hindustani Music: Its History and Technique* (n.d.2)

SAKATA, Hiromi Lorraine. *Music in the Mind: The Concept of Music and Musicians in Afghanistan*. Ohio: Kent State University Press, 1983.

SANYAL, Amiyanath. *Ragas and Raginis*. Calcutta: Longmans, 1959.

SARMADEE, Shahab ed. *Tarjuma-i-Manakutuhala and Risala-i-Ragdarpana by Faqirullah* (Kapila Vatsyayan gen. ed. Kalamulashastra Series). New Delhi: Indira Gandhi National Centre for the Arts and Motilal Banarsidass, 1996.

SATYAMURTHY, T. V. ed. *Region, Religion, Caste, Gender and Culture in Contemporary India*. New Delhi: Oxford University Press, 1996.

SCHWARTZBERG, Joseph E. ed. *A Historical Atlas of South Asia*. Chicago: University of Chicago Press, 1978.

SCHWEINITZ, Karl de (Jr). *The Rise and Fall of British India: Imperialism as Inequality*. New York: Methuen, 1983.

SEAL, Anil. *The Emergence of Indian Nationalism: Competition and Collaboration in the Later 19th Century*. London: Cambridge University Press, 1968.

SEEGER, C. 'Semantic, Logical and Political Considerations Bearing upon Research in Ethnomusicology' in *Ethnomusicology*, May 1961, VOL. 5, no. 2, pp. 77–80.

SENGUPTA, Pradip Kumar. *Foundations of Indian Musicology: Perspectives in the Philosophy of Art and Culture*. New Delhi: Abhinav, 1991.

SHANKAR, Rajendra. 'Ustad Alauddin Khan' in *Sangeet Natak*, 1973, no. 29, pp. 9–16.

SHARAN Rani. *The Divine Sarod: An Ancient Indian Musical Instrument (Antiquity, Origin and Development from c 200 B.C.)*. New Delhi: Sangeet Kala Bhawan, 1992.

SHARAR, Abdul Halim. *Lucknow: The Last Phase of an Oriental Culture* [E. S. Harcourt and Fakir Hussain tr. and ed.]. London: Paul Elek, 1975.

SHARMA, B. L. 'Contribution of Rajasthan to Indian Music' in *Indian Musicological Society Journal*, 1971, VOL. 2, no. 2, pp. 32–47.

SHRIVASTAVA, Ashirbadi Lal. *The First Two Nawabs of Oudh: A Critical Study based on Original Sources*. Lucknow: The Upper India Publishing House, 1983.

SHRIVASTAVA, Indurama. *Dhrupada: A Study of its Origin, Historical Development, Structure and Present State*. New Delhi: Motilal Banarsidass, 1980.

SILVER, Brian. 'On Becoming an Ustad: Six Life Sketches in the Evolution of a Gharana' in *Asian Music*, 1976, VOL. 7, no. 2, pp. 27–58.

SINGER, Milton. *When a Great Tradition Modernizes*. New York: Praeger, 1972.

SINGH, Thakur Jaidev. 'Contribution of Acharya Alauddin Khan to Hindustani Music' in *JDIM*, 1982, VOL. 2.

SINHA ROY, Ajoy. 'The Swarode: An Indian Musical Instrument' in *Sangeet Research Academy Journal*, August 1988, VOL. 9, no. 1.

SLOBIN, Mark. *Music in the Culture of Northern Afghanistan*. Tuscon: University of Arizona, 1972.

SOLIS, Theodore. *The Sarod: Its Gat-Tora Tradition with examples by Amir Khan and three of his students*. Unpublished MA thesis, University of Hawaii, 1970.

SOPHER, David E. 'Rohilkhand and Oudh: An Exploration of Social Gradients across a Political Frontier' in R. G. Fox ed. *Realm and Region in Traditional India* (Comparative Studies Monograph no. 14). Durham: Duke University, 1977.

SPAIN, James W. *The Pathan Borderland*. The Hague: Mouton & Co., 1963.

SRINIVAS, M. N. *Social Change in Modern India*. California: University of California, 1966.

STEPHENS, Ian Melville. *Horned Moon: An Account of a Journey through Pakistan, Kashmir and Afghanistan*. Bloomington: Indiana University Press, 1955.

STOLLER, Paul. *The Taste of Ethnographic Things*. Philadelphia: University of Pennsylvania Press, 1989.

SUBRAMANIAN, Lakshmi. Paper delivered at the conference *Music in the Age of Reproduction: Tradition, Innovation and Enterprise* organized by the Centre for Studies in Social Sciences, Calcutta, 1999.

SUNDAR, Pushpa. *Patrons and Philistines: Arts and the State in British India*. New Delhi: Oxford University Press, 1995.

TAGORE, Sourindra Mohun. *Public Opinion and Official Communications about the Bengal Music School and its President*. Calcutta: Panchanun Mookherjee, 1876.

—. *Hindu Music from Various Authors*. Benaras: Sanskrit Series Office, 1965 [first ed. Part 1, Calcutta: 1875; reprint with Part 2, Calcutta: 1882].

—. *Yantrakosha or A Treasury of the Musical Instruments of Ancient and of Modern India, and of Various Other Countries*. New York: AMS Press, 1976 [first ed. 1875].

TAYLOR, David and Malcolm Yapp. *Political Identity in South Asia*. London: Curzon Press, 1979.

VAN DER MEER, Wim. *Hindustani Music in the Twentieth Century*. New Delhi: Allied Publishers, 1980.

VATSYAYAN, Kapila. *A Study of Some Traditions of Performing Arts in Eastern India: Margi and Deshi Polarities*. Gauhati: University of Gauhati, 1981.

VATUK, Sylvia. *Kinship and Urbanization: White Collar Migrants in North India*. Berkeley: University of California Press, 1972.

VERMA, S. P. 'Ensigns of Royalty at the Mughal Court in the sixteenth century' in *Islamic Culture*, January 1976, VOL. 50, no. 1, pp. 41–45,

VERMA, Vijay. *The Living Music of Rajasthan: A Census of India Monograph*. New Delhi: Office of the Registrar General, 1987.

VYAS, Vidyadhar. 'The Decline of Gharanas' in Bimal Mukherjee and Sunil Kothari eds. *Rasa: The Indian Performing Arts in the Last Twenty-five Years*. Calcutta: Anamika Kala Sangam 1995, VOL. 1: Music and Dance.

DICTIONARIES

APTE, Varman Shivram. *The Student's Sanskrit-English Dictionary*. New Delhi: Motilal Banarsidass, 1976.

CHATURVEDI, M. and B. N. Tiwari. *A Practical Hindi–English Dictionary* (tenth edition). New Delhi: National Publishing House, 1984.

QURESHI, Bahir Ahmad. *Standard Twentieth Century Dictionary: Urdu into English*. New Delhi: Delhi Educational Publishing House, 1985.

INTERVIEWS

DASGUPTA, Buddhadev. Interviewed by Dipali Nag for Calcutta Doordarshan, 1982.

MOITRA, Radhika Mohan. Interviewed by B. C. Deva. New Delhi: Sangeet Natak Akademi (SNA-1267), 1972.

PERSONAL COMMUNICATIONS/RECORDED INTERVIEWS

Anindya Banerjee (1998)

Jon Barlow (1998)

Buddhadev Dasgupta (1986, 1998, 1999)

Somjit Dasgupta (1998)

Ali Akbar Khan (1983, 1990)

Amjad Ali Khan (1986, 1987)

Illyas Khan (1982)

Irfan Khan (1997–2001)

Mohammad Ali Khan (1986)

Musharrat Khan (2000)

Nurullah Khan (1998)

Yakub Ali Khan (1984–87)

Michael Kinnear (1982)

Mukund Lath (1988)

Kalyan Mukherjee (1982, 1999–2001)

Brij Narayan (Melbourne 1987, Mumbai 1999)

Stanley Pereira (1986)

A. Roy (1990)

Sachindra Nath Roy (1998)

Subroto Roy Choudhury (1985–86)

Ravi Shankar (1985)

Radhika Mohan Moitra interviewed by B. C. Deva for the Sangeet Natak Akademi (SNA-1267: 1972)

Index